BISTROS
OF PARIS

BISTROS OF PARIS

ROBERT AND BARBARA

HAMBURGER

THE ECCO PRESS

An Imprint of HarperCollins*Publishers*

BISTROS OF PARIS. Copyright © 2001 by Robert and Barbara Hamburger. All rights reserved. Printed in the United States of America. No part of this book may be used or reproduced in any manner whatsoever without written permission except in the case of brief quotations embodied in critical articles and reviews. For information, address HarperCollins Publishers Inc., 10 East 53rd Street, New York, NY 10022.

HarperCollins books may be purchased for educational, business, or sales promotional use. For information please write: Special Markets Department, HarperCollins Publishers Inc., 10 East 53rd Street, New York, NY 10022.

FIRST EDITION

Designed by Cassandra J. Pappas

Library of Congress Cataloging-in-Publication Data
has been applied for.
ISBN 0-06-095688-7

01 02 03 04 05 RRD 10 9 8 7 6 5 4 3 2 1

For Sequoyah, Sylvanwillow, and Dylan

CONTENTS

PART TWO

ACKNOWLEDGMENTS

WE WOULD LIKE to thank Ellen Baumwoll, Susan Dreyer, Colleen and David Hamburger, Meryl Salzinger, Larry Saphire, Robert and Michele Seass, Jerry and Rita Schneiderman, Louise Sklar, and Melissa Tollefson.

With special thanks to Joel Baumwoll.

INTRODUCTION

PARIS IS a fascinating city offering the visitor a never-ending array of pleasures. One of the most irresistible enticements is the cuisine. There is an age-old commitment to culinary excellence. Celebrated chefs and illustrious restaurants have made the city synonymous with fine food and wine, but it is the bistro that gives Paris its heart and soul.

Always sensitive to current social and economic trends, France's gastronomic reputation is based on constant change. Not long ago, the restaurant world was transformed by a whole new generation of gifted young chefs who, having been classically trained in some of the most prestigious kitchens, began challenging the culinary orthodoxy of French cuisine. Venturing out on their own, many of these chefs chose to open bistros instead of luxury restaurants. These are the places where the most innovative cooking is taking place today, where a new kind of bistro has evolved.

Taking their inspiration from France's diverse regional heritage, these young chefs are bringing refinement and imagination to classic bistro fare by integrating the best products of the countryside with exotic ingredients and global flavors, enhancing basic bourgeois food with the stylish flourish of contemporary haute cuisine. To keep prices down, expensive products are used as garnishes, and time-consuming preparations are abandoned. Menus are determined by the season and market availability, allowing not only maximum freshness but a minimum of waste. To showcase the special talent of the chef, the menu-carte was introduced. This is a greatly expanded version of the *prix-fixe* menu and offers the diner numerous choices from among the top specialties of the particular bistro at a significant saving. Yet there is nothing "budget" about these stylish modern bistros, and the idiom continues to attract other young chefs, resulting in a continual flowering of new addresses.

Meanwhile, the traditional bistros of the city remain firmly entrenched in the hearts of Parisians. Impervious to changing fashions, these legendary places continue to thrive precisely because they maintain and produce the familiar dishes that are the essence of French cuisine. While seasonal and special dishes may be presented, it is the classic preparations that bring a highly critical and discerning clientele back year in and year out.

There are the sausages of the Lyonnaise, the *gigots de prés-salés* of Brittany, the *gratins* of the Dauphiné, the *brandades* of Provence, the *choucroutes* of Alsace, the *cassoulets* of Languedoc, the open tarts and *potées* of Lorraine, *entrecôte* from Bordeaux, *bouillabaisse* from the Riviera, and *coq au vin*, *escargots*, and *boeuf bourguignon* from Burgundy. Less well known are the *marmites* and *andouilles* from Normandy, *rillettes* and *matelots* from the Loire, *truffades* and *aligots* from Auvergne, *garbures* from the Pyrenees, and *poulets au vin jaune* from the mountains of the Jura. Traditional bistros take pride in preparing these lusty dishes so central to French identity. They may refine and update them to suit modern tastes, but innovation is always tempered by tradition.

WINE BISTROS (*bistrots-à-vins*) gained a foothold in Paris many years ago and have become a special part of the bistro scene. In the beginning most were dimly lit, smoke-ridden haunts patronized by the owners' wine-loving cronies. In some places such a description is still pretty accurate, but in others you will find a substantial range of fine food and wine in a tasteful setting. There is nothing excessive in the way of gastronomy; but if you want to lunch well but quickly or dine early in a congenial atmosphere, the wine bistro is ideal.

Today it is not easy to discover a comparatively unknown bistro. Any place serving consistently good food soon becomes popular. We have designated a handful of places as "discoveries," bistros patronized by a discerning Parisian clientele but as yet relatively unexplored by foreign visitors. We have pinpointed these restaurants as worth special consideration for the more adventurous traveler.

This guide is organized around the arrondissement plan and divided into two parts. Part One contains individual listings, which describe the characteristics that make each establishment unique; it includes special dishes, wines, and places of interest in the area. Part Two provides a cross-reference to locate the particular dish you want at the place that prepares it best; and a list of bistros open on Sunday. Finally, there is an alphabetical index of all the listed establishments.

TODAY THE BISTRO reigns supreme. Both traditional and modern bistros are widely popular, so advance reservations are necessary. You should also be warned that between the time this guide was written and your visit, a restaurant may change (closing dates are especially variable), so be sure to telephone to check whether the information in this guide is still valid. In the fall of 2000, the currency rate of exchange was 7.5 francs to the dollar.

There is a persistent fiction that one can eat well almost anywhere in Paris. The fact is that many places are surprisingly mediocre. We hope this highly selective guide will lead you to some of the enjoyable experiences bistro dining has given us.

PART ONE

THE BISTROS BY
ARRONDISSEMENT

PARIS IS DIVIDED into twenty arrondissements (districts) spiraling clockwise around the first, which marks the center of the city. Each arrondissement has its own atmosphere and distinctive landmarks, so to know the number of the arrondissement is to know the style and character of the district.

The 1er (meaning *premier*) includes part of the Île de la Cité and the areas around the Louvre and Palais-Royal. This is a tourist, shopping, and business district with many hotels, restaurants, travel agencies, specialty shops, banks, and government buildings.

The 2e (*deuxième*) is a curious mix of old streets and beautifully renovated glass-roofed *passages*. Originally built in the early nineteenth century, these picturesque galleries still recall the romantic atmosphere of a bygone era.

The 3e and 4e (*troisième* and *quatrième*) include the areas of Les Halles (the old produce markets), Beaubourg, and the Marais. The old narrow, slummy streets and court-yards have been turned into a large pedestrian area with a shopping mall, and many new apartments, all dominated by the gigantic glass-and-steel Pompidou Center. Many of the old *hôtels* (mansions) of the Marais are being used to house museums, schools, libraries, and luxury apartments. Trendy boutiques, antique shops, cafés, and restaurants attract a yuppy crowd.

The 5e and 6e (*cinquième* and *sixième*) on the Left Bank comprise the areas of St-Michel and St-Germain-des-Prés. They are among the liveliest and most picturesque sections of the city. The 5e is student Paris—the Quartier Latin and the Sorbonne. The 6e is intellectual and literary Paris, snobbish and avant-garde. The narrow mazes of streets are lined with bookshops, publishing houses, antique stores, art galleries, and boutiques of every description.

The 7e (*septième*) is on the Left Bank but has nothing in common with the 5e or 6e. It is a residential area, conservative and wealthy, where the historic monuments—the Tour Eiffel, the Invalides, Napoleon's Tomb, and the Musées d'Orsay and Rodin—are found.

The 8e (*huitième*) is the most diverse arrondissement. It is the district of the Étoile, the Arc de Triomphe, the Champs-Élysées, and the place de la Concorde. It encompasses the luxury areas around the Madeleine and Faubourg-St-Honoré and the middle-class student and commercial areas around Gare St-Lazare and boulevard Haussmann.

The 9e (*neuvième*) is the *arrondissement* of the Gaillion-Opéra, Pigalle, and the grand boulevards. It is a shopping, theater, and business district, with big department stores, boutiques, cafés, brasseries, and movie houses. The smart end is near the Opéra; it gets seedier as you go east. The areas around Place Pigalle abound with sex shops, prostitutes, porn films, and porn bookstores.

The 10e (*dixième*) is largely unspoiled; it is dominated by two large train stations, the Gare du Nord and the Gare de l'Est.

The 11e, 12e, and 13e (*onzième, douzième,* and *treizième*) are middle- and working-class areas, crowded with high-rise developments and small industries. A visit to the Bois

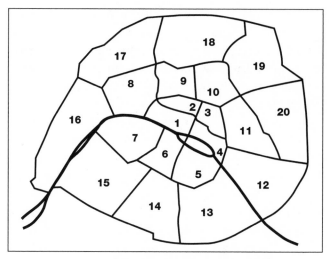

A diagram of Paris showing the arrondissements

de Vincennes is certainly worth a detour to the 12e, and the Asian restaurants in the 13e are among the best in Paris.

The 14e and 15e (*quatorzième* and *quinzième*) are the old districts around Montparnasse and have in the last several years undergone much development. The cafés, brasseries, and movie houses continue to attract a lively, hip crowd.

The 16e (*seizième*) contains the *quartiers* of Passy and Auteuil. Here the rich and superchic live on private, tree-lined streets, behind closed doors and ivy-covered walls.

The 17e (*dix-septième*) is also a luxury area, although not as posh as the 16e. It is not a tourist area, but in rue Poncelet there is a lively market with an astounding choice of produce.

The 18e (*dix-huitième*) contains the slopes of Montmartre. The area is overshadowed by the great white basilica of Sacré-Coeur and has largely escaped reconstruction because of the steep and narrow streets of the Butte. The Goutte d'Or (Drop of Gold) is a commercial and working-class area of mixed nationalities. The Arab groceries and the Afro-Antilles restaurants are considered the best in the city.

The 19e and 20e (*dix-neuvième* and *vingtième*) are the most remote arrondissements. Waves of immigrants have settled here. There is an exotic mixture of food, shops, newspapers, cafés, and so on. The main tourist attractions are the Parc de Villette in the 19e and Père-Lachaise cemetery in the 20e.

RANKINGS

Here is the key to the symbols used in *Bistros of Paris.*

Key to Symbols

Traditional Bistros (pot � represents traditional bistro.
Number of pots is rating for traditional bistros)

    ☞ ☞ ☞   The Best

    ☞ ☞   Exceptional

    ☞   Very Good

Modern Bistros (chef's hat ♕ represents modern bistro.
Number of hats is rating for modern bistros)

    ♕ ♕ ♕   The Best

    ♕ ♕   Exceptional

    ♕   Very Good

    ▭▭▭   metro stop

    ☎   phone number

    Fax   fax number

    Ø   hours/days closed

PRICE RANGE

$	20 to 40
$$	40 to 80
$$$	80 to 120
$$$$	120 to 180

[VISA] [MasterCard] [Diners Club] [Amex]   shows which credit cards are taken

[card] NONE   does not accept any credit cards

♈ wine bistro

※ discovery

🍶 best wine choices

From the hundreds of bistros we have visited on our most recent trips to Paris, we have selected what we consider the best and most representative of two groups: traditional and modern. We have ranked each group according to four basic criteria: consistency, quality, generosity, and warmth of welcome. Our rankings are "Best," "Exceptional," and "Very Good." In the list below, within each category and ranking the restaurants are listed alphabetically by arrondissement. Even those in the lowest category were solid bistros with some dishes of outstanding merit.

TRADITIONAL BISTROS

🍲 🍲 🍲

L'Ami Louis   3^e

Au Bascou   3^e

Benoît   4^e

Chez Dumonet
(Joséphine)   6^e

Le Florimond   7^e

La Fontaine de Mars
7^e

Chez Catherine   9^e

La Grille   10^e

Auberge Pyrénées
Cévennes   11^e

Le Repaire de Cartouche
11^e

À Sousceyrac   11^e

La Régalade   14^e

Restaurant du Marché
15^e

☞ ☞

Chez Pauline 1er	Le P'tit Troquet 7^e
La Tour de Monthléry 1er	Le Boucoléon 8^e
Chez la Vieille 1er	Casa Olympe 9^e
L'Ange Vin 2^e	Le Parmentier 10^e
Chez Georges—Le Jeu du Mail 2^e	Au C'Amelot 11^e
	Cartet 11^e
Le Grizzli 4^e	Chardenoux 11^e
Le Vieux Bistro 4^e	Auberge le Quincy 12^e
Les Fontaines 5^e	À la Biche au Bois 12^e
Chez René 5^e	Le Petit Marguery 13^e
Chez Maître Paul 6^e	Au Vins des Rues 14^e
La Rôtisserie d'en Face 6^e	Le Gastroquet 15^e
	Chez Pierre 15^e
Auberge Bressane 7^e	Le Troquet 15^e
Auberge "d'Chez Eux" 7^e	Le Petit Boileau 16^e
	Caves Pétrissans 17^e
L'Oeillade 7^e	Marie-Louise 18^e
Au Petit Tonneau 7^e	La Boulangerie 20^e

☞

Lescure 1er	Aux Charpentiers 6^e
Le Relais Chablisien 1er	Marie et Fils 6^e
Clémentine 2^e	Wadja 6^e
Baracane (Bistrot de l'Oulette) 4^e	Chez l'Ami Jean 7^e
	Le Calmont 7^e
Au Bourguignon du Marais 4^e	Berrys 8^e
	Ma Bourgogne 8^e
Les Fous d'en Face 4^e	L'Alsaco Winstub 9^e
Mauzac 5^e	L'Oenothèque 9^e
Moissonnier 5^e	Le Pétrelle 9^e
Allard 6^e	Le Bouledogue Bistrot 10^e
Le Réveil du Xe 10^e	Les Coteaux 15^e
Astier 11^e	Le Père Claude 15^e
Le Passage 11^e	Le Bistrot d'à Côté Flaubert 17^e
Le Square Trousseau 12^e	

Chez Paul   13e La Côte de Boeuf   17^e
Le Terroir   13e Le Baratin   20^e

MODERN BISTROS

🎩🎩🎩

Le Pamphlet   3e Jean-Pierre Frelet   12^e
Le Réminet   5e L'Avant-Goût   13^e
L'Épi Dupin   6e L'Os à Moelle   15^e
Chez Michel   10e Le Troyon   17^e
Les Amognes   11^e

🎩🎩

L'Ardoise   1er Baptiste   17^e
L'Argenteuil   1er L'Affriolé   7^e
Willi's Wine Bar   1er Au Bon Accueil   7^e
Le Hangar   3e Velly   9^e
Les Bookinistes   6e Les Jumeaux   11^e
La Villaret   11e Café d'Angel   17^e
L'Anacréon   13e L'Étrier Bistrot   18^e
Virgule   13e La Cave Gourmand   19^e
Le Bistro d'Hubert   15e Les Allobroges   20^e

🎩

Le Dauphin 1er A & M Le Bistrot   16^e
Chez Toutoune   5e Le Bistrot de l'Étoile
La Bastide Odéon   6e "Niel"   17^e
Dame Jeanne   11e Le Zéphyr   20^e

DISCOVERIES

ON OUR MOST RECENT trip to Paris, we tracked down a small group of neighborhood bistros that are relatively unknown even to the most knowledgeable travelers. These delightful restaurants offer the adventurous gourmet an opportunity to explore and enjoy some truly wonderful places before they are included in the best-selling tourist guides. Most have been opened by dedicated and talented chefs in rather obscure areas without fanfare or publicity; and although each has a unique approach to cooking, all offer outstanding dishes in a warm, friendly atmosphere. One word of caution, however—these bistros may be undiscovered by the general public, but they are extremely popular in their local districts, so it is always prudent to reserve. We have listed these discoveries by arrondissement.

1ᵉʳ	*5ᵉ*
L'Argenteuil	Le Réminet
Le Dauphin	
3ᵉ	*7ᵉ*
Le Hangar	Le Florimond
Le Pamphlet	Le Boucoléon

Ier ARRONDISSEMENT

L'ARDOISE

L'ARGENTEUIL

LE DAUPHIN

LESCURE

CHEZ PAULINE

LE RELAIS CHABLISIEN

LA TOUR DE MONTHLÉRY
(CHEZ DENISE)

CHEZ LA VIEILLE

WILLI'S WINE BAR

LOUVRE–LES HALLES–PALAIS-ROYAL

L'Ardoise

M. Pierre Jay

28, rue du Mont-Thabor, 75001 (off rue de Rivoli;
the nearest cross street is rue Rouget de Lisle) |
🚋 Concorde or Tuileries
☎ 01-42-96-28-18
Ø Monday; one week in May; and three weeks in August
$ $ | 💳 💳
👨‍🍳👨‍🍳

L ocated in the heart of Paris, the *premier arrondisse-ment,* this intimate restaurant is the solo debut of Pierre Jay, formerly of La Tour d'Argent and Chez Jean. Going into his third year, M. Jay has established a devoted following who appreciate his originality and his dedication to using only the freshest and best-quality foods for his *cuisine de marché.*

The modern glass facade leads into a small dining room painted white and furnished with rush-seated chairs surrounding comfortably large square or round tables set in white linen. The walls are decorated with black-and-white photos in a contemporary minimalist style. There's nothing minimalist, however, about the imaginative, tasty entrées and *plats* M. Jay has created. On the day we visited, a blackboard carte (at 175 francs) offered no fewer than eleven entrées, ten *plats,* and eight desserts.

Entrées included crab flan in a creamy parsley emulsion, a salad of squid and langoustine with grated carrots and celery with ginger dressing and a tartare of red tuna, and M. Jay's signature dish: foie gras and whipped artichoke enclosed in a flaky philo envelope.

Among the main course listings were such imaginative creations as *fondant de joue de boeuf* (beef cheeks); fresh cod on a bed of mashed potatoes with chorizo sausage chips;

roasted pigeon, boned with the innards cooked to a confit and spread on toast; and grilled sea bass with fennel.

Desserts were also given much attention; they included a *ballon de fraises* (a caramelized dessert, cream and strawberries served in a champagne glass), a superb *feuillantine au citron* (sugar-glazed pastry leaves filled with lemon), and *pain perdu* with vanilla ice cream and caramelized apples.

M. Jay, a native of Macon in Burgundy, has selected interesting, sensibly priced wines.

Up-to-the-minute, appealing food, attentive service, and reasonable prices keep this new, small jewel perpetually busy, so reservations are necessary. (L'Ardoise can sometimes be noisy.)

RECOMMENDED DISHES

Gallette de Foie Gras et Artichaut. Open tart filled with foie gras and whipped artichoke puree.

Miroir de Tourteau au Cresson. Crabmeat salad with watercress.

Raviolis de Langoustines au Beurre de Xérès. Ravioli stuffed with prawns in a sherry-flavored butter sauce.

Aile de Raie Poêlée aux Câpres Rémoulade de Céleri. Panfried skate with capers served with a spicy mayonnaise on celery root.

Épaule d'Agneau Rôtie. Roast lamb shoulder served with a stew of tiny onions.

Pigeon Rôti, Galette de Pommes de Terre. Roast squab served with a potato cake.

Cocotte de Homard aux Lard Fumé et Pommes Charlotte. Casserole of lobster and bacon with pureed apple mousse baked in a pastry shell.

Bar Entier Grillé aux Graines de Fenouil. Whole grilled European sea bass flavored with wild fennel seeds.

Clafoutis aux Abricots. Batter cake with apricots.

Feuillantine au Citron. Sugar-glazed strips of puff pastry filled with lemon cream.

🥄 Particularly strong in white burgundies. The Morgon of Guy Breton is outstanding.

MENU-CARTE | 175 francs.

L'Argenteuil

M. Bruno Schaeffer
Mme. Martine Schaeffer
Chef: Bruno Schaeffer

9, rue d'Argenteuil, 75001 (between rue des Pyramides and rue de l'Échelle) | 🚋 Pyramides or Palais-Royal

☎ 01-42-60-56-22

Ø Saturday and Sunday lunch

$$$ | 🏧 VISA MasterCard ⑩

♟♟ | ☼

Just two steps from the Palais-Royal, chef-patron Bruno Schaeffer has created an homage to the cuisine of his native Lorraine. As you pass between two potted cedar trees and enter the small, minimally elegant setting, there is little that will signal the range and variety of unusual preparations offered by this meticulous and imaginative chef.

M. Schaeffer, who was born in Lunéville, is devoted to the rich dishes of his native province but carefully balances each dish with a lightness and a finesse that are the hallmark of his cooking. Risotto with frogs' legs and lime is the undisputed specialty of the house, but there is a great deal more here. All the pork products come from one farm in the Lorraine. Particularly delicious is the fillet of pork cooked with bacon and potatoes or sometimes served with white haricot beans. The fish and shellfish are especially excellent. Tuna, cod, monkfish, sea bream, scallops, swordfish, rouget—anything that comes out of the sea is exquisitely fresh and beautifully prepared. The blanquette of monkfish and shrimp with a light curry sauce and the wheat risotto with calamari and shellfish sauce are among the favorites. Desserts are a delight; especially tempting are bergamot orange *crème brûlée;* iced soufflé with prunes and Armagnac; and stewed rhubarb with orange, strawberries, and rosemary honey.

Wines are reasonably priced and include a Pinot noir from the Côtes de Toul and a *vin gris* from the Lorraine, two wines rarely seen in Paris.

RECOMMENDED DISHES

Risotto de Grenouilles à Citron Vert. Italian rice dish with minced frogs' legs and lime juice.

Truite Fumée avec sa Crème de Raifort. Smoked trout served with a horseradish cream sauce.

Tartelette de Filets d'Anchois Frais, Tomate Confite et Pistou. Puff pastry tartlet with fillets of anchovies, tomato, and pesto sauce.

Noix de Saint-Jacques Poêlées aux Topinambours. Panfried scallops with Jerusalem artichoke in a sauce flavored with foie gras.

Lasagnes d'Aubergines et Filet d'Espadon Tapenade et Tomate Confite. Lasagna of eggplant and fillet of swordfish with tapenade and tomato preserve.

Effeuillé de Haddock aux Endives Émulsion à la Moutarde de Charroux. Smoked haddock with melted endives sauced with mustard.

Mouclade de Cabillaud au Curry. Fresh cod in a creamy mussel sauce spiced with curry.

Bourride de Lotte et Grenailles de la Baule. Monkfish stew with aioli (garlic sauce) and tiny new potatoes from La Baule.

Fraîche Poêlée d'Ananas Flambée au Rhum et son Granité. Fried fresh pineapple flamed with rum and topped with water ice sprinkled with sugar.

Poêlée de Figues de Sollies à la Canelle. Hot panfried figs from Sollies with cinnamon.

🥄 Côtes de Toul, St. Pourçain, Saumur-Champigny.
MENU | 165 francs.

Le Dauphin

M. Didier Oudill
M. Edgar Duhr

167, rue St-Honoré, 75001 (cross street rue de l'Échelle
   at place André Malraux) | 🚋 Louvre-Palais-Royal
☎ 01-42-60-40-11 | Fax 01-42-60-01-18
Ø Open every day all year
$ $ $ | 💳 VISA 💳 Ⓓ
🍴 | ☀

In 1999 chefs Didier Oudill and Edgar Duhr arrived from the Café de Paris in Biarritz to take over this onetime brasserie situated in a touristy area near the Comédie Française. It did not take long to refresh the two dining rooms with warm touches of beige and brown, paint the old columns, clean the maroon banquettes, polish the antique fluted light fixtures, and cover the tables with fresh linen.

The two partners met in the kitchens of Michel Guérard, where they learned the craft of contemporary cuisine. The flavors of the Basque-Béarn region dominate many of the wonderful dishes to be enjoyed here. The best-quality ingredients are used to prepare smoked salmon accompanied by American-style coleslaw, a marbled foie gras, white asparagus with pungent ham, copious platters of assorted meats, grilled fish and vegetables covered with tangy homemade barbecue sauce, beef chunks with vegetables in a flavorful light bouillon, and a *cassoulet* of jumbo beans in a *pistou*. Desserts vary from a hazelnut *dacquois* and pear sorbet to a spectacular bittersweet chocolate cake with raspberry sauce. The wine list includes many choices from the vineyards of the southwest.

Le Dauphin was designated the best bistro of the year (2000) by the critic Claude Lebay.

RECOMMENDED DISHES

Coleslaw de Chou à l'Anguille Fumée et Coquilles Saint-Jacques. Coleslaw in a salad with smoked eel and scallops.

Vinaigrette de Lentilles et Pommes de Terre à la Tête de Cochon. Lentil and potato salad in a vinaigrette dressing with a slice of headcheese.

Terrine Paysanne "du Vieux Garçon." Hearty country terrine.

Recuite de Légumes et Thon Confit à l'Huile d'Olive. Ricotta and vegetables with preserved tuna, drizzled with olive oil.

Parilladas de Viandes, Poissons, ou Légumes. Assorted meats, fish, or vegetables presented on large platters.

Cassoulet aux Haricots Gambas au Pistou. Southwestern casserole made with giant beans and flavored with pesto sauce.

Dos Épais de Cabillaud Cuisinée à la Louisiane. Saddle of fresh codfish in a thick, hot tomato sauce.

Joues de Cochon Mitonnées à la Mode de Tonneins. Slow-cooked stew of pig's cheeks cooked and served in a cooking pot (*cocotte*).

Dacquoise aux Avelines et Sorbet à la Poire. Layer cake of whipped cream and hazelnut meringue accompanied by a scoop of pear sorbet.

Gâteau Moelleux au Caramel et Poires. Soft cake with caramel sauce and pears.

Small but carefully chosen assortment of southwestern wines.

MENU | 140 francs.

Lescure

M. DENIS LASCAUD

7, rue de Mondovi, 75001 (at the foot of the place de
   la Concorde and the arcades of the rue de Rivoli) |
   🚃 Concorde
☎ 01-42-60-18-91
∅ Saturday and Sunday; three weeks in August
$ | VISA MasterCard
🍲

D enis Lascaud represents the third generation of
the family that has served traditional home cooking in this rustic restaurant since 1919. The food is
simple, the prices are reasonable, and the amiable staff are
quick to make you feel welcome as you are seated among
the tourists and faithful regulars who fill the place at lunch.

   Lescure is hidden away in a quiet corner just behind the
rue de Rivoli, and you might prefer one of the tony fair-
weather tables to eating inside sitting *coude à coude* (elbow
to elbow) under ropes of garlic and country sausages dan-
gling from the rafters. The menu changes every two
weeks, and the best dishes appear on a slate as "specials of
the day." The house carte offers a hot *pâté en croute,* mackerel marinated in white wine, preserved duck, a fine *boeuf
bourguignon,* veal kidneys Auvergne-style, and a copious
poule-au-pot farcie Henri IV (stuffed chicken poached with
vegetables in the style of Béarn). A fresh fruit tart or the
warm chocolate profiteroles would be a good choice for
dessert.

RECOMMENDED DISHES

Maquereaux Marinés Maison. Mackerel fillets poached in
   white wine.

Pâté en Croûte Chaud avec Salade. Pâté nestled in a hollowed-out slice of bread, served over salad greens.

Onglet au Bleu Sauce Noix. Skirt steak served rare in a walnut sauce.

Poule au Riz Sauce Basquaise. Chicken with rice, covered in a tangy tomato and green pepper sauce.

Boeuf Bourguignon Garni. Beef stewed in Burgundy wine with bacon, small onions, and mushrooms.

Haddock Poché à l'Anglaise. Poached haddock served English-style with a beurre blanc sauce.

Poule-au-Pot Farcie Henry IV. Stuffed chicken poached with vegetables.

Confit de Canard "Comme en Limousin." Grilled preserved duck accompanied by potatoes sautéed in oil.

Cabécous des Causses de Rocamadour. Small round goat cheese from the southwest.

Tarte aux Fruits de Saison. Shallow pastry shell variously filled with sweetened fruits of the season.

Cahors, Touraine, Gaillac (you pay only for what you drink)

MENU | 115 francs, a demi-carafe of red or white wine included.

Chez Pauline

M. ANDRÉ GÉNIN

5, rue Villedo, 75001 (off rue de Richelieu) |
Palais-Royal

☎ 01-42-96-20-70 | Fax 01-49-27-99-89

Ø Saturday lunch and Sunday

$ $ $ |

☞☞

nchangeable and dependable, this quintessential bistro is one of a diminishing number of family-owned places that have evolved from humble origins into polished, comfortable, expensive restaurants. Currently, André Génin is the owner and chef of Chez Pauline, and his top-quality Burgundy-inspired cuisine is an example of the best that the bistro repertoire can offer. Even though Génin's food rarely exhibits the inventive flair exemplified by today's top young chefs, his dishes do have occasional luxurious flourishes. Alongside down-to-earth bourgeois classics, he presents many elaborate preparations such as a whole truffle in a bed of delicious foie gras, priced at 500 francs; an old-fashioned fillet of sole at 450 francs; and a roasted Bresse chicken for two, the wings served with *gratin dauphinoise* and the legs with salad, at 400 francs. In contrast there is a beef bourguignon with tagliatelle at 130 francs, and a warm *tête de veau* salad (the best in Paris) at 90 francs.

At lunch you are likely to meet businesspeople on expense accounts, attached to their *portables* (cell phones), eating and talking with great purpose. Dinner brings a more relaxed, eclectic mix of well-heeled tourists and local regulars. They dine in a chic, unhurried atmosphere surrounded by mirrored walls, polished brass, plush banquettes, and lots of fresh flowers.

There are some very good and very expensive wines from Burgundy and Bordeaux, but the reasonably priced house Beaujolais is a perfectly satisfactory accompaniment to the food.

RECOMMENDED DISHES

Salade Tiède de Tête de Veau, Sauce Gribiche. Warm calf's head salad in a mayonnaise sauce with chopped hard-boiled eggs, capers, and mixed herbs.

Terrine de Foie Gras Frais de Canard Mi-Cuit. Fresh duck liver pâté, half cooked.

Salade de Homard Breton Cuit à la Nage. Brittany lobster poached in aromatic liquid and served on a bed of tiny new vegetables.

Jambon Persillé comme en Bourgogne. Parsleyed ham in white wine aspic.

Gibiers. Large selection of wild game available seasonally: pheasant, deer, partridge, rabbit.

Boeuf Bourguignon aux Tagliatelles. Beef stewed in Burgundy wine with onions and mushrooms, served with fresh noodles.

Lièvre à la Royale (in season). Braised, boned hare stuffed with foie gras and truffles.

Poulet de Bresse Rôti. Roast Bresse chicken (for two).

Ris de Veau en Croute à la Façon du "Père Genin." Calf's sweetbreads served in a hollowed-out pastry.

Grosse Sole Poêlée "à la Belle Meunière." Fillet of sole floured and panfried in butter (for two).

Gâteau de Riz aux Fraises. Rice pudding with strawberry confit and vanilla custard sauce.

Baba au Cognac, Mendiant, Chantilly. Sponge cake soaked in cognac and served with a *mendiant* (nut biscuit) and whipped cream.

Beaujolais, Burgundy, Sancerre.

MENUS | Lunch 220 francs, dinner 250 francs.

Le Relais Chablisien

M. CHRISTIAN FAURÉ

4, rue Bertin-Poirée, 75001 (off quai de la Mégisserie) |
🚋 Châtelet or Pont Neuf
☎ 01-45-08-53-73 | Fax 01-45-08-53-73
Ø Saturday and Sunday; first three weeks of August
$$ | VISA MasterCard
⌒ | ♉

Tucked away on a side street beside the mammoth department store Samaritaine, this auberge, with its rustic oak beams, transports you to the countryside. Le Relais Chablisien is the creation of Christian Faure, a warm, merry bon vivant who makes a celebration of his native Burgundy, paying particular homage to his hometown, Auxerre. The popular bar is packed with locals, artists from the opera house, and regulars who attend the nearby Théâtre de la Ville. This is an appealing place to sample Faure's wide choice of little-known wines from Burgundy and Chablis. To accompany the wine, fabulous sausages, cheeses, and sandwiches are offered downstairs at the bar. Moving to an upstairs table, you may order from a menu that varies with the season but always features such traditional regional favorites as parsleyed ham, perfectly poached eggs covered with a rich wine sauce, *coq au vin* made with a luscious pinot noir from Auxerre, and a creamy veal stew. In good weather the little terrace is a pleasant spot for a quiet evening meal.

RECOMMENDED DISHES

Oeufs en Meurette. Eggs poached in red Burgundy with pieces of bacon and small onions.

Cochonailles (Assiette de Charcuteries). Assortment of sausages and pâtés.

Salade de Pieds de Veau Farci d'une Langue en Ravigote. Salad of veal trotters stuffed with tongue in a cream sauce with shallots, herbs, and spices.

Andouillette de Chablis aux Échalotes Blondes. Tripe sausage braised in Chablis wine and served on a bed of sautéed shallots.

Coq au Vin d'Irancy. Cockerel cooked slowly in red Irancy wine with onions, garlic, mushrooms, and pieces of bacon.

Blanquette de Veau. Veal stewed in a white roux sauce with onions and mushrooms.

Aiguillettes de Canard au Vinaigre de Cassis. Thin slices of duck breast cooked with a sauce made from black currant vinegar.

Filet de Daurade Rôti à la Crème Safranée. Roast sea bream in cream sauce flavored with saffron.

Époisses. Perfectly matured cow's milk cheese produced in the village of Époisses in Burgundy.

Gratin de Fruits. Baked dessert of fruit with a top crust.

From the north Burgundy region in and around Chablis and Irancy.

La Tour de Monthléry (Chez Denise)

M. RAYMONDE BENARIAC
MME. DENISE BENARIAC

5, rue des Prouvaires, 75001 (between rue Berger and
   rue St-Honoré) | 🚋 Louvre-Rivoli or Châtelet-
   Les Halles
☎ 01-42-36-21-82 | Fax 01-45-08-81-99
Ø Saturday and Sunday; July 10 through August 15
$$ | VISA MasterCard
🍲🍲

C hez Denise, as it is called these days, is an all-
night institution in the area of Les Halles that
continues to maintain an atmosphere of old-
world conviviality and unchangeable hearty cuisine. Din-
ers are packed shoulder to shoulder in a noisy series of
rustic rooms stretching back from the traditional zinc bar
on the left as you enter. A black-and-white tile floor, brass
rails, posters, lithographs, and red-and-white checked
tablecloths complete the scene. Good-natured, patient
waiters maneuver among the closely set tables with
hearty platters of duck foie gras, garlicky lamb, grilled
hanger steak, and steaming chunks of boiled beef with
vegetables. More adventurous eaters order the delicious
tripe, served Normandy-style, or the grilled *andouillettes*. A
carefully prepared braised salmon with mustard sauce will
please any fish eater. The house Brouilly is fresh, fruity,
and the best accompaniment to this hearty food. If you
have room, the cheese tray provides a satisfying finish to
your meal, especially if you save some wine for it.

RECOMMENDED DISHES

Cochonnailles (Assiette de Charcuteries). Assorted terrines, sausages, and other pork products.

Gâteau de Foie de Volaille. Savory cake of chicken livers.

Onglet de Boeuf Grillée, Frites. Grilled flank steak with outstanding *pommes frites.*

Rognons de Veau, Sauce Moutarde. Grilled veal kidneys in mustard sauce.

Lapin à la Moutarde. Rabbit in mustard sauce.

Pot-au-Feu. Boiled beef with vegetables and broth (Thursdays).

Pieds de Porc Grillé. Grilled pig's feet.

Tripes au Calvados. Tripe cooked in cider brandy.

Chou Farci. Rolled, stuffed cabbage.

Côte de Boeuf Grillée, à la Moêlle. Grilled ribs of beef in a bone marrow sauce accompanied by pommes frites (for two).

Civet de Cerf Grand Veneur. Slow-cooked venison stew in a brown sauce with red currant jelly (game season).

Crème Caramel. Custard baked in a mold, coated with caramel.

Baba au Rhum. Yeast cake steeped in rum syrup.

 Brouilly.

Chez la Vieille

M. Marie-José Cervoni
M. Gérard Besson

1, rue Bailleul or 37, rue de l'Arbre-sec, 75001
    (between rue de Rivoli and rue St-Honoré) |
    🚋 Louvre-Rivoli
☎ 01-42-60-15-78 | Fax 01-42-33-85-71
∅ Saturday and Sunday, evenings except Thursday
$ $ $ | [card] [VISA]
🍲🍲

C hez La Vieille was the domain of the indomitable Adrienne Biasin, the celebrated patron-chef who presided over it for 45 years. Fortunately, the new owners have maintained the two traditions that made this tiny bistro a mecca for Parisian gourmets—warm, welcoming service and huge portions of delicious bourgeois cooking.

You may start your meal by choosing from a superb array of pâtés, hams, terrines, cooked vegetables, stuffed tomatoes, foie gras, smoked herring, and stuffed cabbage left beside your table on a cart. We suggest restraint at this point, for the main courses require a hearty appetite. "Generous" and "satisfying" best describe the portions of veal kidneys with mushrooms, steak with a marrow bone in butter and wine sauce, duck breast in pepper sauce, and pike dumplings with Lyonnaise potatoes.

The cosy dining room, with a timbered ceiling and a lovely tile floor, is as homey and inviting as the food, and if you accompany your meal with a simple *vin de pays,* you will have a true taste of old-fashioned bistro dining.

RECOMMENDED DISHES

Chariot de Hors-d'Oeuvre. Choice of stuffed tomatoes, terrines, marinated herring, and assorted salads.

Foie Gras de Canard Mi-Cuit en Terrine. Homemade duck
foie gras, semicooked and served in its earthenware
terrine.

Jarret de Porc Caramélisé au Four. Hock of pork caramelized in the oven.

Quenelles de Brochet Lyonnaise Maison. Pike dumplings in a
cream sauce with pureed crayfish.

Daube de Boeuf. Braised beef stew with vegetables.

Rognon de Veau Rôti Entier. Roast whole veal kidney served
with eggplant gratinée and mashed potatoes.

Pot-au-Feu. Boiled beef with vegetables and broth (in the
winter).

Blanquette de Veau. Veal stew in a white cream sauce with
onions, carrots, and mushrooms.

Chou Farci. Rolled, stuffed cabbage.

Crème Caramel. Vanilla-flavored custard flan floating in
soft caramel. Huge bowl, seconds invited.

Mousse au Chocolat. Classic dessert of meringue and
whipped cream folded into melted chocolate.

Saumur-Champigny, Brouilly.

MENU | 160 francs.

Willi's Wine Bar

M. MARK WILLIAMSON

13, rue des Petits-Champs, 75001 (between avenue de
l'Opéra and place des Victoires) |
🚋 Bourse, Pyramides, or Palais-Royal
☎ 01-42-61-05-09 | Fax 01-47-03-36-93
Ø Sunday
$ $ | VISA MasterCard
♟♟ | 🍷

B y now most people know they will get more than a
glass of good wine at Willi's. This perfect "English-
style" wine bar, strategically located behind the
Palais-Royal, is the creation of two Englishmen, Mark
Williamson and Tim Johnston, and continues to be a rendezvous for upscale Britons and fashionable Parisians.

Light polished wood floors, a long golden oak bar, and
two small tables are an attractive entrance leading into the
larger dining room, which is furnished with inviting round
tables. Large posters and comfortable chairs add the right
touch of color to the monochromatic background. The
atmosphere is relaxed, casual, and very chic, and one is
never made to feel rushed while leisurely perusing the fascinating list of wines.

The daily menu is seasonal and might feature such
things as pumpkin soup with oysters; curried shrimp and
foie gras; mushroom ravioli with fresh goat cheese; grilled
sea bream with sweet peppers, capers, and cumin; fillet of
beef with crispy shredded potatoes; roasted Lozère lamb;
or chicken fricasseed with balsamic vinegar. Desserts are
indulgent; one listing, *Spécialité du collège de Cambridge,* is
a dish popular in Britain since the seventeenth century
under the English name "burnt cream" and popularized in
France two centuries later as *crème brûlée.*

RECOMMENDED DISHES

Terrine de Pintade. Terrine of guinea hen served with stewed red onions.

Salade de Caille Vinaigre Balsamique. Breast of quail on salad greens sprinkled with vinaigrette dressing.

Tartare de Thon. Chopped raw tuna seasoned and garnished with raw egg yolk, capers, and chopped onion and parsley.

Gigolette de Lapereau Rôti en Fricassée d'Artichauts. Roast leg of young rabbit in a stew with artichokes.

Caneton de Challans. Roast Challans duck with four spices.

Filet de Boeuf Sauté Ragoût de Primeur au Poivre. Tenderloin of beef sautéed and served in a stew of baby vegetables and crushed peppercorns.

Pavé de Cabillaud Rôti au Lard, Petits Oignons Confits, au Xérès. Roasted piece of fresh cod with bacon and preserved onions cooked in sherry wine.

Ragoût d'Agneau aux Épices et Abricots. Lamb stew with spices and apricots.

Feuilleté aux Poires Caramélisées. Flaky pastry filled with cream and caramelized pears.

Terrine de Chocolat Amer. Terrine of bittersweet chocolate.

Very good selection of sherries and a number of Côtes du Rhône by the glass.

MENUS | Lunch 158 francs, dinner 195 francs.

2ᵉ ARRONDISSEMENT

L'ANGE VIN

CLÉMENTINE

CHEZ GEORGES—LE JEU DU MAIL

BOURSE–TURBIGO

PLACES OF INTEREST

Bourse (stock exchange)

Cabinet de Médailles
(museum of coins, medals, artifacts,
and royal treasures)

Covered passages
(Vivienne, du Grand-Cerf,
du Bourg-l'Abbé de la Trinité,
Basfour, Beauregard, des Panoramas,
des Princes)

Place du Caire

Quartier de la Presse

Rue des Petits-Carreaux and
rue Montorgueil

Sentier (garment district)

Tour de Jean-sans-Peur

Place des Victoires

L'Ange Vin

M. Jean-Pierre Robinot
Chef: Olivier Pierpaoli

168, rue Montmartre, 75002 (between rue St-Marc
   and rue d'Uzès | 🚋 Grands-Boulevards
   (rue Montmartre) or Bourse
☎ 01-42-36-20-20 | Fax 01-42-36-20-62
∅ Sunday and Monday
$$ | VISA MasterCard
🍶🍶 | 🍷

Jean-Pierre Robinot has two passions. The first is for
the wines of the Loire Valley, particularly those
from the Jasnières, where he was born; and the sec-
ond is for wines that are naturally grown, unfiltered, and
nonchaptalized.

In 1997, when M. Robinot gave up his little wine bar on
rue Richard Lenoir to move into a much larger space on
rue Montmartre, he brought with him the old Richard
Lenoir street sign as a souvenir. Once you step inside his
new place, you are surrounded by the world of the 1930s.
Everything is authentic and beautifully preserved. The
zinc bar on the right as you enter is by Nectoux; the geo-
metric tile floors are original; but the most outstanding
features in the restaurant are the metal staircase and the
fabulous balustrade that encloses the mezzanine.

The new young chef, Olivier Pierpaoli, presents a cui-
sine that is somewhat sophisticated for a wine bistro,
adapting many of his recipes to include the regional wines
M. Robinot is so fond of. The foie gras in aspic is made
with a Coteaux du Layon, the fricassee of chicken with a
Jasnières, and beef and sweetbreads with an Anjou. Dur-
ing the game season, partridge, wild boar, and rabbit are
prepared.

The blackboard menu changes daily, and an ambitious six-course *dégustation* menu is offered in the evening at 500 francs for two (not including wine).

RECOMMENDED DISHES

Petit Gâteau d'Aubergines et Concassé de Tomates. Baked savory tart of crushed (in a mortar) eggplant and tomato.

Filets de Sardines Fraîches Marinées au Basilic. Fillets of fresh sardines marinated with basil.

Terrine de Foie Gras et Gelée de Coteaux du Layon. Terrine of foie gras in an aspic made from naturally sweet white Loire wine.

Filet de Sandre Laqué aux Graines de Sésame. Fillet of pike perch sprinkled with sesame seeds.

Filet d'Agneau en Croûte de Pommes de Terre et son Jus au Romarin. Tenderloin of lamb baked in the oven, encased in pastry, with potatoes and natural juices flavored with rosemary.

Ragoût de Lapin aux Épices d'Asie et Jeunes Légumes. Rabbit stew with Asian spices and baby vegetables.

Paupiette de Veau aux Champignons. Thin slice of veal rolled, stuffed with mushrooms, larded, and roasted in the oven.

Filet de Boeuf Rôti au Parmesan et Tomates. Roast tenderloin of beef accompanied by a sauce made from Parmesan cheese and tomato pulp.

Tarte Fine aux Pommes et Raisins de Corinthe, Boule de Vanille. Thin apple tart with dried currants and a scoop of vanilla ice cream.

Millefeuilles de Chocolat et Fruits Rouges de l'Époque. Layered flaky pastry filled with chocolate cream and topped with berries.

Coteaux du Layon (apéritif), Jurançon (J. Bousquet), Plume d'Ange (Les Cailloux du Paradis), Jasnières (Cuvée Molière), Bourgueil (Breton), Anjou-Villages (Château Pierre Bise).

Clémentine

M. FRANCK LANGRENNE

5, rue St-Marc, 75002 (across from passage des Panora-
mas, between rue Vivienne and rue Montmartre) |
🚋 Grands-Boulevards (rue Montmartre) or Bourse
☎ 01-40-41-05-65 | Fax 01-45-08-08-77
∅ Sunday
$ $ | 💳 VISA 💳 🅾

☞

The amiable owner-chef, Franck Langrenne, formerly of Lucas-Carton and Clos Longchamps,
can be seen preparing sophisticated seasonal specialties in his charming little bistro located across from the
passage des Panoramas. The beautiful old facade simply
says "Restaurant 5," with the sign "Vins—Plats du Jour"
painted on one of the windows temptingly filled with a
display of regional products. Inside are a small zinc bar,
velour banquettes, and 9 or 10 marble-topped tables covered with red-checked cloths. Wine posters, maps, and
mirrors cover the old walls.

The menu-carte at 145 francs includes a choice of one
entrée, one *plat,* and either a dessert or cheese all selected
from the à la carte menu. Businesspeople from the nearby
stock exchange rapidly fill the room for lunch. Evenings
are more sedate, with a pleasant intimate atmosphere.
Six Cancale oysters, pieces of veal with a tasty sauce gribiche, and a salad of mussels and red potatoes are typical
starters. Fish is particularly good here, prepared in many
different ways and with many unusual garnishes. Swordfish is served with seaweed salad; *filet de loup* (a kind of sea
bass) is flamed with pastis; trout is sprinkled with chives.
M. Langrenne sometimes likes to use ostrich as an alterna-
tive to beef and serves it panfried with a rich whiskey

sauce. Cheeses come from the house of Michel Gaurel in the Ardèche. For dessert an orange-flavored cheesecake and anise-flavored *crème brûlée* are worth attention. The house wines tend toward the south, with robust discoveries from the Languedoc region. Armagnac and Calvados may be ordered by the glass.

RECOMMENDED DISHES

Foie Gras de Canard Frais. Fresh duck foie gras.

Fraise de Veau, Sauce Gribiche. Fried calf's membrane (similar to tripe) in a cold vinaigrette with gherkins, capers and hard-boiled egg yolks.

Salade de Choux Vert aux Foies de Volaille. Green cabbage salad with chicken livers.

Blanc de Volaille Rôti au Chèvre Frais. Roast chicken breast with fresh chavignol goat cheese.

Cabillaud Rôti aux Agrumes. Roast fresh cod with citrus fruits.

Côte de Boeuf, Jus au Romarin. Roast rib of beef with natural juices flavored with rosemary.

Poêlée de Rognon à la Moutarde. Panfried veal kidney in mustard sauce.

Civet de Biche, Flan au Céleri Rave. Game stew of venison, mushrooms, and red wine served with an open-face celery root tart.

Figues Rôties et Glace Vanille. Roast figs with homemade vanilla ice cream.

Palet Mi-Cuit au Chocolat Amer. Sweet petit flour biscuit with melted bitter chocolate.

Southwest, Languedoc, Rhône Valley, Loire.
MENU-CARTE | 145 francs.

Chez Georges–Le Jeu du Mail

M. BERNARD BROUILLET

1, rue du Mail, 75002 (off place des Victoires) |
🚋 Sentier or Bourse
☎ 01-42-60-07-11
∅ Sunday; August 1 through 21
$$$ | [Amex] [VISA] [MasterCard]
🍲🍲

Opened in 1964 and run by three generations of the Brouillet family, Chez Georges is a charming old-style bistro with a fine reputation founded on classic cooking that rarely changes, to the delight of everyone who comes here. Lunch is always packed with traders from the nearby stock exchange, so if you are planning a shopping trip to the smart place des Victoires and want to lunch here, you must reserve. Evenings are quiet.

This bistro is located behind a lovely square with the statue of Louis XIV in the center. You enter a corridor-like room with the front bar area set apart from the back. A large mural of young couples and minstrels strolling through a medieval garden decorates the entrance. The color scheme—deep wine and cream—lends an elegant simplicity to the small alley-like dining area, lined on each side with banquettes, huge arched mirrors, and decorative wall sconces.

The menu, handwritten in pink and purple ink, lists the dozens of dishes that have made this restaurant popular, but the outstanding favorites are the *oeufs mayonnaise,* the steak with béarnaise sauce served with a plate of fabulous *pommes frites,* and grilled lamb chops served with buttery *haricots verts.* If you are a herring maven, you will want to order the heaping bowl of Baltic herring fillets with *crème fraîche* to start. The house has an extraordinary cellar of

fine old Burgundies and Bordeaux, but you can also order
Beaujolais served by the pitcher.

RECOMMENDED DISHES

Harengs de la Baltique. Deep bowl of marinated herring fillets served with *crème fraîche.*

Jambon Persillé. Parsleyed ham in white wine aspic.

Escargots de Bourgogne. A dozen Burgundian snails served
in their shells with garlic butter.

Sole au Pouilly. Fillet of sole in a sauce of white wine and
cream.

Le Pavé du Mail. Thick-sliced beefsteak in a creamy mustard sauce. Served with *pommes frites.*

Rognons de Veau Grillées, Henry IV. Grilled veal kidneys
with hearts of artichoke.

Steak de Canard aux Girolles. Grilled duck fillet with sautéed
wild mushrooms (*girolles* or *cèpes*).

Filet de Turbot Poché Pâtes et Girolles. Poached turbot and
béarnaise sauce with noodles and *girolle* mushrooms.

Baba au Rhum. Yeast cake steeped in rum syrup.

Tarte Tatin. Caramelized upside-down apple cake.

Extraordinary *carte* of high-price *grand cru* wines, but
the Côte-de-Brouilly and Morgon served by the pitcher
are fine.

3ᵉ ARRONDISSEMENT

MARAIS–TEMPLE

L'Ami Louis

M. LOUIS GADBY

32, rue du Vertbois, 75003 (off rue St-Martin; closest
cross street, rue Vaucanson) |
🚋 Arts-et-Métiers or Temple
☎ 01-48-87-77-48
Ø Monday and Tuesday; July 15 through August 25
$ $ $ $ | 💳 [VISA] [MasterCard] [Ⓓ]
🍲🍲🍲

It is hard to believe that for more than 70 years the
insignificant entrance and red-checked café window
curtains have hidden one of the most famous
Parisian bistros. The tiny dining room, dingy with age,
still houses an old coal-burning stove, overhead coatracks,
little iron-legged marble-topped tables, and a worn-out art
deco trompe l'oeil tile floor.

People still vie for tables so that they can feast on outra-
geously large slabs of foie gras served with Bayonne ham,
the famous roast chicken with shoestring potatoes, tender
roast baby lamb, Breton scallops, and—in season—game
with mushrooms.

The prices are out of sight, but if you can afford a pil-
grimage to this venerable old Parisian institution created
by Louis Pedetos and made famous by Antoine Magnon,
you will be rewarded with copious portions of heartwarming food, some very good wine, and an experience
to add to your memory book.

RECOMMENDED DISHES

Foie Gras Frais de Landes. Fresh duck foie gras (three large
slices) from the Landes.

Grenouilles à la Provençale. Frogs' legs sautéed in olive oil with tomatoes, garlic, and olives.

Cèpes Rôtis en Saison. Roasted wild *cèpes* mushrooms (available fall to early spring).

Coquilles Saint-Jacques à la Provençale. Scallops sautéed with garlic and tomatoes (October to May).

Côte de Veau à la Crème. Grilled veal chop in a rich cream sauce accompanied by shoestring potatoes and mushrooms.

Poulet de Challans Rôti. Roasted free-range chicken with *pommes frites* (for two).

Côte de Boeuf Grillé avec Pommes Allumettes. Grilled ribs of beef with shoestring potatoes (for two).

Rognons de Veau Grillées à la Crème. Grilled veal kidney in a rich cream sauce.

Gigot d'Agneau de Lait Rôti. Roast leg and hind quarter of suckling lamb (spring only).

Gâteau au Chocolat Maison. Rich chocolate cake.

Extensive list of high-priced Burgundies and Bordeaux, but the house Beaujolais (Fleurie) is fine.

Au Bascou

M. Jean-Guy Loustau

38, rue Réaumur, 75003 (closest cross street, rue Volta) | Arts-et-Métiers

01-42-72-69-25 | Fax 01-42-72-69-25

Ø Saturday lunch and Sunday, August

$ $ |

Jean-Guy Loustau, a former sommelier who worked with Alain Dutournier at Trou Gascon and Carré-de-Feuillants, specializes in earthy Basque country cuisine and the best of the region's little-known wines.

M. Lousteau, who comes from the Basque village St-Jean-Pied-de-Port, insists on using only the best and the freshest regional products. The menu is small but choice. If you happen to be at Au Bascou in the winter, don't miss the delectable roasted baby lamb from the Pyrenees (available from November to March), served with a puree of white beans and potatoes and garnished with a slice of ham. The perfect way to begin a meal here is with a glass of Pacherenc du Vic-Bilh, a sweet white wine that is a nice aperitif to accompany a dish of finely spiced black and green olives and little slices of sausage and ham. The *pipérade* is a savory dish of scrambled eggs, sweet peppers, tomatoes, and onions served with cured ham. The *chipirons* are crisp baby squid served on a bed of rice; the red peppers from Espalette are roasted and stuffed with cod; and the braised beef with anchovies is accompanied by polenta and *cèpes* (mushrooms). The cheese appears under the name ardi gasna and consists of thin slices of provolone-type cheese aged for six months and served with a confit of cherries soaked in sherry. The dessert duo combines a slice of lemon custard pie with a slice of cherry pie and vanilla ice cream.

The atmosphere at Au Bascou is rather contemporary despite a few rustic touches: sunny ocher walls, beamed ceilings, large cracked-tile floors, and an odd assortment of chairs surrounding well-spaced tables covered in mauve linen. The restaurant was voted best bistro of the year in 1995 and is popular with both Parisians and tourists.

RECOMMENDED DISHES

Pipérade Basquaise. Beaten eggs with tomatoes, onions, sweet peppers, and Bayonne ham.

Pimentos del Piquillo Farcis. Grilled red peppers stuffed with a puree of salt cod.

Foie Gras Frais Maison de Canard. Homemade duck foie gras.

Axoa de Veau Comme à Espelette. Ground veal cooked with onions, garlic, and chili peppers.

Agneau de Lait des Pyrénées Rôti. Roast suckling lamb.

Chipirons Sautés à la Luzienne. Sautéed tiny squid on a bed of rice with minced almonds.

Morue Pil-Pil. Baked salt cod with garlic.

Lapin de Garenne en Crépinette, Lentilles et Chorizo. Stewed wild rabbit encased in a sausage membrane served with lentils and sliced chorizo sausage.

Fromage de Brebis et sa Confiture de Cerises. Sheep cheese with cherry preserves.

Duo de Gâteaux Basques. Pastry filled with custard and cherries.

➣ Extraordinary selection of Irouléguy wines from the Pays Basque. Also Jurançon and Pacherenc du Vic-Bilh.

MENU | Lunch 90 francs.

Le Hangar

MME. SYLVIE CERCUEL
CHEF: JACQUES ANTÈLME

12, impasse Berthaud, 75003 (in an alley next to the doll museum close to the Centre Georges Pompidou) | 🚌 Rambuteau

☎ 01-42-74-55-44

Ø Sunday and Monday lunch, August

$$ | ▭ NONE

👨‍🍳👨‍🍳 | ☀

idden behind a glass-screened terrace on a quiet impasse steps away from the frenetic pace of Beaubourg, Le Hangar once housed the carts that transported fruits and vegetables to the stalls of the old Les Halles markets. Today the owner, Sylvie Cercuel, welcomes an upscale clientele into an attractive modern interior nicely carpeted and brightened by many bouquets of flowers. All the tables are spaced comfortably apart and nicely appointed with white linen, little dishes of sea salt, and pepper mills.

Everything here is homemade, absolutely fresh, and exquisitely presented. Crunchy *haricots verts* are drizzled in olive oil, panfried foie gras is served on a creamy bed of lentils, little raviolis turn up in an eggplant cream sauce, fillet of beef is served in a rich sauce of *morilles,* risotto is served with tender pieces of asparagus and Parma ham, and fresh cod comes with eggplant caviar. A few sweet wines by the glass (sherry, *vin jaune,* Sauternes, and Jurançon moelleux) are suggested to accompany the stunning desserts. Fresh fruit *clafoutis* are cooked to order, and orange crepes are slathered in a sauce flavored with Grand Marnier; but the crowning dessert is a *gâteau* filled with warm chocolate that oozes over two small marbles of homemade vanilla ice cream, the whole dusted with confectioners' sugar.

RECOMMENDED DISHES

Foie Gras de Canard aux Lentilles. Fresh duck foie gras in a salad of creamed lentils.

Tartare de Saumon au Basilic. Raw chopped salmon garnished with onions, capers, and basil.

Bavarois d'Asperges aux Morilles. Fresh asparagus in a smooth custard with morel mushrooms.

Filet de Boeuf aux Morilles. Grilled tenderloin of beef in a brown mushroom sauce.

Morue Fraîche Poêlée. Fried salt cod with mashed potatoes.

Sauté de Veau au Citron, Riz Basmati. Veal lightly browned with lemon juice, accompanied by basmati rice.

Escalope de Foie Gras de Canard Poêlé, Purée à l'Huile d'Olive. Slice of panfried foie gras in a rich puree of mashed potatoes and olive oil.

Filet de Boeuf Stroganoff. Lean beef sautéed and served in a sour cream sauce with onions and mushrooms.

Petit Gâteau Mi-Cuit au Chocolat. Hot chocolate cake with melting chocolate center.

Glace au Lait de Brebis. Sheep's milk ice cream.

A wide variety of first-rate wines, over 60 in all, some of which are inexpensive.

Le Pamphlet

M. ALAIN CARRÈRE
M. FRED ARNIAUD
CHEF: ALAIN CARRÈRE

38, rue Debelleyme, 75003 (between rue de Bretagne and rue de Turenne) | 🚌 Filles-du-Calvaire

☎ 01-42-72-39-24

Ø Saturday and Sunday; August 8 through 23

$$ | VISA MasterCard

♟♟♟ | ☼

After cooking in several fine restaurants, including Ledoyen, chef Alain Carrère decided to open his own place and in 1998 created this lovely bistro, reminiscent of an inn one might find in his native city, Pau.

Two pretty dining areas are elegantly furnished with comfortably spaced round and square tables covered with peach linen. A Spanish bullfight theme is evident in nicely framed prints by Picasso, Cocteau, and Ducalle. Hanging red peppers, a display of regional products and wine, and fresh flowers are a colorful contrast to the dark ceiling beams and wainscoting.

The short "market menu" at 160 francs—four starters, four main courses, and desserts—demonstrates M. Carrère's genius at choosing fresh products and devising tantalizing combinations of meat, seafood, and vegetables. Each day Le Pamphlet offers a new soup, two fish and two meat choices, and fresh fruit tarts, fruit crumbles, and pots of vanilla cream, ice cream, and sorbet for dessert. Fresh pea soup is made with mussels or lobster, lentil soup with shrimp. Warm foie gras is made with apples; cooked cabbage may accompany skate one day and fillet of beef with reblochon cheese on another day; lemon sole may be served with cumin-scented carrots or asparagus, fresh cod with potatoes and chorizo sausage, lamb with zucchini and green peppers, and veal kidneys with a mousseline of celeric.

Le Pamphlet has already made a hit with Parisian gourmets, so reservations are advised.

RECOMMENDED DISHES

Raviolis de Tourteaux à la Crème de Pois Frais. Ravioli stuffed with crabmeat in a cream sauce with fresh peas.

Vinaigrette de Lentilles Saucisson Pistaché de Lyon Pissenlits en Salade. Lyonnaise sausage studded with pistachio nuts in a lentil salad dressed with vinaigrette and dandelion greens.

Poêlée de Pommes Granny Smith Escalopes de Foie Gras Rôtie, Jus de Cumin. Fried slices of green apples with roast sliced foie gras flavored with extract of caraway seeds.

Dos de Lieu Jaune Rôti Jeunes Carottes Cuisinées à la Truffe. Roast pollack cooked kitchen-style with baby carrots and truffles.

Parmentier de Pieds de Cochon. Baked casserole of suckling pig's feet and mashed potatoes.

Carré d'Agneau Rôti Polenta Crémeuse au Chèvre Frais. Roast rack of lamb with a creamy goat cheese polenta.

Foie de Veau Poêlé Fine Mousseline de Céleri. Panfried calf's liver, whipped puree of celery root.

Rôti de Cabillaud Ecrasée de Pommes de Terre à l'Andouille Basque. Roast fresh cod with crushed potatoes accompanied by a Basque pork sausage.

Onglet de Boeuf d'Aubrac Poêlé et sa Truffade de Pommes de Terre. Pan-cooked skirt steak with an Auvergne pancake made of shredded potato and *tomme* cheese.

Ananas Caramélisé aux Épices, Glace Vanille. Caramelized pineapple slices with spices and homemade vanilla ice cream.

➤ Small but moderately priced and well-selected wine list.

MENUS-CARTES | Lunch 120 francs, dinner 160 francs.

4e ARRONDISSEMENT

BARACANE (BISTROT DE L'OULETTE)

BENOÎT

AU BOURGUIGNON DU MARAIS

LES FOUS D'EN FACE

LE GRIZZLI

LE VIEUX BISTRO

HÔTEL DE VILLE

PLACES OF INTEREST

Bastille ("July Column")

Cathédrale de Notre-Dame (Musée Notre-Dame)

Centre Pompidou (Beaubourg)

Eglise Saints Gervais et Protais

Église St-Paul–St-Louis

Hôtels de Sully, Sens, Beauvais, Lambert,
Lauzin, Aumont

Hôtel de Ville

Île de la Cité

Île St-Louis

Marais (southern half)

Musée Victor Hugo

Odéon (Théâtre de France)

Place des Vosges (3e, 4e)

Pont Marie

Baracane (Bistrot de l'Oulette)

M. Marcel Baudis
M. Alain Fontaine
Chef: Alain Fontaine

38, rue Tournelles, 75004 (close to place des Vosges) |
🚌 Bastille or Chemin Vert
☎ 01-42-71-43-33 | Fax 01-40-02-04-77
Ø Saturday lunch and Sunday
$ | VISA MasterCard

🍳

Just a few steps from the magnificent place des Vosges, this small, narrow unpretentious bistro specializes in the wines and hearty food of the southwest. Marcel Baudis and his partner, Alain Fontaine, have conceived a winning combination of menus that offer tremendous value for the money. The least expensive, at 52 francs (available at lunch only), includes the *plat du jour* from the daily slate with wine and coffee. The 82-franc menu adds an entrée and dessert. The most expensive formula is a three-course menu-carte, which begins with an aperitif and includes a half bottle of wine per person and coffee. The wine list, although short, is wisely conceived, with regional wines offered to complement the food. You might choose a Madiran to accompany the grilled duck breast or duck confit with parsley potatoes, a Cahors to go along with the *cassoulet,* and the Pacherenc du Vic-Bihl sec as the perfect match for the grilled sea bream with fennel and tomatoes.

There are no surprises here, but if you plan to be in the vicinity of the place des Vosges, Baracane is the perfect place for an inexpensive lunch. It is always crowded, so you will need a reservation.

RECOMMENDED DISHES

Salade Quercynoise Aux Gésiers Confits. Regional salad with duck gizzards and hearts.

Hure de Cochon Fait Maison, Vinaigrette aux Herbes. Home-made pork headcheese in an herbed oil and vinegar dressing.

Tartare de Maquereaux, Crème de Moutarde. Chopped fresh mackerel in a mustard cream sauce.

Magret de Canard des Landes Rôti. Grilled fattened duck breast.

Cassoulet Maison aux Confits. Toulouse-style casserole ragout with preserved duck and goose and beans from Tarbes in the Pyrenees.

Poêlée d'Encornets "à la Catalane." Panfried squid with olive oil, tomatoes, eggplant, garlic, and red pepper.

Daube de Boeuf. Braised beef stew with vegetables.

Confit de Canard, Pommes de Terre Persillées. Preserved duck with sliced potatoes seasoned with chopped parsley and garlic.

Pavé de Rumsteck aux Échalotes Confites. Thick piece of grilled beef with a shallot sauce.

Tourtière aux Pommes. Landes apple tart.

Nougat Glace aux Mendiants. Nougat ice cream in a dessert of raisins, figs, hazelnuts, and almonds.

Cahors (Château la Coustarelle), Tursan (Gascon de Dulucq), Gaillac (Domaine des Terrisses), Pacherenc du Vic-Bihl Sec (Domaine de Diusse).

MENUS | Lunch 82 francs; lunch or dinner "market menu" 135 francs.

MENU-CARTE | 215 francs including aperitif, wine, and coffee.

Benoît

M. Michel Petit

20, rue St-Martin, 75004 (close to place Georges
   Pompidou) | 🚇 Châtelet-Les-Halles or
   Hôtel-de-Ville
☎ 01-42-72-25-76 | Fax 01-42-72-45-68
∅ August
$$$$ | 💳
🍲🍲🍲

Opened in 1912 and still run by the same family,
Benoît continues to be one of the smartest and
most expensive bistros in Paris, still maintaining
a modest old-world charm and a Michelin star. Benoît,
with its polished wood facade and red-and-gold awning,
was once surrounded by the old Les Halles produce markets but now stands in the middle of a trendy pedestrian
mall. Inside, light oak paneling is set off with mirrors, old
photographs, plush red banquettes, brass railings, and parquet floors. Lots of fresh flowers and potted plants are
scattered throughout the two rooms. A marble bar at the
entrance glistens with glasses and bottles.

The menu, which arrives in an old leather frame, lists
seasonal specialties and superb classic dishes inspired by
Lyonnaise cuisine. Garlicky burgundy snails and a *ballottine* of duck fois gras head the list of hors d'oeuvres. There
are steaming tureens of crab or mussel soup, creamy
and delicious. The plates that follow are a roster of traditional bourgeois fare interpreted with a lighter touch than
you might expect—beef made in rich red wine, poached
chicken with mounds of morel mushrooms, saddle of
lamb, knuckle of veal provençal, and a casserole of duck.
The seasonal specialties are more contemporary—a salad
of medallions of langouste and artichoke hearts stuffed

with an artichoke mousse, a sauté of scallops on a puree of potatoes, and chicken cooked in salt crust accompanied by *beurre blanc* and asparagus. Lavish desserts include a frozen Grand Marnier soufflé. The short wine list is as expensive as everything else.

RECOMMENDED DISHES

Compotier de Boeuf en Salade à la Parisienne. Beef salad with a varied choice of hors d'oeuvres.

Soupe de Moules. Copious tureen of mussel soup.

Ballottine de Canard au Foie Gras. Boned duck rolled and stuffed with foie gras.

Boeuf Mode Braisé à l'Ancienne aux Carottes. Marinated beef braised in Beaujolais wine with carrots, onions, and root vegetables.

Rognon de Veau Entier en Cocotte. Veal kidney pot-roasted in a casserole.

Cassoulet Maison. White bean and meat stew cooked and served in a large earthenware casserole.

Blanquette de Veau. Veal stew in a white cream sauce.

Steak de Lotte au Poivre. Baked monkfish steak in a demi-glace whole peppercorn sauce.

Boeuf à la Ficelle. Beef tied with a string and poached in broth.

Poulet Fermier en Croûte de Sel. Free-range chicken cooked in a salt crust, garnished with asparagus, and accompanied by *beurre blanc* sauce.

Gâteau à la Ganache. Rich chocolate cake with its ganache of heavy cream, butter, and liqueur flavoring.

Soufflé Glacé au Grand Marnier. Frozen Grand Marnier soufflé.

Chiroubles, Morgon, Brouilly; except for the Beaujolais, the *carte* can be pricey.

MENU | Lunch 200 francs.

Au Bourguignon du Marais

M. Jacques Bavard
Mme. Christine Bavard

52, rue François-Miron, 75004 (off rue de Rivoli at rue
   Tiron) | 🚋 St-Paul or Pont Marie
☎ 01-48-87-15-40 | Fax 01-48-87-17-49
Ø Saturday and Sunday; middle of July through middle
   of August
$$ | [cards]
☕ | 🍷

Jacques Bavard, who hails from Puligny-Montra-
chet, has created a chic wine bistro dedicated exlu-
sively to the region of Burgundy. An amazing
selection of bottles from the Côte de Beaune and the Côte
de Nuits line the shelves of this wineshop-cum-restaurant
frequented by an upscale Marais clientele.

Blond wood wainscoting, nicely spaced tables decked
out with cheerful red napkins, and wicker armchairs make
for a relaxed and casual atmosphere. Candles in tin table
lanterns add a festive touch in the evening.

The regular menu is straightforward with regional
accents: eggs poached in wine sauce, parsleyed ham, Bur-
gundian snails, *andouillettes* in an Aligoté wine sauce with
duck confit, and steak always on hand. There is also a daily
blackboard menu offering fresh and seasonal suggestions,
which might include six oysters, a Breton lobster salad, a
fricassee of *cèpe* and *girolle* mushrooms, langoustine served
with ratatouille, turbot on a bed of leeks with a saffron
sauce, and vension in the fall. The special cheese is a strong,
creamy Burgundian cheese known as *Époisses*.

Wine is available by the glass and bottle. If you choose
something from the shop to accompany your meal, there

is a small corkage charge. One final note—the rules of the house require all cell phones to be turned off.

RECOMMENDED DISHES

Six Escargots de Bourgogne Ail et Persil. Six Burgundian snails served in their shells with garlic butter and parsley.

Oeufs Pochés en Meurette. Eggs poached in red Burgundy sauce with onions, carrots, bacon, and mushrooms.

Foie Gras de Canard Mi-Cuit. Half-cooked house foie gras.

Jambon Persillé Maison. Cubes of cooked ham in parsleyed aspic.

Andouillette de Simon Duval à L'Aligot. Grilled tripe pork sausage from Duval served with *aligot* cheese and pureed potatoes.

Tartare de Rumsteak Cru ou Poêlé. Steak tartare or grilled steak with *pommes frites.*

Confit de Canard. Grilled preserved duck legs and thighs.

Noisettes de Filet de Chevreuil. Small tender venison fillets (available in game season).

Marquise au Chocolat. Mousse-like dessert made with melted chocolate and butter to which beaten egg yolks and whites are folded in.

Crème Brûlée. Rich cream-based custard burned under the grill to form a hard coating of caramel.

All-Burgundy selection brought directly in from the vineyards. Many are available by the glass.

Les Fous d'en Face

M. PHILIPPE LLORCA

3, rue du Bourg-Tibourg, 75004 (off rue de Rivoli) |
🚋 Hôtel-de-Ville
☎ 01-48-87-03-75 | Fax 01-42-78-38-03
∅ Open every day, all year
$$ | 𝗩𝗜𝗦𝗔 MasterCard
🥘 | 🍷

I n the summer everyone tries to get a table on the
lovely terrace of Phillippe Llorca's rustic wine bistro
situated on a leafy square near the Hôtel de Ville.
Tourists and residents from the nearby Marais vie for the
dozen or so tables gaily set with red-and-white cloths and
surrounded by huge potted plants and flowers.

M. Llorca is passionate about his food and wine and
encourages his customers to experiment by taking advan-
tage of the many interesting wines offered by the glass. He
might suggest a vin jaune with the foie gras or a hearty
Corsican red to accompany the delicious Corsican and
Spanish ham carved directly from the bone. Much of the
large menu is oriented around unpretentious bistro fare:
country terrines, onion soup, fricassees of rabbit or chicken,
roast leg of lamb, a tasty bavette steak, and a substantial
pot-au-feu. Seasonal fish and vegetables are offered as *plats
du jour,* and there are some very good cheeses. During the
winter, the interior rooms house a changing art exhibition
and are always crowded with regular customers, so reser-
vations are suggested in the evenings.

RECOMMENDED DISHES

Assiette de Charcuteries. Outstanding selection of ham,
sausages, and pork pâtés.

Oeufs Cocotte au Bleu-d'Auvergne. Eggs cooked and served in an individual dish with butter, cream, and blue cheese.

Foie Gras de Canard Maison. Generous serving of fattened duck liver pâté.

Pot-au-Feu. Slowly cooked dish of meat and root vegetables presented in two services: first the seasoned broth, followed by the boiled beef and vegetables.

Magret de Canard au Citron Vert. Grilled fattened duck breast with lime.

Filet de Sandre aux Amandes. Baked pike perch with almonds.

Fricassée de Lapin aux Tagliatelles Safranées. Rabbit stewed in a white cream sauce accompanied by tagliatelli (pasta).

Tian d'Agneau à la Crème d'Ail. Lamb stew in a potato and vegetable gratin in garlic cream sauce.

Gratin au Miel et Fruits de Saison. Casserole of fresh fruits and honey baked until a golden crust forms on the surface.

Clafoutis aux Cerises, Sauce Griotte. Traditional batter tart with cherries, covered in a dark bitter cherry sauce.

➤ Very adventurous selection of more than 180 country wines, many available by the glass.

MENUS | Lunch 85 francs and 109 francs.

Le Grizzli

M. BERNARD ARÉNY

7, rue St-Martin, 75004 (close to Tour St-Jacques) |
🚌 Châtelet or Hôtel-de-Ville

☎ 01-48-87-77-56

∅ Sunday

$$ | 🔳 VISA MasterCard

🍲🍲

Originally opened in 1902, this authentic belle epoque bistro (only a stone's throw from Benoît) gets its name from the little grizzly bears at the foot of the nearby Tour St-Jacques. As you enter the two-level interior, you are keenly aware of the historic surroundings. There are cream-colored mirrored walls, green moleskin banquettes, lace curtains, and on top of a lovely old zinc bar a delicious smoked ham from the Auvergne is being sliced.

Bernard A</br>ény, who became the proprietor in 1990, takes great pride in the consistency of his fine menu, which has never declined in quality or changed very much over the years. The cold ratatouille (an appetizer) is still topped with a warm poached egg; the tender lamb stew is still served with carrots, turnips, and *cèpes* (mushrooms); and the roast guinea hen is still served with braised cabbage. For those who come here for meat, the favorites remain lamb and beef cooked Ardoise-style, on a slate, the way they are still prepared in the Auvergne. Salmon and sole are also cooked à l'Ardoise. There is a savory dessert croustade filled with prunes and doused in Armagnac; but many regulars opt for the perfectly aged farm-raised Saint-Nectaire cheese, slices of crusty rye bread, and a pitcher of Côte du Marmandais—a pleasant, soft, fruity wine from the Lot region.

In the summer, dinner on the terrace of this old Les Halles classic is a picturesque and lovely way to spend an evening.

RECOMMENDED DISHES

Terrine de Canard aux Noisettes et Confiture d'Oignons. Duck pâté with hazelnuts served in an earthenware terrine.

Jambon au Couteau. Smoked Auvergne ham, sliced off the bone.

Foie Gras de Canard. Duck foie gras.

Fricot de Veau aux Cèpes Séchés. Veal shoulder stew simmered with dried *cèpes* (mushrooms), white wine, herbs, and vegetables.

Cassoulet aux Haricots Tarbais. A casserole of broad beans, sausage, duck, and mutton.

Agneau de Lait des Pyrénées. Roast milk-fed baby lamb (served in the spring).

Confit de Canard, Pommes Sautées à l'Ail. Grilled preserved duck with sautéed sliced potatoes and garlic.

Faux-Filet de Boeuf Cuit sur l'Ardoise. Thick sirloin steak cooked over the fire on a slate.

Saumon à l'Ardoise. Salmon grilled over the fire on a slate.

Saint-Nectaire—Brebis des Pyrénées. Two outstanding farm cheeses from the Pyrenees.

Croustade Chaude aux Pruneaux à l'Armagnac. Hot pastry filled with prunes and flamed with Armagnac brandy.

Madiran (Château Peyros), Buzet (Baron d'Ardeuil), Corbières (Château Cros), Bergerac blanc (Domaine de Conti).

MENUS　|　Lunch 120 francs, dinner 160 francs.

Le Vieux Bistro

M. Éric Trompier

14, rue du Cloître-Notre-Dame, 75004 (opposite Notre Dame cathedral)　|　Cité

☎ 01-43-54-18-95　|　Fax 01-44-07-35-63

Ø Open every day, all year

$ $ $　|　VISA MasterCard

In December 1999, Éric Trompier, who owns the highly acclaimed seafood restaurant Le Marée (8e), took over this wonderful old bistro with the intention of refreshing the decor but maintaining the quality and fine traditional cuisine for which it is renowned.

Standing in the shadow of Notre Dame cathedral, Le Vieux Bistro personifies the refinements of the past. The small front room is a quiet refuge hidden from the noisy street and the dozens of souvenir stands filled with tourists. The larger room in the back is beautifully furnished with original mirrors, dark wood paneling, and comfortable banquettes.

The menu is a roster of time-honored renditions: Lyonnaise sausages, Baltic herring in cream, Burgundian snails, Provençal scallops, calf's liver sautéed in raspberry vinegar, fillet of beef flamed in cognac, homemade profiteroles drizzled with hot dark chocolate, and a perfect tart Tatin flamed in Calvados and served with *crème fraîche.*

Evenings feature candlelight and well-dressed Parisians.

RECOMMENDED DISHES

Harengs de la Baltique, Crème Fraîche. Fillets of Baltic herring in cream.

Pâté De Tête à l'Ancienne Maison. Terrine of calf's head pâté in aspic.

Rillettes de Saumon et ses Toasts. Cubed pieces of salmon cooked with herbs pounded in a mortar and preserved, accompanied by toast.

Boeuf Bourguignon. Beef chunks cooked in red wine with bacon, small onions, and mushrooms.

Coeur de Filet de Boeuf à la Moelle. Beef fillet of mignon garnished with poached bone marrow (for two).

Foie de Veau au Vinaigre de Framboise. Calf's liver sautéed in raspberry vinegar.

Carré d'Agneau à la Provençale. Roast rack of lamb with tomatoes, garlic, and olives (for two).

Coquilles Saint-Jacques Fraîches à la Provençale. Scallops
   sautéed in olive oil, white wine, and garlic.

Profiteroles au Chocolat Chaud Maison. Small pastry balls
   made with *chou* paste encased in meltingly hot bittersweet chocolate.

Tarte Tatin Maison Flambée au Calvados et sa Crème Fraîche.
   Upside-down apple cake flamed at the table with Calvados. Accompanied by a thick, rich, sweetened cream
   sauce.

Nice selection of *grands crus* of Bordeaux and Burgundy, Brouilly, Fleurie, Saint-Nicholas-de-Bourgueil,
Sancerre.

5ᵉ ARRONDISSEMENT

LES FONTAINES

MAUZAC

MOISSONNIER

LE RÉMINET

CHEZ RENÉ

CHEZ TOUTOUNE

QUARTIER LATIN– PANTHÉON

PLACES OF INTEREST

Boulevard St-Michel (Place St-Michel)

Institut du Monde Arabe

Jardin des Plantes et Musée National d'Histoire Naturelle

La Mosquée de Paris (mosque)

Musée de l'École Supérieure des Beaux-Arts

Musée de Sculpture en Plein Air

Musée des Thermes et l'Hôtel de Cluny (Cluny Museum)

Panthéon

Rue Mouffetard and Place de la Contrescarpe

Sorbonne

Val-de-Grâce

Les Fontaines

M. Jean-Marie Plas-Debecker

9, rue Soufflot, 75005 (at place du Panthéon) |
🚋 Maubert-Mutualité or R.E.R. Luxembourg
☎ 01-43-26-42-80 | Fax 01-44-07-03-49
Ø Sunday; first three weeks in August
$$ | VISA MasterCard

🍲🍲

Many knowledgeable Parisian gourmets breathed a sigh of relief when the new owner-chef, Jean-Marie Plas-Debecker, successfully took over this nondescript neighborhood café, which they had come to know as one of the best values in the city for traditional cuisine. Nowhere can you find better cuts of aged prime meats or game, with portions so generous that they are served on platters rather than plates.

The former owner, Roger Lacipière, spent several months before the turnover introducing M. Plas-Debecker to all his kitchen secrets, sharing his recipes, and taking him out to the wholesale markets in Rungis to personally acquaint him with his well-cultivated resources for meats, seafood, and cheeses.

Selecting a meal at Les Fontaines can be a challenge since there are at least 20 meat and fish preparations alone; but some special dishes stand out. The most popular meats are the fabulous *côte de boeuf* (ribs of beef), the *steak au poivre,* and the panfried veal kidneys in either sherry or mustard sauce. The favorite fish dishes are the fricassee of monkfish with herbs and the famous fifteen-spice Saint-Pierre.

First-time visitors should not be put off by the plastic, chrome, and neon decor: once you are introduced to it, we assure you that this popular bistro will be on your short list of favorites.

RECOMMENDED DISHES

Terrine de Foie Gras de Canard Maison. Duck foie gras served in an earthenware terrine.

Salade de Homard. Lobster salad.

Steak Tartare, Frites. Raw seasoned ground beef with *pommes frites.*

Côte de Boeuf. Roast ribs of beef (for two).

Gigot d'Agneau de Limousin Rôti aux Herbes. Roast leg of lamb with herbs.

Rognons de Veau Dijonnaise. Panfried veal kidneys in a mayonnaise-like mustard sauce.

Escalope de Saumon au Confit d'Échalotes. Thin slices of salmon with preserved shallots.

Pigeon Farci aux Champignons de Bois. Squab stuffed with wild mushrooms.

Tarte aux Pommes à l'Ancienne. Sliced cooked apples in a pastry crust.

Crème Brûlée à l'Ancienne. Cream-based custard with topping of brown sugar burned under the grill to form a hard caramel crust.

Roussillon rouge (Sarda-Malet), Anjou (Pierre Blanche), Côtes de Bourg (Château de la Tour Bidou).

Mauzac

M. Jean-Michel Delhoume
Mme. Christine Delhoume
Chef: Laurent Guillard

7, rue de l'Abbé-de-l'Épée, 75005 (between rue St-Jacques
and rue Gay-Lussac) | 🚃 R.E.R. Luxembourg
☎ 01-46-33-75-22
∅ Saturday evening and Sunday; three weeks in August
$ | VISA MasterCard
☕ | 🍷

When Jean-Michel Delhoume and his wife, Christine, moved from their former wine bar, Les Pipos,
into their delightful new bistro, they brought
with them not only a passion for wine and tasty country
food but also a substantial following of loyal customers.

Mauzac takes its name from a grape variety found in
the Gaillac region of the southwest, so it is not surprising
to find several of the sparkling white wines of that region
on the wine list. M. Delhoume was awarded the coveted
Coupe de Meilleur Pot in 1993, honoring his expertise as
a bistrotier (wine bar owner) who is dedicated to find-
ing, promoting, and bottling country wines from small
producers.

Mauzac is located on a quiet, tree-lined square near the
Luxembourg Gardens; its brightly lit interior is decorated
with 1950s-style tables, many pieces of bric-a-brac, and
such fanciful touches as Ionic pilasters and a rectangular
wall pillar disguised as a tree. The cooking is handled by a
young chef, Laurent Guillard, whose hearty specialties
include terrines, regional sausages, thick soups, stews, shepherd's pie, and juicy steaks accompanied by tapenade and
homemade *frites*. Dinner, which is served on Thursday
and Friday, is by reservation only. If you decide to visit,

don't fail to strike up a conversation with the convivial host, who will guide you to his latest discoveries and will be pleased to take you through his entertaining wine cellar.

RECOMMENDED DISHES

Terrine de Foie Gras et son Céleri Fondant. Foie gras served in an earthenware terrine topped by a celery croquette.

Mouclade de Bouchot. Mussels cooked in white wine with parsley and shallots and served in their sauce with cream, egg yolk, and butter added.

Filets de Harengs et Pommes à l'Huile. Marinated herring fillets with sliced potatoes in oil.

Entrecôte à la Moelle, Pomme au Four. Grilled beef rib steak garnished with bone marrow sauce and accompanied by a baked potato.

Parmentier de Queue de Boeuf, Salade Verte. Shepherd's pie: minced oxtail and mashed potatoes baked in a casserole, also made with blood sausage (*boudin noir*); accompanied by a green salad.

Carré d'Agneau à la Crème d'Ail. Lamb stew in a creamy garlic sauce with baby vegetables.

Blanquette de Veau. Veal stew in a white sauce thickened with egg yolks and cream.

Dorade à l'Huile d'Olive Pommes Écrasées. Sea bream cooked in olive oil and accompanied by crushed potatoes.

Clafoutis aux Cerises. Black cherry batter tart, a specialty of the Limousin region.

Crumble aux Pommes. Apple crumble.

Mauzac (Robert Plageole), Touraine (Puzelat), Anjou (Angeli), Coteaux du Layon (Lecointre), Minervois (Clos de l'Escandil).

Moissonnier

M. PHILIPPE MAYET

28, rue des Fossés-St-Bernard, 75005 (between boulevard
   St-Germain and rue Jussieu) |
   🚌 Cardinal-Lemoine or Jussieu
☎ 01-43-29-87-65
∅ Sunday evening; Monday, August
$ $ $ | 💳 💳
☞

I t looks as though the very experienced young chef,
Philippe Mayet, who has taken over this venerable
Lyonnaise bistro will be able to return it to its former
brilliance. Already, without materially changing the decor
or the specialties, he seems to have infused the place with
new spirit and energy. The food has been brought up a
notch or two, and the welcome provided by Mme. Mayet
is warm and inviting. Don't, however, be seated in the
tacky room upstairs, where it can be hot, noisy, and
smoky. The downstairs room is more upbeat, with fresh
flowers, pleasant lighting, a high ceiling, and comfortable
banquettes.

The house specialties written in red ink on the menu
list among the entrées a daunting selection called *saladiers
lyonnais*—12 meat, fish, and vegetable dishes rolled to your
table on a trolley. Heaping bowls of terrines, rillettes,
sausages, herring in cream sauce, potatoes in oil, Greek
mushrooms, pickled calf's feet, and beef with greens are
among the choices. If you wish to try one of the wonderful and copious Lyonnaise specialties, skip the salads—
which are very filling—and order the chicken liver terrine
or the *brési,* the air-dried beef from the Franche-Compté;
then go on to the pan-roasted skirt steak, the classic *tablier
de sapeur* (breaded tripe), the *boeuf miroton* (sliced boiled

beef with onions), the pike dumplings, or the blood sausage (*boudin noir*) with fried apples.

The Beaujolais wines served in the "pot" bottles are fine, and lately some lovely Jura wines have been added to the carte.

RECOMMENDED DISHES

Saucisson Chaud Pommes à l'Huile. Large hot Lyonnaise sausage, sliced thin and served with potato salad in olive oil.

Oeufs en Meurette. Eggs poached in red wine with pieces of bacon and tiny onions.

Saladiers Lyonnais. Variety of meat, fish, and vegetable salads.

Quenelle de Brochet Soufflé Maison. Seasoned pike dumplings in cream sauce.

Boeuf Miroton. Sliced leftover beef and sautéed onions topped with Lyonnaise sauce.

Petit Salé aux Lentilles. Lean salt pork with lentils.

Tablier de Sapeur Sauce Gribiche. Ox tripe dipped in egg and bread crumbs and grilled.

Onglet Poêlé à la Lyonnaise. Panfried flank steak with sautéed onions in white wine sauce.

Oeufs en Neige. Composed dessert of meringue poached in milk and served with custard sauce.

Gâteau de Riz. Molded rice pudding.

Mâcon-Villages blanc, Chiroubles, Beaujolais (Louis Tête).

MENU | Lunch 150 francs.

Le Réminet

M. Hugues Gournay

3, rue des Grands-Degrés, 75005 (off the quai de
    Montebello) | 🚋 Maubert-Mutualité
☎ 01-44-07-04-24 | Fax 01-44-07-17-37
Ø Monday and Tuesday lunch; first three weeks of
    January and last two weeks of August
$$ | VISA ●
♟♟♟ | ☼

L
e Réminet is only steps away from the Seine in
the shadow of Notre Dame cathedral. It is quite a
surprise to find this little oasis of calm surrounded
by fast-food eateries packed with tourists. Le Réminet
(meaning "the small rooster") is the concept of a talented
young couple, Hugues and Anne Gournay, who in a very
short time have attracted a fanatical group of supporters
who would be happy to keep this little gourmet inn to
themselves.

The minuscule restaurant is installed in a sixteenth-
century structure modernized to some extent by the
Lampréia brothers, who later departed for the 15e arron-
dissement. When the Gournays took over in 1997, they
painted the inviting facade a deep wine color and set about
decorating the ancient stone interior with elegant mirrors,
four baroque crystal chandeliers, red velvet, and ten small
tables to seat 25. Recently, because of Le Réminet's great
popularity, a vaulted room in the basement was reno-
vated, doubling the size of the bistro.

Chef Gournay was classically trained and made a name
for himself at the Hyde Park Hotel in London. He is noted
for a fusion of traditional provincial French foods with
ideas picked up from his travels in Asia. He combines

preserved ginger, hot Szechwan pepper, saffron, fresh Provençal herbs, cumin, and truffles in his earthy yet sophisticated cuisine. Cooked carpaccio of tuna with ginger, shrimp sautéed in garlic butter sprinkled with chicory, blue cheese and walnuts, duck breast with prunes, crusty tarts of pig's trotters, beef fillets in béarnaise sauce with tomato puree, and scallops stewed with morel mushrooms are just a few of the tempting possibilities. The deceptively simple desserts are delicious, and the coffee is served with exquisite little meringues.

RECOMMENDED DISHES

Foie Gras de Canard Mi-Cuit en Terrine. Semicooked home-made duck foie gras in an earthenware terrine.

Galette de Râpé de Pommes de Terre et Saumon Fumé Crème Fouettée aux Oeufs de Saumon et Ciboulette. Potato pancake with smoked salmon and whipped cream with red caviar and onions.

Tarte Fine au Caviar d'Aubergine Gambas Sautées. Thin tart filled with mashed eggplant and sautéed jumbo shrimp.

Poêlée de Saint-Jacques aux Têtes de Morilles et Monbazillac. Panfried scallops with mushroom heads and sweet white wine.

Joues de Porc Braisées Sauce au Xérès Carottes Vichy. Braised pig's cheeks in sherry sauce with sliced carrots, reduced to a syrupy consistency, garnished with chopped parsley.

Dos de Lapin au Boudin Noir. Roast saddle of rabbit and blood sausage.

Rouget Poêlé avec Pipérade de Courgettes et Aubergines. Panfried red mullet with eggplant and zucchini sautéed in oil with tomatoes and onions.

Magret de Canard aux Pruneaux avec son Écrasée de Radis Noir Ailée. Duck breast with prunes and mashed radishes flavored with garlic.

Crème Brûlée aux Gousses de Vanille Bourbon. Cream custard caramelized with flavored vanilla beans.

Nougat Glace aux Mendiants Coulis d'Abricots. Nougat ice
   cream on a dessert of raisins, figs, and hazelnuts with a
   puree of apricots.

🥄 Sancerre, Bourgogne Aligoté, Bergerac rouge,
   Madiran.

MENUS | Lunch 85 francs, dinner 110 francs.

Chez René

M. JEAN-PAUL CINQUIN

14, boulevard St-Germain, 75005 (at rue du Cardinal
   Lemoine off quai de la Tournelle) |
   🚇 Maubert-Mutualité or Cardinal-Lemoine
☎ 01-43-54-30-23 | Fax 01-43-26-43-92
Ø Saturday lunch and Sunday; August
$$$ | VISA
🍳🍳

This fine old Burgundian bistro was created by
   the father of present owner, Jean-Paul Cinquin, in
   1957, partly as an outlet for the splendid wines
grown in the family's extensive vineyards in Beaujolais.
Since that time nothing has changed. The kindly waiters
in long aprons, the moleskin banquettes, the lumpy sau-
sages hanging from the ceiling, the handsome mirrors, the
simple wooden bistro tables and chairs, and the darkening
cream-colored walls seem frozen in time.

The unvarying *plats du jour* and grand Burgundian à la
carte classics are still cooked in the original copper pots
and pans in an unrenovated kitchen with absolute fidel-
ity to the original recipes created by Mme. René. These
include a homey *coq au vin* cooked in Burgundy, a heady
rich *boeuf bourguignon*, a thick *entrecôte Bercy* with sautéed

potatoes, a tender rosy rack of lamb for two, succulent frogs' legs, a wonderful gratin of Swiss chard, and a down-to-earth rice pudding in a pool of caramel. With such fine nostalgic food, the only thing to drink is a house Beaujolais, either the Chénas or the Juliénas. The owners are always ready with a friendly welcome, and you will be sent on your way with fond memories of a bygone era.

RECOMMENDED DISHES

Assiette de Cochonnailles. Assorted pork sausages and pâtés.

Rillettes de Canard Fumées. Smoked, shredded duck used as a spread.

Cuisses de Grenouilles Fraîches à la Provençale. Fresh frogs' legs sautéed in olive oil with tomatoes, onions, and garlic.

Coq au Vin. Cockerel cooked in thickened Beaujolais wine with mushrooms, onions, and bacon chunks.

Boeuf Bourguignon, Tagliatelles Fraîches. Beef cooked in Beaujolais with button mushrooms, pearl onions, and bacon, accompanied by fresh noodles.

Entrecôte Bercy, Pommes Sautées. Broiled rib steak in a shallot sauce with white wine, lemon juice, and butter, sautéed sliced potatoes (for two).

Carré d'Agneau Garni. Rack of lamb (for two).

Quenelles de Brochet à la Crème. Poached pike dumplings in cream sauce.

Gâteau de Riz. Molded rice pudding cake with vanilla sauce.

Profiteroles. Small pastries filled with vanilla ice cream and covered with hot bitter chocolate sauce.

Beaujolais of the patron "Louise Cinquin."

MENU-CARTE | Lunch 170 francs.

Chez Toutoune

MME. COLETTE DEJEAN

5, rue de Pontoise, 75005 (between quai de la Tournelle
   and boulevard St-Germain) |
   🚋 Maubert-Mutualité
☎ 01-43-26-56-81 | Fax 01-40-46-80-34
Ø Monday lunch; August
$ $ $ | 💳 VISA 💳
♟

C hefs come and go, but the indomitable Toutoune
   (Colette Dejean) runs her ship with astonishing
   consistency, and her regulars are as loyal as any
in Paris.

The decor of Chez Toutoune reflects the shimmering
Provençal landscape—brilliant sunshine and yellow flowers. The cuisine, sometimes delicate, sometimes powerful, is always true to its regional origins, with many dishes
touched with olives, sweet tomatoes, pungent garlic, peppers, onions, eggplant, artichokes, rosemary, and thyme.
Once you are comfortably seated in the little country dining room, you will choose your meal from the 198-franc
menu-carte, which always begins with a soup course
served from a large *soupière* with as many additional helpings as you desire. Starters generally include country terrines, salads, foie gras, snail, and raw salmon. The main
courses feature hearty stews in winter and a variety of
Provençal meat and fish dishes the rest of the year. The
fourth and last course is a choice between the goat cheese
platter and the selection of cakes, tarts, ice cream, and
stewed fruits from the dessert list. The wine carte is rather
varied, with a number of expensive Bordeaux wines; but
there are some lovely wines from Côtes de Provence and

Bandol that are both affordable and perfect complements to this sort of cooking.

RECOMMENDED DISHES

Caviar d'Aubergine au Jambon Serrano et Oeuf Poché. Mashed eggplant with cured, smoked ham slices topped with a poached egg.

Supions Sautés à la Coriandre. Tiny squid sautéed in coriander.

Terrine de Lapin à la Sarriette, Maison. Rabbit pâté flavored with summer sage.

Carrée d'Agneau, Rôti au Thym, Purée aux Olives Vertes. Roast rack of lamb with thyme and green olive puree.

Onglet de Veau Sauté aux Citrons Confits et Pâtes Fraîches. Veal flank sautéed with preserved lemons accompanied by fresh noodles.

Noix de Saint-Jacques Blondies Tomates Fraîches, Ail, et Persil. Grilled scallops and tomatoes flavored with garlic and parsley.

Morue Fraîche en Aioli et ses Légumes. Fresh cod served with garlic mayonnaise and fresh vegetables.

Petite Marmite de Provence aux Poissons du Marché. A hearty Provençale fish soup selected in the market according to availability.

Tarte Chaude au Chocolat Glace aux Truffes. Hot tart with chocolate ice cream and bittersweet chocolate truffles.

Petits Chèvres au Lait Cru. Assortment of farm-fresh goat cheese made from raw milk.

Côtes de Provence, Bandol, Loire Valley.

MENUS-CARTES | Lunch 138 francs, dinner 198 francs.

6ᵉ ARRONDISSEMENT

ALLARD

LA BASTIDE ODÉON

LES BOOKINISTES

AUX CHARPENTIERS

CHEZ DUMONET (JOSÉPHINE)

L'ÉPI DUPIN

CHEZ MAÎTRE PAUL

MARIE ET FILS

LA RÔTISSERIE D'EN FACE

WADJA

ST-GERMAIN–LUXEMBOURG

PLACES OF INTEREST

Boulevard St-Germain, Place St-Germain,
and Église St-Germain-des-Prés

École des Beaux-Arts and Hôtel de Conti

Église St-Suplice (Delacroix mural)

Fontaine des Medicis

Institut de France

Jardin et Palais du Luxembourg
(Musée Luxembourg)

Musée Zadkine

Place Furstenberg
(Atelier Eugène Delacroix)

Place de l'Odéon

Rues de Seine, St-André-des-Arts,
Buci, Jacob

Allard

M. Claude Layrac

41, rue St-André-des-Arts, 75006 (on the corner of rue
   de l'Éperon) | 🚋 Odéon or St-Michel
☎ 01-43-26-48-23 | Fax 01-46-33-04-02
∅ Sunday; August
$$$ | 💳 VISA 💳 💳
☞

Originally a sixteenth-century mail-coach inn named
À la Halte de l'Eperon (The Spur Stop), Allard
became one of the most renowned traditional
bistros in Paris. Founded by André Allard's father and con-
tinued by André and his wife, Fernande, the restaurant
became famous for a menu of extraordinary dishes pre-
pared by Fernande, the most celebrated being roast duck
smothered in olives. Unfortunately, upon their deaths, Allard
went into a period of slow decline, but then in 1998 the
Layrac brothers took over. These experienced restaura-
teurs have skillfully revived the place and faithfully dupli-
cated the menu, down to the purple ink. Now one can
again feast on the famous duck with olives, Burgundian
snails, braised beef with carrots, scallops in *beurre blanc,*
and *coq au vin,* all complemented by superb Beaujolais
wine. The old front room has more character than the
room in the rear, but the low ceiling and uninhibited con-
versation can make it rather noisy and smoky.

Eating here is truly an excursion into a bygone era.
Allard should be on the list of any serious gourmet.

RECOMMENDED DISHES

Escargots de Bourgogne. Vineyard snails in garlic butter.
Jambon Persillé. Cubes of cooked ham in parsleyed aspic.

Frisée aux Lardons. Curly lettuce salad with chunks of bacon in a vinaigrette sauce.

Entrecôte Marchand de Vin. Grilled rib steak in a sauce prepared with red wine and shallots.

Coq au Vin. Slow-cooked chicken in Beaujolais wine with onions, garlic, mushrooms, and bacon.

Petit-Salé. Lightly salted pork tenderloin.

Canard aux Navets/Olives. Roast duck with turnips in the spring, and with olives during the rest of the year.

Saumon Frais Grillé au Beurre Blanc. Grilled salmon in a white wine butter sauce.

Cassoulet Toulousain. White bean casserole with tomatoes, sausage, pork, and goose.

Paris-Brest. Large *choux* (cream puff) pastry ring filled with almonds and butter cream.

Crème Caramel. Custard baked in a mold, coated with caramel.

Tarte Fine Chaude aux Pommes. Thin apple tart served hot.

🍷 Morgon, Moulin-à-Vent.

MENUS | Lunch 150 francs, dinner 200 francs.

La Bastide Odéon

M. GILLES AJUELOS

7, rue Corneille, 75006 (off place de l'Odéon close to Luxembourg Gardens) | 🚋 Odéon or R.E.R. Luxembourg

☎ 01-43-26-03-65 | Fax 01-44-07-28-93

Ø Sunday and Monday; three weeks in August

$$ | 💳 VISA MasterCard

♟

This extremely popular two-story bistro decorated in the style of an elegant Mediterranean auberge is situated across from the beautiful Luxembourg Gardens. White terra-cotta tile floors, large windows, stone walls, beamed ceilings, attractive bouquets of dried flowers, and a fine old floor-to-ceiling fireplace transport you to the southern countryside.

The Bastide is the concept of Gilles Ajuelos, a young chef trained by two chefs who received Michelin stars: Michel Rostang and Jacques Maximin. Strictly speaking, the bistro is a Provençal restaurant; it offers many Mediterranean dishes, such as grilled eggplant, raw salmon with anchovy sauce, and roasted cod with pesto, white beans, and pine nuts. However, chef Ajuelos is more comfortable with, and excels at, thoughtfully executed contemporary dishes, using Provençal herbs and spices to dress up his preparations. Two of his favorite dishes are roasted chicken with whole garlic cloves, and veal kidneys with mushrooms and candied shallots. Three pasta choices—gnocchi with snails, penne with spicy sausages and black olives, and cheese ravioli in a fresh tomato sauce—may be substituted for either the entrée or the main course on the 194-franc menu.

There is a nice list of regional wines to choose from. Always save room for the signature dessert, *moelleux mi-cuit au chocolat Valrhona, glace vanille*—a hot bitter chocolate cake with vanilla ice cream. Rhubarb tart served with almond ice cream is another winner.

RECOMMENDED DISHES

Mille-Feuille Tiède aux Aubergines Grillées Façon Riviera. A flaky pastry filled with grilled eggplant.

Achoïade de Saumon Cru et Salade Tiède de Pommes de Terre Rattes. Raw salmon with anchovy sauce, warm potato salad in oil.

Tarte Feuilletée à la Tomate et Chèvre Cabichou à la Sariette Salade Riquette. Pastry tart with tomatoes and soft goat cheese accented with savory, served on salad greens.

Pavé de Thon Poivrons et Tomates Confites. Grilled tuna steak with preserved bell peppers and tomatoes.

Volaille Rôtie à l'Ail Confit, Pommes de Terre. Roast poultry with whole sweet garlic and potatoes.

Pieds et Paquets d'Agneau à la Provençale. Mutton tripe rolled into packets and cooked with sheep's trotters.

Lapin Farci aux Aubergines avec Toasts à la Tapenade et Vinaigrette au Balsamique. Roast rabbit stuffed with eggplant accompanied by a puree of capers, black olives, anchovies, and herbs dressed with balsamic vinegar on toast.

Cochon de Lait Farci en Porchetta. Whole stuffed suckling pig, spit-roasted.

Moelleux Mi-Cuits au Chocolate Valrhona. Velvety soft cake half-cooked with bittersweet chocolate and vanilla ice cream.

Sablé de Poire Épicée et Crème Brûlée à la Pistache. Spiced shortbread and pear on caramelized custard and pistachio nuts.

Fine selection of Mediterranean and Provençal wines.

MENUS | 154 francs and 194 francs.

Les Bookinistes

M. GUY SAVOY

CHEFS: WILLIAM LEDEUIL AND ERIC BRUYELLE

53, quai des Grands-Augustins, 75006 (overlooking Notre Dame cathedral) | R.E.R. St-Michel

☎ 01-43-25-45-94 | Fax 01-43-25-23-07

Ø Saturday lunch and Sunday lunch

$ $ $ |

♟♟

This, the most successful bistro annex of the famous chef Guy Savoy, is perfectly located in front of the Left Bank bookstalls along the Seine, with a view of Notre Dame cathedral.

When the bistro opened in 1994, Savoy brought in a chef de cuisine, William Ledeuil, who made a success at Le Bistro de l'Étoile "Lauriston" in the 16e. His cuisine is light and airy, and the contemporary decor—originated by Leopold Gest and the jazz musician and muralist Daniel Humair—is a fine match for it. Pale yellow walls are delightfully accented with large mirrors and wall lamps covered with bright-colored shades. The yellow theme, carried out in the table linen, is stunningly contrasted by black banquettes, minimalist chairs, and lovely floral table arrangements in blue and charcoal vases. The playing cards displayed on the ceiling are part of a magician's act performed here on Thursday nights.

Chef Ledeuil's downstairs kitchen produces a good selection of original but simple dishes skillfully blending different tastes and flavors, which constantly play against one another. Two of the many original creations are paper-thin slices of raw tuna on a bed of spring vegetables dribbled with anchovy extract and delicately covered by a Parmesan-flavored pastry wafer; and a *terrine de foie de volaille* accompanied by apple chutney.

A romantic evening meal could cost as much as 300 francs, but the good-value lunch menu, augmented by a few blackboard specials at 160 francs, is a bargain, considering the quality of the food and service.

RECOMMENDED DISHES

Tartare de Bar et Daurade au Gingembre Compotée de Poivrons. Chopped and seasoned raw sea bass and sea bream with fresh ginger and stewed bell peppers.

Fricassée de Chipirons et Langoustines Rôties Jus Émulsionnée. A light stew of roast squid and prawns in a blend of juices.

Chausson d'Aubergine Farci de Tomate et de Féta. A pastry turnover stuffed with cooked tomato and Greek feta cheese.

Agneau de Lait Rôti Haricots Noirs au Jus, Légumes Grillés. Roast milk-fed lamb with black beans and garden vegetables in natural juices.

Fricassée de Sot-l'y-Laisse et Ailerons de Volaille Cappelini. A thickened white stew of chicken oysters and wings on angel hair pasta.

Entrecôte Poêlée à la Bordelaise Ragoût de Pommes de Terre de Noirmoutier et Fèves. Pan-roasted rib steak in a red wine sauce served with a stew of potatoes and broad beans.

Collier d'Agneau Farci Mijoté, Pommes Boulangères au Foie Gras et Romarin. Stuffed neck of lamb with baked potatoes garnished with foie gras and rosemary.

Travers de Porc Mariné et Grillé au Romarin Frit. Grilled spareribs with fried rosemary.

Salade d'Oranges Sanguines et Écorce Farci de Crème Brûlée. Blood-orange salad and caramelized flan topped with orange rinds.

Crêpes Tièdes Farcies de Pomme Cannelle Glace Caramel. Hot apple pancakes, cinnamon-spiced, accompanied by homemade caramel ice cream.

Well-balanced moderately priced wine list. Bordeaux by the pitcher.

MENUS | Vegetarian lunch menu 140 francs, lunch 160 francs, dinner 180 francs.

Aux Charpentiers

M. Pierre Bardèche
Mme. Colette Bardèche

10, rue Mabillon, 75006 (opposite Marché St-Germain) |
🚋 Mabillon or Odéon
☎ 01-43-26-30-05 | [Fax] 01-46-33-07-98
Ø Open every day, all year
$ $ | [cards]

☞

The very modern Marché St-Germain is directly across the street from this authentic old bistro, originally opened in 1856, which once was the rendezvous for the Parisian guild of carpenters and cabinet-makers.

Pierre Bardèche and his wife, Colette, acquired this famous St-Germain "hangout" in 1976 and set about furnishing it with memorabilia in keeping with its historic past. The bistro has a fascinating collection of photographs and prints depicting carpenters at work, an elegant zinc bar, bare wood floors, Victorian lighting fixtures, and displayed behind the front door, an old-fashioned napkin ring cabinet.

Chef Bardèche continues to prepare the hearty *plats du jour* and bistro specialties for which the restaurant is famous. Veal with tomatoes, garlic, and mushrooms on Monday; beef stew with carrots on Tuesday; salt pork with lentils on Wednesday; *pot-au-feu* with veal and vegetables on Thursday; cod with aioli on Friday; and stuffed cabbage on Saturday. Typical desserts include chocolate mousse, *clafoutis,* and lemon tart, and several flavors of sorbet are always available. There are a number of country wines, with Beaujolais topping the list.

There is no pretension about this conservative little bistro, which begins service at noon and stays open until 11 P.M.

RECOMMENDED DISHES

Foie Gras de Canard Frais Maison. Homemade duck liver pâté, served in slices and accompanied by a glass of Sauternes.

Jambon Labellisé du Pays Corrèzien. Certified cured ham from the Limousin region of central France.

Escargots de Bourgogne. Snails served in their shells with garlic butter.

Poulard de Bresse, Sauce Suprême. Roast Bresse chicken in a white flour-based cream sauce.

Carré d'Agneau Rôti à la Gousse d'Ail. Roast rack of lamb with garlic cloves (for two).

Filet de Boeuf à la Ficelle. Roast beef tied with string and poached in broth.

Bar Rôti au Fenouil et Flambé. Roast sea bass with fennel, flamed at the table.

Caneton Rôti Sauce Olives et Porto. Roast duckling in a port sauce with olives.

Mousse au Chocolat. Whipped chocolate cream dessert.

Clafoutis. Traditional batter tart with cherries.

Bourdeaux, Côtes du Rhône, Beaujolais

MENUS | Lunch 120 francs, dinner 158 francs (wine included).

Chez Dumonet (Joséphine)

M. Jean-Dominic Dumonet
M. Jean-Christian Dumonet
Chef: Jean-Christian Dumonet

117, rue du Cherche-Midi, 75006 (off boulevard du
    Montparnasse) | �car Duroc or Falguière
☎ 01-45-48-52-40 | Fax 01-42-84-06-83
Ø Saturday and Sunday; August
$ $ $ | ▄▄ VISA MasterCard

🍲 🍲 🍲

*A*nyone who remembers this famous old bistro,
established in the early 1900s, still calls it Chez
Joséphine, although Jean Dumonet and now his
sons have been the owners for decades.

The large, comfortable dining room is sectioned into
three distinct areas by etched-glass-and-wood dividers.
Multicolored cracked-tile floors, polished blond wood,
large mirrors, and pretty hanging lights with antique shades
create a lovely old-fashioned ambience. The long bar at
the entrance is tastefully decorated with a huge bouquet
of fresh flowers.

The absolutely classic cuisine—which leans toward the
Landes, the pine-planted stretch of coast south of Bordeaux—is prepared by Jean-Christian Dumonet. There is a
curious mix of inexpensive bourgeois dishes such as herring salad with warm potatoes at 58 francs, juxtaposed
with things like an exquisite puff pastry *feuilleté* filled with
truffles, listed at 961 francs. In season, the chef prepares
truffles 17 different ways and encourages sharing or half
portions. Do as we did recently for lunch and share the luscious fresh duck foie gras with raisins followed by a perfectly prepared truffle omelet, accompanied with one of
the Burgundy treasures from a *cave* that is considered

among the finest in Paris. Other classic specialties worth trying are the roast leg of lamb, served on Wednesdays for lunch; the marvelous *boeuf bourguignon;* the savory lamb stew; and the *cassoulet* with duck confit. If you can manage dessert, there is a Grand Marnier soufflé (for two), which must be ordered at the beginning of the meal.

RECOMMENDED DISHES

Escalope de Foie Gras aux Raisins. Thin slice of foie gras served hot with dried grapes.

Omelette aux Truffles. Omelette with fresh truffles.

Pot d'Harengs, Salade de Pommes Tièdes. Pickled herrings with potato salad.

Boeuf Bourguignon aux Tagliatelles. Beef stewed in red wine, onions, and mushrooms, served with fresh noodles.

Gigot Duranton, et ses Mojettes Piattes. Roast leg of lamb with white beans (Wednesday lunch).

Châteaubriand Grillé, Sauce Béarnaise. Fillet of grilled tenderloin steak (served rare) accompanied by an emulsion sauce of shallots, tarragon, and vinegar combined with beaten egg yolks and whisked in butter.

Petit Canard Sauvageon Rôti. Roast wild duckling.

Confit de Canard Maison. Preserved duck seasoned with duck fat and served with sautéed potatoes (*pommes landaises*).

Soufflé au Grand Marnier. Hot, puffed-up soufflé with orange-flavored brandy (for two).

Nougat Glace au Coulis de Framboises et ses Tuiles aux Amandes. Nougat ice cream with a puree of raspberry and almond-flavored petits fours.

Beaujolais and a superb selection of Bordeaux wines—one of the richest in Paris.

L'Épi Dupin

M. FRANÇOIS PASTEAU

11, rue Dupin, 75006 (between rue de Sèvres and rue
du Cherche-Midi) | 🚋 Sèvres-Babylone
☎ 01-42-22-64-56 | Fax 01-42-22-30-42
Ø Saturday and Sunday; three weeks in August
$$ | 💳 VISA 💳
♟♟♟

Exposed stone, half-timbered walls, ceiling beams,
and large terra-cotta floor tiles add a rustic touch to
the little rooms of this sophisticated bistro not far
from the Bon Marché department store. L'Épi Dupin has
become such a success that reservations are required days
in advance—at least two or three days ahead for lunch and
a week or so for dinner.

François Pasteau, who worked under François Clerc
in Maisons Laffitte, was one of the first young chefs to
devise a clever, inventive, upscale menu at a very afford-
able price. His lunch for 115 francs offers an appetizer and
main course or a main course and dessert with wine in-
cluded. Dinner at 175 francs, with all three courses, is a
bargain. There is no à la carte menu.

Pasteau focuses on French classics, always using fresh
ingredients and adding a creative touch to the meat and
fish dishes, which change every month. Fresh bread is
baked twice a day, and all the pastries are homemade. Mar-
ket vegetables are skillfully employed to harmonize with
basic produce. Shredded oxtail is coupled with eggplant,
skate with an artichoke cream sauce, guinea fowl with fen-
nel, and duckling with *girolles* (mushrooms).

The wine list is small: only about 50 bottles, all priced
under 175 francs. We had a very fine white Languedoc
wine (Domaine la Chevalière 1997) for 110 francs.

RECOMMENDED DISHES

Tatin d'Endives et Chèvre Frais. Braised endives in a pie topped with fresh goat cheese.

Tartare de Bulots et Croustillant de Tête et Langue de Veau. Raw ground sea snails accompanied by veal head and tongue.

Tartine de Sardines à la Provençale. Thick slice of bread with fresh sardines in a tomato sauce in the style of Provence with garlic and olives.

Déroulé d'Entrecôte et Pied de Veau aux Herbes. Beef rib steak coupled with herbed calf's trotters.

Caille Rôtie à la Gousse d'Ail et Girolles. Roast quail with garlic cloves and wild mushrooms.

Souris d'Agneau et Fenouil Confit au Citron. Lamb shank with preserved fennel and lemon sauce.

Paupiette de Raie à la Crème d'Artichaut. Flattened, braised skate in cream sauce with hearts of artichoke.

Moelleux de Poitrine de Porc, Julienne de Légumes et Raisins Secs. Roast pork breast with vegetables cut up in thin strips and raisins.

Dariole au Coulant de Chocolat, Sauce Pistache. Pastry filled with chocolate and topped with pistachio sauce.

Pastilla de Pommes et Fenouil Anisés Glace au Thym Citron. Anisette-flavored apple puff pastry with thyme-flecked lemon ice cream.

Well-chosen, varied selection of wines under 175 francs.

MENUS-CARTES | Lunch 115 francs, dinner 175 francs.

Chez Maître Paul

M. Jean-François Debert

12, rue Monsieur-le-Prince, 75006 (closest cross streets:
rue C. Delavigne and rue A. Dubois, off boulevard
St-Germain) | 🚋 Odéon

☎ 01-43-54-74-59 | Fax 01-46-34-58-33

Ø Open every day, all year

$ $ | 💳 VISA MasterCard 💳

🍲🍲

J ean-François Debert is one of the foremost ambas-
sadors promoting the cuisine of the Franche-Comté,
an isolated region in the eastern part of France.
Delightful, unusual wines and produce are used in the
sumptuous dishes of this mountainous area.

The restaurant is noted for several specialties, but the
most famous is chef Debert's classic *poulet au vin jaune avec
morilles,* a rich preparation of free-range chicken and
morel mushrooms cooked in a creamy sauce made with
sweet golden wine fermented from late-harvested grapes.
Somewhat reminiscent of sherry, *vin jaune* (yellow wine)
is produced from the sauvignon grape and aged in oak
barrels for a minimum of six years. The best-known,
Château-Chalon, has its own appellation.

Other regional produce shows up in dishes made with
montbéliard sausages, smoked *brési,* and Comté cheese.
The cellar provides a selection of wines from the Côtes du
Jura and Arbois rarely seen in Paris.

The ambience is refined and comfortable, with nicely
spaced tables covered in white linen and set with fresh
flowers. This is one of the few good restaurants open on
Sunday; and if you want one of the coveted downstairs
tables, you must reserve early in the week.

RECOMMENDED DISHES

Saucisse de Montbéliard Chaude, Pommes à l'Huile. Hot cumin-flavored sausage with sliced potatoes in oil.

Escargots de Bourgogne en Coquille Maison. Classic snails, cooked and served in the shell with garlic butter.

Salade Comtoise Mélangée, Comté, Jambon Fumé et Noix. Mixed country salad with Gruyère cheese, smoked ham, and walnuts.

Poulet au Vin Jaune avec Morilles. Chicken with morels in creamy sauce made with potent yellow Jura wine.

Entrecôte Poêlée à la Vigneronne. Panfried rib steak, "wine-grower" style, with grapes, brandy, and wine.

Rognons de Veau à la Comtoise. Veal kidneys bread-crumbed and baked with cheese and ham.

Filets de Sole au Château-Chalon. Grilled Dover sole in a white wine sauce made from the celebrated *vin jaune*.

Poulette à la Crème Gratinée. Young chicken in a rich white sauce sprinkled with grated cheese and bread crumbs and crusted in the oven.

Gâteau aux Noix (Grenoblois). Rich walnut cake.

Mont Blanc. Pureed chestnut dessert topped with whipped cream.

✎ Arbois, Château-Chalon, *vin jaune,* vin de Paille.

MENUS | 165 francs and 195 francs (wine included).

Marie et Fils

MME. MARIE STEINBERG

34, rue Mazarine, 75006 (nearest cross streets: rue J. Callot
   or rue Guénégaud) | 🚋 Odéon
☎ 01-43-26-69-49 | [Fax] 01-43-26-11-99
Ø Sunday and Monday lunch; August
$ $ | 💳 [VISA] [MasterCard]
☞

M arie Steinberg, whose refined little restaurant
Chez Marie we so admired, opened this chic belle
epoque–style bistro in the heart of St-Germain.
This new venture is run in collaboration with her son
Guillaume. It has quickly become very fashionable and is
frequented by the jet set and famous fashion models and
designers. Although it is a "see and be seen" place, first-
time clients are treated with great warmth and hospitality
by the endearing Marie and her staff of elegant, young,
attractive women.

One goes through a glass-roof conservatory into a mirrored room casually decorated with antique sideboards,
old prints and posters, and rustic objects, with subtle and
subdued lighting provided by pretty globe lamps.

The delicious family-style food includes everybody's
favorite: the roast beef platter with the most delectable
mashed potatoes served in Paris. Another favorite is the
juicy grilled tuna steak. For the calorie-conscious a number of uncomplicated salads are on hand. The daily specials are inspired by the sunny cuisine of Provence. Light,
tasty Loire wines are featured.

RECOMMENDED DISHES

Terrine de Chèvre aux Tomates Confites. Terrine of goat cheese and preserved tomatoes.

Salade de Lentilles au Pied de Veau. Lentil salad with veal trotters.

Salade de Calmars Provençale. Squid salad with tomatoes, garlic, olive oil, and inky vinegar.

Roast Beef Purée de Pommes de Terre. Roast beef with mashed potatoes and gravy.

Steak de Thon à la Coriandre. Grilled tuna steak with coriander flavor.

Filets de Rouget à la Tapenade. Grilled red mullet fillets in a puree of capers, black olives, anchovies, and herbs.

Joue de Boeuf aux Épices, Carottes Fondantes. Braised beef cheeks with spices and carrot puree.

Râble de Lapin au Basilic. Roast saddle of rabbit with basil.

Chou Farci. Stuffed cabbage.

Pain Perdu Glace au Miel. French toast with honey ice cream.

Côtes de Bourg, Côtes du Rhône, Beaujolais, Sancerre.

MENU | 120 francs.

La Rôtisserie d'en Face

M. JACQUES CAGNA

2, rue Christine, 75006 (off rue Dauphine) |
Odéon or St-Michel

☎ 01-43-26-40-98 | Fax 01-43-54-22-71

Ø Saturday lunch and Sunday

$$ |

ince its opening in 1992, this first rotisserie annex of the famous chef Jacques Cagna, located opposite (*en face*) his main restaurant, was an instant success. Although the service is uneven and the noise level high, a very Parisian clientele of all ages continues to enjoy the grilled meat, fish, and poultry that have made this place a Left Bank institution. Sponged apricot walls, high-tech lighting, and black chairs in a setting with both modern and antique touches create an attractive, relaxed country feeling. There is no à la carte menu; but the three-course formula at 159 francs offers a wide range of choices, beginning with a terrine of avocado and leeks, a tartare of salmon and sea bream with mint, and *petits gris* (snails) in a pastry shell. Grilled Scotch salmon with sautéed spinach, *entrecôte* with béarnaise sauce, rotisserie free-range chicken with mashed potatoes, and rack of lamb with thyme are a few of the main courses. Desserts are good, typical of bistro fare. The wine list is adequate.

Over the last few years, Cagna has opened two other rotisseries—La Rôtisserie d'Armaille, 6 rue d'Armaille, 01-42-27-19-20, and La Rôtisserie Monsigny, 1 rue Monsigny, 01-42-96-16-61—and a seafood restaurant, L'Espadon Bleu, 25 rue des Grands-Augustins, 01-45-33-00-85.

RECOMMENDED DISHES

Saumon d'Écosse Fumé par Nos Soins. Home-smoked Scottish-style salmon.

Tartare de Petits Maquereaux au Gingembre. Raw baby mackerel ground and seasoned with ginger.

Friture d'Éperlans, Sauce Tartare. Deep-fried smelts and tartar sauce.

Petit Bar Breton Grillé, Huile d'Olive Vierge, et Purée de Fenouil. Grilled sea bass, cold-pressed olive oil, and pureed fennel.

Pastilla de Pintade, Aubergines, Oignons, et Épices Douces. Crispy pastry filled with guinea fowl, onion, eggplant, and sweet spices.

Galette Vonnassienne de Saumon, Fondue de Poireaux, et Crème à l'Oseille. Savory salmon and potato fritter with stewed leeks and a creamy sorrel sauce.

Poulet Fermier, Purée de Pommes de Terre à l'Ancienne. Spit roasted free-range chicken with home-style mashed potatoes.

Entrecôte Grillée, Sauce Béarnaise, et Pommes Pont Neuf. Grilled sirloin steak, thick reduction sauce of beaten egg yolks, shallots, vinegar, and tarragon served with *pommes frites.*

Vacherin Glacé au Caramel et aux Noix. Caramel and walnut ice cream cake.

Moelleux au Chocolat Valrhona et Glace Vanille. Soft-center bittersweet chocolate cake with vanilla ice cream.

Beaujolais (Jean-Charles Pivot), Alsace Pinot noir (Beyer), Gamay de Touraine (Marionnet).

MENUS | Lunch 135 francs, 159 francs, dinner 240 francs.

Wadja

MME. DENISE LEGUAY
CHEF: DIDIER PANISSET

10, rue de la Grande-Chaumière, 75006 (off boulevard du Montparnasse) | ▆▆▆ Vavin

☎ 01-46-33-02-02

Ø Sunday and Monday lunch; August

$ | VISA ●●

☞

This wonderful old art deco place is intimately associated with the life and history of Montparnasse. For many years, until its decline, it nurtured the young artists of the neighborhood, displaying their work and feeding them hearty, affordable food. In the summer of 1997, Denise Leguay had the foresight and courage to revitalize the place and install a fine young chef, Didier Panisset, whose modernized versions of French regional classics have gone a long way toward returning Wadja to its original splendid reputation. Certainly, the 89-franc menu will ensure that no young artist with more appetite than money will go hungry.

The blond wood entrance, grape motif, and lace curtains beckon from the outside; inside, the stunning geometric floral tile floor, classic zinc bar, red banquettes, and new art deco lighting fixtures recapture the original atmosphere. The yellow walls provide a background for changing displays of art, and Mme. Leguay is always ready with a warm, maternal welcome.

One outstanding dish, which should not be missed, is the classic version of seven-hour leg of lamb (*gigot de sept heures et sa côte rosée pommes à l'ail*), so tender that it melts in your mouth; it is accompanied by potatoes cooked in garlic. The *carte des vins* is rich in proprietor wines, many of which are available by the glass.

RECOMMENDED DISHES

Mille-Feuille de Chèvre aux Artichauts et Pistaches. Layered flaky pastry stuffed with artichokes, goat's milk cheese, and pistachio nuts.

Carpaccio de Thon et Salade de Poivrons Grillés. Thin slices of raw cured tuna with grilled bell peppers.

Tarte Fine aux Oignons, Bacon, et Andouille Blanche. Thin tart of onions, bacon, and slices of pork sausage, served hot.

Filet de Boeuf Poêlé en Croûte d'Herbes, Jus au Romarin. Panfried tenderloin of beef encased in pastry with aromatic herbs in natural juices.

Vapeur de Perche à la Coriandre Fraîche Fondue de "Poriaux." Steamed freshwater perch spiced with fresh coriander and topped with vegetables steamed to a pulp.

Gigot de Sept Heures Pommes à l'Ail. Braised leg of lamb with garlic potatoes.

Poulet Fermier Sauté au Gingembre et Citron. Free-range chicken lightly browned with ginger and lemon.

Salmis de Palombe, Galette de Châtaignes. Wood pigeon, first roasted then finished in a red wine sauce with a thick pancake topped by chestnuts.

Soufflé Glacé au Chocolat. Chocolate iced dessert resembling a soufflé.

Figues Rôties aux Épices Douces, Glace Vanille. Spiced, roasted figs with vanilla ice cream.

Carefully chosen selection of growers' wines.

MENU-CARTE | Lunch 89 francs.

7e ARRONDISSEMENT

L'AFFRIOLÉ

CHEZ L'AMI JEAN

AUBERGE BRESSANE

AUBERGE "D'CHEZ EUX"

AU BON ACCUEIL

LE CALMONT

LE FLORIMOND

LA FONTAINE DE MARS

L'OEILLADE

AU PETIT TONNEAU

LE P'TIT TROQUET

TOUR EIFFEL

L'Affriolé

M. THIERRY VEROLA

17, rue Malar, 75007 (between rue de l'Université and rue St-Dominique) | 🚋 Invalides or Latour-Maubourg

☎ 01-44-18-31-33 | Fax 01-44-18-91-12

Ø Saturday lunch and Sunday

$$ | VISA MasterCard

♟♟

ince opening this smart modern bistro in 1996, the original owner-chef Alain Atibard, and now his successor, Thierry Verola, have charmed a fashionable, almost exclusively French clientele with sophisticated, inventive cuisine. L'Affriolé has small colorful mosaic-tile tables (made by an artisan in Nantes), muted cream-colored walls, beige banquettes, and lightly frosted hanging light fixtures. The stylish modern decor is a bit of Greco-Roman whimsy with faux marble moldings and columns, wall planters, mirrors, and two large ostrich eggs prominently displayed in the rear.

M. Verola, trained in the prestigious kitchens of Cagna, Senderens, and Duquesnoy, strikes a tone of originality and style that has earned him a reputation for food of a quality associated with more serious restaurants. Some of the most outstanding dishes we recently enjoyed included a richly prepared pressed rabbit with ginger and lemon, a sumptuous roast saddle of lamb infused with lemon thyme and accompanied by ratatouille, a grilled breast of wild duck accented with exotic spices, and a perfectly prepared tuna steak garnished with cannelloni stuffed with eggplant. The homemade chocolate desserts are outstanding and the superb country bread loaf from master baker Poujauran is the perfect accompaniment to a small but first-rate selection of cheeses. The excellent *vins de pays,* from hand-picked grapes with no chemical additives, completes a truly memorable meal.

RECOMMENDED DISHES

Feuilleté d'Escargots. Puff pastries filled with snails and whipped potato puree.

Tarte à la Tomate, Anchois, Basilic, et Parmesan. Provençale tart with grilled tomato, anchovies, sweet basil, and Parmesan cheese.

Pâté Pantin au Coquelet et Foie Gras. Savory patty of duck liver and chicken folded and cooked in a crusty pastry.

Selle d'Agneau Rôtie au Thym-Citron Artichault Poivrade et Ratatouille. Roast saddle of lamb with stewed peppers and artichokes.

Poitrine de Canette aux Épices Torréfiées. Grilled duck breast stuffed with spices.

Cannellonis de Saumon Marinés à l'Aneth. Pasta stuffed with pickled salmon and fresh dill.

Thon de Saint-Jean-de-Luz, Poivrons Doux Confits. Grilled tuna Basque-style with hot peppers and chorizo sausage.

Meunière de Saint-Jacques Poêlée de Légumes d'Ailleurs aux Baies de Ronce. Scallops, floured and panfried, flavored with wild blackberries.

Gaufre à la Crème Chocolat et Glace Pistache. Waffle covered in chocolate cream and topped with pistachio ice cream.

Chèvre Cendré. Goat cheese coated with ashes.

A well-chosen selection of naturally grown, unfiltered wines from small-scale growers.

MENUS-CARTES | Lunch 120 francs, dinner 190 francs.

Chez l'Ami Jean

M. Pierre Pagueguy

27, rue Malar, 75007 (between rue de l'Université and
rue St-Dominique) | 🚃 Invalides or Latour-
Maubourg
☎ 01-47-05-86-89
∅ Sunday; month of August
$ $ | VISA MasterCard
☞

∫ ince its origin in 1931, this rustic little bistro has
  been a bastion of the highly spiced cuisine of the
  Basque region. Garlic, chili peppers, tomatoes, and
onions show up in numerous meat, fish, and egg dishes.
Bayonne ham and chorizo sausages are combined with
vegetables to make a hearty *garbure,* which is always
served in the evenings, along with many other unpretentious Basque specialties. The most popular dishes include
poulet basquais, chicken cooked with mixed vegetables;
paella valenciana, a saffron-rich dish of chicken, seafood,
and sausages; and *chipirons farcis,* tiny squid cooked in a
spicy sauce with black squid ink. The menu also offers a
wide range of familiar classic bistro dishes as well as salads, omelets, *pommes frites,* steak, and sole or trout *meunière.* The *mystère flambé à l'Izarra* is an ice cream dessert
flamed with a chartreuse-like liqueur from Bayonne.

Pierre Pagueguy is an amiable host and can usually be
found behind the bar recapping the latest soccer game
with a group of neighborhood customers. The rooms are
dimly lit by small hanging lanterns. Dark banquettes,
small tables covered with red cloths protected by paper,
and walls filled with mementos and paintings related to
rugby and jai-alai create pleasant, intimate surroundings.

RECOMMENDED DISHES

Terrine de Lapin au Foie de Canard. Rabbit and duck liver terrine.

Salade Landaise. Gizzards, Bayonne ham, preserved meats, and foie gras served on salad greens with vinaigrette sauce.

Chipirons à la Basquais. Tiny stuffed squid with stewed squid's ink added to the preparation.

Garbure Béarn. Vegetable soup served in an earthenware *toupin* with cabbage and goose confit (dinner only).

Pipérade. Basque omelet with peppers, ham, tomatoes, and garlic.

Poulet Basquais. Chicken cooked with tomatoes, peppers, chorizo sausage, mushrooms, and red wine.

Truite aux Amandes. Sautéed trout with almonds.

Confit de Canard des Landes, Pommes Sarladaises. Grilled preserved duck served with sliced sautéed potatoes and truffles.

Gâteau Basquais. Flaky-crust pastry filled with vanilla custard.

Mystère Flambé à l'Izarra. Ice cream dessert flamed with Izarra, a chartreuse-like liqueur made in Bayonne.

🐟 Madiran, Cahors, Irouléguy.

MENU | 99 francs.

Auberge Bressane

M. Jérôme Dumant
M. Stéfane Dumant

16, avenue de la Motte-Picquet, 75007 (off boulevard de
la Tour Maubourg) | 🚋 La Tour-Maubourg
☎ 01-47-05-98-37 | Fax 01-47-05-92-21
Ø Saturday lunch; two weeks in August
$ $ | 💳 VISA 💳

☞☞

T his neo-Gothic Burgundian inn established in the
1930s is replete with medieval kitsch—lots of dark
wood paneling and wrought iron. It was taken over
by the Dumant brothers several years ago and has since
become a trendy hangout for a well-to-do young clientele
who pack the place in the evenings to enjoy the robust
dishes and heady wines of the Burgundian region. The
atmosphere can become a bit close, and the room is often
smoky, so ask to be seated as near the front as possible.

All the classic dishes of Burgundy are to be found:
superb Bresse chicken in a rich cream sauce full of flavorful morel mushrooms; a gratin of pike dumplings garnished with a velvety puree of crayfish tails and truffles;
Lyonnaise sausages with warm potatoes; and a powerful
rendition of *coq au vin* made with Juliénas wine. Soufflés
are a specialty of the house, and several versions are available, including an airy cheese soufflé served as an appetizer and, for dessert, a luscious Belgian chocolate soufflé.
There is an inexpensive lunch menu, which does not
include any of the regional dishes but does offer crisp salads; a house terrine; a choice of chicken, meat, or fish; and
a large selection of desserts. Wine is included.

The inn is located near the Invalides, and on warm days
there is a mad scramble for the terrace seats.

RECOMMENDED DISHES

Jambon Cru et Persillé Comme en Bourgogne. Cold pressed cured ham layered with parsley and white wine aspic.

Salade de Ris et de Pieds d'Agneau Croustillants. Salad of lamb sweetbreads and trotters served in a pastry case.

Oeufs en Meurette à la Mode du Beaujolais. Eggs poached in Beaujolais wine with onions, garlic, and herbs, then garnished with bacon bits.

Quenelles de Brochet Gratinées comme à Nantua. Pike dumplings in a crayfish cream sauce.

Coq au Vin de Juliénas. Cockerel stewed in Beaujolais wine with button onions and mushrooms.

Poulet Fermier à la Crème et aux Morilles. Free-range chicken in a rich cream sauce with morel mushrooms.

Civet de Sanglier aux Châtaignes et aux Airelles. Rich wild boar stew with chestnuts and bilberries, served in the fall.

Entrecôte au Grill Sauce Béarnaise. Grilled beef rib steak accompanied by a hot sauce made with white wine, vinegar, shallots, and spices to which egg yolks and butter are added.

Crêpes Suzette. Hot crepe dessert, flamed with Curaçao liqueur.

Soufflé au Grand Marnier. Baked soufflé made with orange liqueur.

➤ Brouilly (Chateau du Thivin), Mâcon-Lugny, Burgundies.

MENU | Lunch 149 francs, wine included.

Auberge "d'Chez Eux"

M. Jean-Pierre Court

2, avenue de Lowendal, 75007 (between avenue de
   Tourville and avenue Duquesne) |
   🚍 École Militaire
☎ 01-47-05-52-55 | Fax 01-45-55-60-74
Ø Sunday; first three weeks of August
$$$$ | 💳 VISA 💳 💳

🍲🍲

This impressive family-run rustic auberge is famous
for the rich and varied cuisine of the southwest
and the Landes. Jean-Pierre Court, the amiable
host, delights in making sure that you take full advantage
of the best he has to offer, so it is imperative to approach
the table with a hearty appetite. He might suggest that
you begin with the homemade goose liver pâté accompanied by a glass of sweet Bordeaux wine, or thick slices of
serrano ham and garlic sausage from a basket of *cochonnailles,* which is filled with a dozen or so sausages and
dried pork products. There is also a two-tier appetizer trolley brimming with bowls of meat, seafood, and vegetable
salads. A few seasonal daily specials are available, but most
regular customers usually opt for the chef's classics, which
include *cassoulet* made with duck confit, sausage, and
pork, in a light tomato sauce; poached free-range chicken
in broth with aromatic vegetables; crispy duck confit with
garlic potatoes; roasted duck breast garnished with
poached pears in red wine sauce; and a delicious blood
sausage with caramelized apples.

A cheese platter follows the meal; there is also a selection of desserts, all served with vanilla ice cream. A special
chariot de la farandole offers a tasting of all the desserts
for 72 francs a person. The cellar contains a tremendous

selection, including some of the finest Bordeaux; and as you would expect from a southwestern auberge, there is a fabulous collection of vintage Armagnacs to choose from.

The decor is that of a typical country inn. There are several small dining areas with red-checkered tablecloths, wine-colored velour seats, and dark wood paneling.

RECOMMENDED DISHES

Foie Gras d'Oie à l'Ancienne. Fresh homemade goose liver pâté served with hot toast.

Sélection des Cochonnailles de l'Auberge. Large selection of pork products: terrines, pâtés, sausages, ham, blood sausage.

Cuisses de Grenouilles Provençale. Panfried frogs' legs in garlic butter.

Carré d'Agneau Rôti, Gratin Dauphinois. Roast rack of lamb with a gratin of creamed potatoes with bacon bits (for two).

Cassoulet de l'Auberge en Marmite avec le Confit de Canard. White bean stew with sausage, pork, and preserved duck in a light tomato sauce.

Fricassée de Volaille Fermière aux Morilles. Free-range chicken in a creamy white wine sauce with morels.

Cuisse de Confit de Canard, Pommes à l'Ail. Salted, cured duck leg roasted until crispy and served with garlic potatoes.

Côte de Boeuf Grillée d'Chez Eux. Grilled rib of beef served with béarnaise sauce.

Escalopes de Saumon Poêlées et Coulis d'Échalotes. Panfried salmon slices in a shallot puree.

Farandole de Tous les Desserts. Assorted desserts wheeled out on the chariot.

Brouilly, Chiroubles, Cahors, Chinon, Sancerre.

MENUS | Lunch 180 francs; lunch 220 francs, wine included; dinner *menu gastronomique* 600 francs.

Au Bon Accueil

M. Jacques Lacipière

14, rue de Monttessuy, 75007 (between avenue de la
   Bourdonnais and avenue Rapp) |
   ⬛ Alma-Marceau or R.E.R. Pont de l'Alma

☎ 01-47-05-46-11

∅ Saturday and Sunday

$$$ | VISA MasterCard

♟♟ | 🏆

E ven though Au Bon Accueil offers service until
11 P.M., one often has to wait for a reserved table
to become available. The popularity of this chic
contemporary bistro with a sophisticated neighborhood
crowd and upscale tourists is understandable, as Jacques
Lacipière offers a refined fixed-price menu and well-priced
wines.

A pink neon sign out front welcomes you to this sober
but elegant bistro, decorated in tones of ivory and peach
with panels crafted from crates of the great wines, neo-
classic columns showing Bacchus and grapevines, and
lighting fixtures covered in faux leaves. Wooden chairs,
banquettes, elbow-to-elbow seating, and waiters in long
black aprons create a cheerful, friendly atmosphere. In the
rear, brown upholstered chairs around tightly squeezed
tables are set against ivory stucco walls.

Each morning, M. Lacipière shops for produce, and the
daily menu always includes uncompromisingly fresh fish
and shellfish. Plump line-caught sea bass cooked in olive
oil and turbot with balsamic vinegar are simple and savory.
The charcuterie and meat come from the Auvergne, a
region in central France renowned for beef. Hefty ribs
of beef served with savory butter and beef tenderloin in
truffle sauce are popular favorites. During game season

a hearty potato puree accompanies roast pheasant and the famous rabbit preparation *lièvre à la royale*—a rich compote with foie gras and *cèpes*. The classic tarts are especially delicious, but all the desserts are simple, subtle blends of flavor with an emphasis on toppings of cream and ice cream.

At night, the view of the Eiffel Tower from the little terrace out front is breathtaking.

RECOMMENDED DISHES

Salade de Homard Breton. Lobster salad served with grated raw vegetables in a vinaigrette sauce.

Etuvé d'Écrevisses aux Petits Légumes. Braised crayfish with baby vegetables.

Duo de Foie Gras de Canard Chaud et Froid. Duck foie gras served two ways, hot and cold.

Pigeon Rôti à la Fricassée de Morilles. Roast squab in a thickened white sauce with morel mushrooms.

Compotée de Lièvre à la Royale au Foie Gras et aux Cèpes. Boned hare braised in red wine and brandy, stuffed with foie gras and *cèpes* (mushrooms).

Entrecôte Façon Côte du Boeuf, Petits Pois, et Carottes à la Française. Grilled beef rib steak accompanied by a pastry case filled with carrots and peas.

Fricassée de Ris d'Agneau aux Céleris et Champignons. Fricassee of lamb sweetbreads with sautéed mushrooms and celery.

Tranche de Thon au Piment d'Espelette. Grilled tuna steak with Basque chili peppers.

Profiteroles Vanille et Chocolat Chaud. Vanilla profiteroles with warm chocolate sauce.

Rocher de Châtaigne Mousse à l'Abricot. Chestnut cake in a whipped apricot mousse.

Côtes du Roussillon (Sarda-Malet), Saumur-Champigny.

MENUS | Lunch 155 francs, dinner 175 francs.

Le Calmont

M. Michel Battut

Chef: Alexandre Battut

35, avenue Duquesne, 75007 (corner of avenue Duquesne
and avenue de Ségur) | 🚊 St-François Xavier or
École Militaire

☎ 01-47-05-67-10

∅ Saturday evening and Sunday; three weeks in August

$$ | [credit card logos] [VISA] [MasterCard]

☞ | 🍷

Michel Battut is the patron of this spacious, color-
ful wine-bar-cum-restaurant located just behind
the imposing École Militaire; the natural wood
and glass facade spans the corner of avenue de Ségur and
avenue Duquesne. Le Calmont was honored as the best
wine bistro in Paris in 1995. When Battut is not behind his
bar chatting with customers about wine, he is traveling
the countryside, tasting and buying from his *vigneron*
friends the special Beaujolais he serves in his restaurant.

The large dining area is neo–art deco with blond wood
walls, mirrors, booths upholstered in dark green, and
many tables covered with bright wine-colored cloths. The
meat and fish *plats du jour* change daily, but regulars prefer
to order the copious platters of beef from the à la carte
menu. There is a large selection of wine by the glass; there
is also excellent draft beer. Le Calmont is a family affair,
with M. Battut's wife, Marie-Andrée, helping in the front,
and their son Alexandre behind the stove in the kitchen.

RECOMMENDED DISHES

Caille Farcie de Foie Gras, Pain Grillé. Quail stuffed with
foie gras and served on toast.

Oeufs en Meurette à Notre Façon. Eggs poached in red wine with bacon and tiny onions.

Assiette de Cochonnailles de l'Aveyron. Assortment of pork sausages and pâtés from the Aveyron region of central France.

Confit de Canard, Pommes à l'Ail. Preserved duck grilled and accompanied by potatoes sautéed with garlic.

Pavé de l'Aubrac au Roquefort. Thick piece of prime Salers beef accompanied by a Roquefort cheese sauce.

Tripoux de Laguiole. Highly seasoned little stuffed cushions of mutton tripe.

Saint-Jacques aux Trompettes Beurre de Romarin. Pan-roasted scallops with dark brown wild mushrooms and rosemary butter.

Andouillette AAAAA* à la Dijonnaise avec des Pommes de Terre Sautées. Grilled pork sausage in mustard sauce with sliced sautéed potatoes.

Tarte Maison aux Fruits. Freshly baked seasonal fruit tarts.

Pruneaux d'Agen à l'Armagnac et sa Boule de Glace. Stewed Agen prunes in Armagnac brandy with a scoop of ice cream.

Beaujolais, Sancerre, Chinon.

MENU | 140 francs for lunch, wine included.

*AAAAA The *Association Amicale des Amateurs d'Authentique Andouillettes* (The Amicable Association of Appreciators of Authentic Pork Tripe Sausages). An exclusive gourmet group that awards its diploma to a few restaurants serving what it considers to be the best tripe sausages. The ideal is made of pig's intestines filled with strips of choice innards mixed with pork fat and seasonings. It is fleshy without too much fat.

Le Florimond

M. PASCAL GUILLAUMIN

19, avenue de la Motte-Picquet, 75007 (at rue Bougainville
across from rue Duvivier) | 🚋 École Militaire
☎ 01-45-55-40-38 | Fax 01-45-55-40-38
∅ Saturday lunch and Sunday; first three weeks of August
$$ | VISA MasterCard

🍲🍲🍲 | ☀

L e Florimond is one of those fabulous little sleepers
rarely mentioned in guidebooks but consistently
delivering superb cuisine in a comforting atmo-
sphere of intimacy and warmth. Pascal Guillaumin, who
is both host and chef, is proud of his Corrèzienne origin,
which he says has influenced many of his culinary ideas
and recipes. He describes his little 30-seat bistro as a *salle à
manger* (a dining room), and in it you are treated more like
a guest than a customer. The comfortable room is car-
peted and decorated in warm tones of peach, orange,
gold, and wine. Fresh flowers in blue vases on the well-
spaced tables add a bright note. Pretty presentation plates
and gleaming wineglasses are a nice contrast, set on crisp
white linen cloths. An attractive service bar at the entrance
gives the only hint of a restaurant.

The menu is seasonal, and there are daily specialties,
but the lobster ravioli and the stuffed cabbage made from
M. Guillaumin's grandmother's recipe are always on the
menu. It is difficult to choose from such an appetizing
selection, which supports Pascal's theory that the two main
components of a successful meal are taste and presentation.

This marvelous bistro may remain undiscovered by the
critics; but a word of caution—it is extremely popular in
the neighborhood, so reservations are imperative.

RECOMMENDED DISHES

Raviolis de Homard, Brunoise de Légumes. Ravioli squares filled with lobster meat and diced mixed vegetables.

Foie Gras de Canard Maison, Brioche Toastée. Homemade duck foie gras with a toasted bun.

Fricassée de Petits-Gris en Brioche à la Crème d'Ail et Persil. Light stew of small gray snails in a creamy garlic and parsley sauce.

Civet de Biche, Tagliatelles au Beurre. Game stew of doe and buttered tagliatelle pasta. Served in fall and winter.

Chou Farci, Recette de ma Grand-Mère. Rolled stuffed cabbage, considered the best in Paris.

Faux-Filet Poêlé, Sauce à la Moutarde Violette de Brive. Pan-roasted sirloin steak in a spicy mustard sauce.

Mitonnée de Lapereau à l'Oseille, Caviar de Carottes. Slowly stewed young rabbit in sorrel sauce with pureed carrots.

Magret de Canard Rôti, Sauce aux Myrtilles. Grilled fillet of fattened duck breast with bilberry sauce.

Millefeuille à la Vanille. Layered flaky pastry filled with vanilla cream.

Blanc-Manger aux Fruits de Saison. Almond milk with gelatin chilled in a mold with seasonal fruit.

> Beaumes-de-Venise, Branceilles (*vin de pays* de Corrèze), Arbois (Domaine Jacques Tissot).

MENUS | Lunch, Monday to Friday 108 francs; dinner 168 francs.

La Fontaine de Mars

MME. CHRISTIANE BOUDON
M. JACQUES BOUDON
CHEF: ÉRIC LEFÈVRE

129, rue St-Dominique, 75007 (between avenue de la
   Bourdonnais and avenue Bosquet) |
   🚌 École Militaire
☎ 01-47-05-46-44 | Fax 01-47-05-11-13
∅ Open every day all year
$ $ | ▨ ▨ ▨
👒 👒 👒

This charming place is one of a handful of authentic old Paris bistros that have managed to maintain
their romantic appeal. The new owners have
refurbished the interior and revamped the menu without
losing any of the original nostalgia. The animated downstairs is reminiscent of another time, with yellowed walls,
beveled mirrors, long banquettes with chrome rails, tile
floors, an open kitchen, assorted flea market bric-a-brac,
the indispensable faded red-checked tablecloths, and lace
curtains. A narrow winding staircase leads up to two
rooms with round tables, wainscoting, parquet floors, and
oil paintings, a sedate contrast to the floor below.

Christiane Boudon is a vivacious hostess, and her winning smile and genuine warmth make you feel right at
home as she suggests that you might like to begin with
an aperitif—perhaps the famous Boyer pastis or a cardinal (a kir made with red wine, in this case with Cahors).
Many familiar southwestern specialties are listed on the
menu in alternating violet and red ink: *foie gras, confit,*
magret, and a *véritable cassoulet.* There is an assortment
of regional cheeses; there is also a choice of about ten
desserts, among which are a tasty *tarte Tatin* laced with

Calvados and served with cream, and a scrumptious *tourtière* of prunes in Armagnac.

In warm weather, chairs are set outside on the picturesque arcaded square dedicated to the goddess Hygeia.

RECOMMENDED DISHES

Escalope de Foie Gras Frais à la Ventrèche. Slice of fresh foie gras slightly smoked and salted.

Cochonnailles de Laguiole. A selection of southwestern cured meats, sausages, and pâtés.

Salade de Tête de Veau Sauce Ravigote. Calf's head salad served in a vinaigrette sauce with chopped hard-boiled eggs, capers, chopped onions, and mixed herbs.

Filet de Boeuf à la Moelle Sauce Madiran. Beef tenderloin with bone marrow in a red wine sauce.

Magret de Canard à la Crème de Cèpes. Fillet of fattened duck breast in a cream sauce with *cèpes* mushrooms.

Véritable Cassoulet Maison au Canard Confit. Genuine white bean stew with duck confit, Toulouse sausage, and tomatoes.

Poulet Fermier aux Morilles. Free-range chicken with morel mushroom sauce and steamed rice.

Confit de Canard, Pommes Sarladaises. Grilled preserved duck and baked, sliced truffled potatoes.

Boudin aux Pommes Fruits. Grilled blood sausage with cooked apple slices.

Tourtière Landaise aux Pruneaux et Armagnac. Deep-dish Landes pie with prunes and Armagnac brandy.

Crème Brûlée à la Vanille. Custard flan with a caramelized topping.

Cahors, Madiran, Bordeaux.

MENU | Lunch 90 francs.

L'Oeillade

M. Pascal Molto

10, rue St-Simon, 75007 (between boulevard St-Germain
and rue de Grenelle) | ▆▆▆▆ Rue du Bac or Solférino
☎ 01-42-22-01-60
Ø Saturday lunch and Sunday; last two weeks of August
$$ | VISA MasterCard
☞ ☞

Situated on a quiet residential street only steps away
from the turmoil of two boulevards—St-Germain
and Raspail—this lovely little bistro with its terra-
cotta floors and blond wood paneling continues to offer
substantial home-style cooking to the upscale residents of
the 7th and many foreign regulars who are attracted by
the honest cooking and *sympathique* atmosphere.

Tables are covered with crisp white linen, and an ever-
changing display of modern art and fresh flowers add a
bright touch to the sober surroundings. A chunky terrine
and delicious rillettes are passed from table to table
accompanied by country bread supplied by boutique
baker Beauvallat. In addition to a fixed menu, there are
about 20 à la carte offerings of satisfying bourgeois dishes.
Some of the beautifully presented favorites are the stuffed
cabbage, braised calf sweetbreads with morel mushrooms,
fricassee of chicken with foie gras and whole cloves of gar-
lic, *tripe à la mode de Caen,* thick steaks, roast lamb, and veal
shank. Dessert choices include a classic *tarte Tatin* with
vanilla ice cream, a luscious chocolate fondant, pink grape-
fruit with sherbet, and a Balthazar—a parfait made with a
blancmange (a gelatin of almond-flavored milk) and pear
sherbet in caramel sauce.

Reservations are suggested, as this place is always
crowded.

RECOMMENDED DISHES

Foie Gras de Canard Fait au Torchon. Homemade duck foie
gras, tied up in cloth and steeped in brine.

Saucisson Chaud de Lyon et se Petites Rattes. Hot Lyonnaise
sausage with a potato salad made with tiny yellow potatoes.

Papeton d'Aubergines au Coulis de Tomates. Eggplant puree
Provençal with eggs, in a thick tomato sauce.

Épaule d'Agneau Rôtie Piquée à l'Ail. Roast shoulder of
lamb studded with garlic.

Chou Farci. Stuffed cabbage.

Braisée de Ris de Veau aux Morilles. Braised calf sweetbreads with morel mushrooms.

Filet de Boeuf au Poivre Vert. Broiled tenderloin of beef in a
green pepper sauce.

Brandade de Morue. Creamed salt cod.

Pavé de Cabillaud Rôti et sa Purée à l'Huile d'Olive. Roast
fresh cod with pureed potatoes drizzled with olive oil.

Fondant au Chocolat-Amer. Bittersweet chocolate dessert.

Tarte Fine aux Pommes. Thin apple tart.

Saumur rouge, Bordeaux.

MENU-CARTE | 168 francs.

Au Petit Tonneau

Mme. Ginette Boyer

20, rue Surcouf, 75007 (off rue St-Dominique, close to
boulevard de la Tour Maubourg) |
🚃 La Tour-Maubourg
☎ 01-47-05-09-01
Ø Open every day; closed two weeks in August
$$ | 💳 VISA 💳 💳
🍲 🍲

This wonderful little bistro, circa 1910, is the hearth-
stone of Ginette Boyer, an outspoken, brilliant
chef who turns out fabulous, superbly simple
food, the kind that gives meaning to what the French call
cuisine de femme.

Anything eaten here—whether eggs, fowl, meat, mush-
rooms, vegetables, or fish—is personally selected by Mme.
Boyer, and she uses only the very best and freshest ingredi-
ents: organic chickens and eggs, wild mushrooms, line-
caught and *sauvages* fish, and hand-picked first-quality
fruits and vegetables. She'll appear in her tall chef's hat
and white coat to select a handful of wild mushrooms
from the brimming baskets set on the small service bar,
disappear into her tiny kitchen, and several minutes later
reappear with a steaming, creamy mushroom stew or a
brouillade of mushrooms and scrambled eggs.

Mme. Boyer was taught to cook by her grandmother,
and everything here is tempting—the *entrecôte* with shal-
lots, the rumpsteak with Roquefort, the rack of lamb with
gratin dauphinois. When it comes to fish, depending on
what the fishmongers are offering on any given day, she
prepares exquisite salmon, sole, sea bass, and turbot. From
September to April, almost everyone orders her luscious
coquilles Saint-Jacques (scallops). The duck or rabbit terrine

to start and the fresh fruit *clafoutis* or the *tarte Tatin* (caramelized apple tart) to finish are the perfect complements to a Ginette meal.

Service is slow, and the two intimate rooms may be crowded, but the diners never seem to mind as they sip a second pitcher of Loire wine in anticipation of what is to come.

RECOMMENDED DISHES

Assiette de Crudités, selon le Marché. Copious fresh chopped and grated vegetables, market selected and served with a vinaigrette sauce.

Terrine de Volaille Maison. Homemade chicken and chicken liver pâté.

Champignons Sauvages en Fricassée. Wild mushroom stew.

Brouillade aux Champignons Sauvages. Scrambled eggs with wild mushrooms.

Carré d'Agneau au Gratin Dauphinois. Grilled rack of lamb served with scalloped potatoes.

Magret de Canard au Poivre Vert. Grilled fillet of fattened duck breast in a green pepper sauce.

Rognons de Veau Sauce Madère. Veal kidneys cooked in a richly flavored brown sauce made from Madeira wine.

Turbot au Beurre Blanc. Whole turbot served with a buttery cream sauce made with white wine and shallots.

Tarte Tatin, Crème Fraîche. Caramelized upside-down apple cake with lightly soured cream.

Clafoutis aux Cerises. Traditional batter tart with fresh cherries.

Pitcher of Loire wine (white) or Bordeaux (red).
MENU | 120 francs.

Le P'tit Troquet

M. Patrick Vessière
Mme. Dominique Vessière
Chef: Patrick Vessière

29, rue de l'Exposition, 75007 (off rue St-Dominique) |
🚃 École Militaire
☎ 01-47-05-80-39 | Fax 01-47-05-80-39
Ø Sunday and Monday lunch; three weeks in August
$ $ | VISA 💳
🍺🍺

The atmosphere is intimate and friendly in this attractive little bistro located in the shadow of the Eiffel Tower. Two tiny rooms are tastefully fitted out with old tin cigarette signs, syphons, coffeepots, clocks, and a lovely old zinc bar.

Chef Patrick Vessière is an advocate of *cuisine du marché,* and his moderately priced three-course 165-franc menu has earned a reputation for quality and freshness. One could easily become a regular with such a tempting array of well-prepared dishes. Smoked salmon served with potato waffles and acidulated cream, goat cheese quenelles with smoked salmon, terrine of beef and chicken livers, quail salad, free-range guinea fowl, skate with capers, Pauillac (salt-meadow) lamb, calf's liver with port—there are so many appealing dishes that it is difficult to choose a particular specialty. The bread is homemade, and so is the ice cream, which is usually served with a delicious Granny Smith apple crumble for dessert. Many of the wines listed are expensive, but there is always a moderately priced *bouteille du jour.*

RECOMMENDED DISHES

Terrine de Chèvre au Saumon Fumé. Earthenware pot with goat cheese and homemade smoked salmon.

Salade de Boudin Noir aux Pommes. Blood sausage salad with cooked apple slices.

Brioche d'Escargots Coulis Persil Plat. Snails in a bun garnished with a parsley puree.

Fondant de Porc Braisé en Cocotte. Braised pork croquette served in a casserole.

Magret de Canard au Miel. Grilled fattened duck breast with honey.

Râble de Lapin, Sauce à la Moutarde aux Aromates. Saddle of rabbit in mustard sauce with herbs.

Agneau de Pauillac au Four avec son Jus. Oven-baked Pauillac lamb with natural juices.

Noix de Saint-Jacques en Coquille Beurre de Ciboulette. Scallops presented in the shell with chive butter.

Soufflé au Chocolat. Chocolate soufflé.

Crumble aux Pommes Glace Vanille Bourbon. Apple crumble with homemade vanilla ice cream with whiskey.

Bordeaux. Wines of the month are moderately priced.

MENU-CARTE | 165 francs.

8ᵉ ARRONDISSEMENT

BERRYS

LE BOUCOLÉON

MA BOURGOGNE

ÉTOILE–CHAMPS-ÉLYSÉES

PLACES OF INTEREST

Arc de Triomphe

Avenues Montaigne and Matignon

Champs-Élysées

Église de la Madeleine

Gare St-Lazare

Grand Palais

Musée Cernuschi

Musée Jacquemart-André

Musée Nissim de Camondo

Parc Monceau

Petit Palais

Place de la Concorde

Pont de l'Alma (Bateaux Mouches and Vedettes)

Rue du Faubourg St-Honoré

Rue Royale

Berrys

M. PATRICK CIROTTE

44, rue de Naples, 75008 (off boulevard Malesherbes) |
🚋 Villiers
☎ 01-40-75-01-56 | Fax 01-45-61-24-76
Ø Saturday lunch and Sunday
$$ | VISA MasterCard
☞

P atrick Cirotte has dedicated his bistro to two of his passions, the cuisine of his native Berry region and the sport of soccer. Located just around the corner from the Musée Nissim de Camondo (which is not to be missed), Berrys is the little bistro annex of Cirotte's gourmet restaurant Le Grenadin. The atmosphere is cheerful, with twelve tables downstairs and a few more on a small mezzanine. White stucco walls are decorated with colorful displays of rugby jerseys, photographs of sports teams, and a striking Kandinsky-like fresco executed by Daniel Humair, a friend who is a jazz musician.

The food, which is prepared in and served from a kitchen shared with Le Grenadin, recalls the Berry region, south of Touraine in the valley of the Loire. An entire meal prepared by this master chef can cost as little as 100 francs if you opt for one of the formulas from the *menu d'aujourd'hui,* but there is also a larger à la carte listing with a variety of dishes. The perennial hors d'oeuvre specialties are a chicken liver terrine ("Mme. Arlette") with endives, and smoked ham Sancerre with a celery *rémoulade.* Specialties among the main dishes are veal (*viau*) in a wonderfully rich red wine sauce; a fricassee of chicken *à la Berrichone* with cabbage, poached chestnuts, and a glaze of pearl onions; and a dish of *andouillettes* accompanied by a superb gratin of macaroni. Desserts include a thick apple fritter (*chanciau*) with *crème anglaise*, and a pear (*poirat*) glazed in dark chocolate. There are some good, reasonably priced regional wines, light, fruity, and dry.

RECOMMENDED DISHES

Jambon de Sancerre Fumé aux Sarments de Vigne et son Céleri Rémoulade. Regional ham smoked over vine shoots and celery dressed with a spicy oil and vinegar sauce.

Salade Berrichonne. Salad greens, tomatoes, celery and *fromage de chèvre* (goat cheese).

Terrine de "Mme. Arlette," Foies de Volaille, et Salade d'Endives. Chicken liver pâté accompanied by an endive salad.

Paleron de Boeuf Braisé, Topinambours. Braised shoulder of beef with Jerusalem artichokes.

Andouillette et son Gratin de Macaronis. Grilled chitterling pork sausage accompanied by a gratin of macaroni and cheese.

Veau (Viau) au Vin Rouge, Pommes de Terre. Sliced veal in a rich wine sauce, with sautéed potatoes.

Filet de Saumon et Épinards à l'Ail. Grilled salmon with fresh spinach and garlic cloves.

Fricassée de Volaille au Sancerre. Creamed chicken stew made with Sancerre wine.

Poirat Berrichon et Glace au Chocolat. Pear glazed with bittersweet chocolate.

Chanciau aux Pommes et Anglaise Vanille. Apple fritter in vanilla egg custard.

Coteaux de Vendômois (Jean Brazilier), Touraine rouge (Marionnet), Reuilly (Claude Lafond). Trois Monts beer.

MENU │ 100 francs.

Le Boucoléon

M. Jérémy Claval

Chef: Philippe Abraham

10, rue de Constantinople, 75008 (at rue de Naples) |

🚃 Villiers or Europe

☎ 01-42-93-73-33 | Fax 01-42-93-17-44

Ø Saturday and Sunday; August

$ $ | VISA MasterCard

☕☕ | ☼

Here, in an unfashionable neighborhood alongside the railroad yards of the Gare St-Lazare, two professionals with backgrounds in the restaurants of Bocuse, Guy Savoy, and Goumard-Prunier, have taken over a nondescript little place and in short order created one of the best *qualité-prix* bistros in the city.

Jérémy Claval oversees the 25-seat dining room, which is perpetually crowded with regulars who are joyfully squeezed around oilcloth-covered tables in anticipation of the savory cuisine prepared by chef Philippe Abraham. The slate menu is always enticing, with such diversified choices as tiny sardine-filled ravioli in a chive-infused cream sauce; homemade smoked salmon; rib steak with béarnaise sauce and crispy *pommes frites;* a duck *pot-au-feu;* and panfried sea bream with artichokes and fresh coriander. A few inexpensive wines are listed.

If you close your eyes to the decor, you will certainly be treated to some of the most refined and inexpensive food to be found.

RECOMMENDED DISHES

Tartare de Saumon Coupé au Couteau. Raw, seasoned salmon chopped by hand.

Gâteau de Champignons. Savory mushroom tart.

Tatin de Boudin Noir et Poivre Vert. A blood sausage tart with green peppercorns.

Ragoût de Penne aux Gambas. A stew of macaroni and jumbo shrimp.

Entrecôte Béarnaise, Pont-Neuf. Grilled rib steak accompanied by a sauce of shallots, tarragon, butter, vinegar, and egg yolks. Excellent *pommes frites.*

Noisette de Selle d'Agneau et Nage de Cocos. Saddle joint of lamb cooked in its own juices in a bed of large haricot beans.

Filets de Rougets Poêlés et Charlotte Écrasée. Panfried red mullet fillets and crushed vegetables.

Dos de Cabillaud Rôti Ragoût de Légumes. Thick slice of fresh cod, roasted and accompanied by a vegetable stew.

Paleron Braisé au Laurier. Shoulder of beef braised with bay leaves.

Crème Brûlée Sauce au Thé. Caramelized cream custard flavored with tea.

Financier au Chocolat Chaud. Small sponge cake with ground almonds and hot chocolate melted on top.

Coteaux d'Aix (Domaine de la Tuilière-Vieille). Very modest but intelligently conceived *cave.*

Ma Bourgogne

M. Louis Prin

133, boulevard Haussmann, 75008 (off rue de
   Miromesnil) | 🚋 Miromesnil
☎ 01-45-63-50-61 | Fax 01-42-56-33-71
∅ Saturday and Sunday; July15 through August 15
$$ | ■ VISA MasterCard
☞ | 🍷

This is a large, well-established wine bistro that has been serving serious aficionados for more than thirty years. Customers come here to seek the hearty Burgundian daily specials, engage in spirited conversation, and drink the wine of southern Burgundy and the Beaujolais. Since the client base is drawn from the numerous office buildings in the neighborhood, lunchtime can be daunting. Customers sometimes line up two deep at the zinc bar for a quick snack, and the rustic back room and downstairs are usually filled with regulars. Evenings are more sedate: One can sit back and enjoy the solid, traditional list of Burgundian specialties.

When *coq au vin* is on the menu, most Thursdays, it should never be passed up. Here this hearty dish is made with extraordinary Chénas wine and is cooked to perfection. Other time-tested dishes include *oeufs en meurette, escargots de Bourgogne, jambon persillé,* and wonderful fresh foie gras made in the bistro's own kitchen.

Ma Bourgogne is within easy walking distance of the Musée Jacquemart-André, which houses an excellent collection of art and antiques and is considered one of the finest museums in Paris. Why not combine both places in one visit and experience a real treat?

RECOMMENDED DISHES

Oeufs en Meurette. Poached eggs in a red wine sauce with pieces of bacon and tiny onions.

Cassolette d'Escargots de Bourgogne. Burgundian vineyard snails served in their shells with garlic butter.

Jambon Persillé. Chunks of cooked ham in parsleyed aspic.

Entrecôte Beaujolaise. Grilled beef rib steak in a red wine sauce with shallots.

Coq au Vin (Juliénas), Pâtes Fraîches. Chicken cooked in a thickened Beaujolais wine sauce with onions, garlic, mushrooms, and bacon, served with fresh noodles.

Boeuf Bourguignon. Beef cooked in red Burgundy wine with bacon, small onions, and mushrooms.

Pavé de Lieu Jaune Grillé à l'Unilatérale. Thick piece of yellow pollack, grilled on one side only.

Blanquette de Veau aux Morilles. Veal stewed in a white roux sauce with morel mushrooms.

Feuilleté aux Pommes Tièdes. Flaky pastry with apple, served warm.

Crêpes Suzette. Hot crêpe dessert, flamed with curaçao liqueur.

Excellent selection of Beaujolais and Burgundy wines. Pouilly-Fumé, Chénas, Saint-Véran, Morgon.

MENUS | Lunch 165 francs, dinner 195 francs.

9ᵉ ARRONDISSEMENT

L'ALSACO WINSTUB

CHEZ CATHERINE

L'OENOTHÈQUE

CASA OLYMPE

LE PÉTRELLE

VELLY

OPÉRA–TRINITÉ–PIGALLE

L'Alsaco Winstub

M. Claude Steger

10, rue Condorcet, 75009 (off rue de Maubeuge) |
📟 Poissonnière
☎ 01-45-26-44-31 | Fax 01-42-85-11-05
Ø Saturday lunch and Sunday; August
$ | 💳 VISA MasterCard
🍲 | 🍷

Running his little rustic Alsatian "winstub" with warmth and expertise, Claude Steger is a virtual one-man show, disappearing into his kitchen to prepare a course, rushing out to greet a familiar customer, helping another select one of the 250 varieties of regional wines, or extolling the virtues of his rare artisan beers to a new guest.

The comfortable old-fashioned Alsatian decor is highlighted by a marvelous hunting scene on wall panels painted by Edgar Malher, antique beer steins, and country plates. The tables are covered with bright folklorish cloths and set with wine-colored napkins and green-stem Alsatian wineglasses. There is a wonderful old black-and-white tile floor.

Most of the menu consists of authentic versions of dishes for which the Alsace region is so acclaimed. Top-quality smoked meats and sausages are brought in from the Strasbourg area, and the fermented cabbage used in the *choucroute garnie* is produced in Krautergersheim (Cabbageland). Three other delectable dishes are *pipalakass,* a *fromage blanc* with cumin, onions, and herbs; *backaofa,* a stew of mutton, beef, pork, and potatoes braised in Riesling and served every Friday or to order; and *flammakuacha,* an onion tart made with cream and bacon. Météor beer is served on draft, and there is a large selection of regional *eaux-de-vie.* For dessert you might try the cheese platter, a large selection of Muenster cheese in varying degrees of ripeness.

RECOMMENDED DISHES

Pipalakass. *Fromage blanc* accented with cumin, onions, and herbs.

Jambon Cru de la Forêt Noire. Smoked and cured Black Forest ham.

Flammakuacha. Traditional Alsatian "pizza."

Salade de Choucroute Paysanne. Sauerkraut salad with assorted smoked meats and sausages.

Jarret Braisé à la Munichoise. Knuckle of pork braised in beer.

Assiette de Choucroute Garnie Maison. Platter of house sauerkraut with three kinds of smoked pork and sausages.

Backaofa. Traditional Alsatian stew (available Fridays or to order a few days in advance).

Petite Marmite Marcaire du Bruckenwald. Oven-baked dish of smoked pork and potatoes (to order a few days in advance).

Plateau de Münster Varié. Platter of aged Muenster cheeses.

Sorbet au Gewurst Vendanges Tardives et Marc. Sorbet with distilled marc (brandy).

More than 250 Alsatian wines and 60 *eaux-de-vie;* Riesling and Sylvaner stand out.

MENUS | Lunch 87 francs, dinner 95 francs and 190 francs.

Chez Catherine

MME. CATHERINE GUERRAZ

65, rue de Provence, 75009 (off rue de la Chaussée
d'Antin) | 🚇 Chaussée-d'Antin
☎ 01-45-26-72-88 | Fax 01-42-80-96-88
Ø Saturday, Sunday, and Monday evening; August
$$$ | VISA MasterCard ◉

𝕮 𝕮 𝕮

Here is a traditional bistro to be treasured, a rare combination of *cuisine bonne femme* created by the charming, talented Catherine and an exemplary cellar lovingly assembled by her husband, Frédéric.

Catherine Guerraz had the good fortune to be brought up in a Provençal household with her father, a famous Michelin-starred chef, from whom she inherited her culinary talent. When the opportunity came, five years ago, to take over this rather run-down 1950s-style bistro, a meeting place for women of little virtue, she and her husband, who was in advertising, jumped at the chance. It was not long before their tiny 28-seat bistro was requiring reservations several weeks in advance. They have, in fact, recently opened an annex a few doors down the street, which also became an instant success (Le Bouchon de Catherine, 63, rue de Provence, 01-48-78-67-00).

The *carte* seldom changes, as Catherine's classic dishes are all cooked to perfection. Many consider her *steak au poivre* in cream sauce with a touch of cognac to be the best in Paris. Her ravioli, stuffed with either basil or *cèpes* (mushrooms), also served in a cream sauce, are light and bursting with flavor. Equally impressive are the tuna steak with mangoes and *girolles* (mushrooms) and, depending on the season, sea scallops with endives and wild duck with figs.

An exquisite *crème brûlée* with pistachios and pears is the favored dessert.

Frédéric Guerraz has earned a reputation for excellent wines, some of which are served by the glass and carafe. All the wines, including the *grands crus,* are reasonably priced.

RECOMMENDED DISHES

Beignets de Fleurs de Courgette. Deep-fried zucchini fritters.

Ravioles aux Cèpes. Ravioli in cream sauce with *cèpes.*

Gâteau de Foies Blonds, Comme en Bugey. Pounded chicken livers mixed with foie gras, eggs, and cream; steamed and served with a sauce of crayfish tails.

Terrine d'Agneau à la Menthe. Lamb pâté terrine with fresh mint.

Steak au Poivre Flanqué de Pommes Sautées. Panfried steak covered with crushed peppercorns and cream sauce, sliced sautéed potatoes.

Pigeonneaux aux Petits Pois. Braised squab with mixed peas and onions.

Confit de Canard. Duck, cooked and preserved in its own fat.

Thon aux Girolles et aux Mangues. Grilled tuna steak with wild mushrooms and mangoes.

Demi-Canard Sauvageon Rôti "Façon Catherine." Half a roast duck with potatoes and apples.

Saint-Jacques à la Fondue d'Endive. Grilled sea scallops with a pulpy reduction of endive.

Crème Brûlée à la Pistache et aux Poires. Caramelized custard flan in a pear sauce with pistachio nuts.

Extensive cellar of Rhône Valley and little-known country wines.

L'Oenothèque

M. DANIEL HALLÉE

20, rue St-Lazare, 75009 (off rue St-Georges) |
▭▭▭ Notre-Dame-de-Lorette
☎ 01-48-78-08-76 | Fax 01-40-16-10-27
Ø Saturday and Sunday; last two weeks of August
$ $ $ | 💳 VISA 💳 💳
🍳 | 🍷

D aniel Hallée, a former sommelier to Joel Robu-chon, describes his little place—in a building that has housed an eating or drinking establishment since 1847—as a café, a *cave*, or a *traiteur*. Actually, this charming bistro is a sophisticated *restaurant-à-vin*.

Wine bottles are stacked on shelves in the front as you enter a dimly lit interior surrounded by dark wine-and-charcoal walls, floors, and ceilings. Large paintings splashed with color hang on the dark walls; these works by contemporary artists are the only decorations. Although the two small rooms are crowded, there is an atmosphere of serenity.

M. Hallée, a wine and cognac merchant, offers a short daily menu of well-prepared classic terrines, foie gras, grilled meats, and fine game in season. Roast pigeon is a specialty, and there are always one or two simple but fresh fish dishes. First and foremost, however, is the extraordinary selection of wines and cognacs, over 450 in all, and the vibrant personality of the generous host.

RECOMMENDED DISHES

Foie Gras de Canard au Torchon. Duck foie gras cooked tied in a cloth and steeped in brine.

Terrine de Pied de Veau. Calf's foot pâté served in an earthenware terrine.

Casserons Rôtis. Pan-roasted cuttlefish.

Salmis de Faisan. A game stew of boned pheasant slow-cooked in red wine and served in a casserole.

Foie de Veau en Papillotte. Calf's liver seasoned with herbs and baked inside a pouch of parchment paper.

Noix de Saint-Jacques en Coquille, Persillade. Scallops presented in a shell with a condiment of chopped parsley and garlic.

Côte de Boeuf à la Moelle. Roast ribs of beef garnished with poached bone marrow (for two).

Pigeonneau de Racan Rôti. Roast young tender squab.

Soupe de Fraises au Vin. Fresh strawberries steeped in red wine.

Crème Brûlée. Cream-based custard topped with brown sugar and crusted under the grill.

In-depth selection of more than 400 wines and about 50 vintage cognacs.

MENU-CARTE | 180 francs.

Casa Olympe

MME. DOMINIQUE VERSINI

48, rue St-Georges, 75009 (off rue St-Lazare) |
Saint-Georges

☎ 01-42-85-26-01 | Fax 01-45-26-49-33

Ø Saturday and Sunday; first week of May; and first three weeks of August

$$$ | VISA MasterCard

Multicolored cracked-tile floors, a few wine-colored banquettes, deep ocher walls, and yellow and green pottery lend a Mediterranean air to Dominique Versini's newest venture, located a block from the Gustave Moreau museum. Versini, known as Olympe, brings her enormous range of culinary skills to this tiny, sunny bistro. Two minuscule rooms with a few small tables squeezed close together are separated by an attractive wooden appetizing table set with a basket of country bread, mushrooms, fruits, and stacks of yellow and green faience plates.

Olympe is celebrated for *cuisine ménagère* (home-style cooking), which emphasizes fresh produce cooked with simple tasty garnishes. The menu-carte at 200 francs is a windfall yet deceptive, as there are often supplements attached to some of the dishes. Everything is expertly prepared, making it difficult to single out any specialties. Fennel ravioli in a crab cream sauce and crispy pieces of *boudin noir* sausages on a mesclun mix are ideal starters. Particularly good to follow is the free-range chicken in a crayfish-flavored cream sauce served with potato pancakes; the tuna steak with bacon and onions; or the Challans duck in a tangy herbal sauce on a bed of very thin pasta garnished with herbs, vegetables, and accented with ginger.

Olympe remains one of the top chefs on every gourmet's list. It is a pity that this place is so small, making dining a bit close and reservations a necessity.

RECOMMENDED DISHES

Aubergines Grillées avec Tomates et Brousse. Grilled eggplant with tomatoes and fresh goat cheese salted with herbs.
Croustillant de Boudin au Mesclun. Crunchy blood sausage on a bed of greens.
Pipérade à l'Oeuf Poché. A fondue of bell peppers and tomatoes flavored with onion and garlic, topped with a poached egg.

Thon au Lard et aux Oignons. Grilled tuna steak garnished
with onions and bacon.

Canette de Challans avec sa Sauce Acide et Douce aux Épices.
Roast Challans duckling served in a spiced sweet-and-
sour sauce.

Cocotte de Lapin. Slow-cooked rabbit stew, served in its
own casserole.

Turbot Sauvage à l'Huile d'Olive. Line-caught turbot fried
with olive oil.

Épaule d'Agneau de Sisteron, Rôtie au Four. Shoulder of
lamb, oven-roasted.

Crème Brûlée à la Vraie Vanille. Cream-based custard topped
with caramelized brown sugar, then topped with shredded vanilla.

Fondant au Chocolat Amer. Iced bitter chocolate cake.

✎ *Vin de pays* des Coteaux de l'Ardèche.

MENU-CARTE | 200 francs.

Le Pétrelle

M. JEAN-LUC ANDRÉ

34, rue Pétrelle, 75009 (off rue de Rochechouart) |
🚌 Poissonnière

☎ 01-42-82-11-02 | Fax 01-40-23-05-69

Ø Saturday lunch, Sunday, Monday lunch; July 25
through August 25

$ $ $ | VISA MasterCard

☞ | ☀

Jean-Luc André, the owner-chef of this charming
neighborhood bistro, treats his customers to rich
and generous portions of home-style cooking using
the best produce the market and season have to offer.

Upon entering Le Pétrelle one is greeted by an odd collection of whimsical bric-a-brac that does not detract from the nicely set tables and bouquets of fresh flowers. The menu has a sophistication that one might not expect, with entrées such as wild asparagus, sushi-style Breton langoustine, and warm rabbit salad with fava beans dressed in walnut oil. The *plat du moment* might be milk-fed veal with *girolles* (mushrooms) and the fish of the moment line-caught sea bass with fennel. During the fall all sorts of game appear, accompanied by seasonal vegetables, mushrooms, and truffles. A classic *entrecôte bordelaise* with marrow is usually available. Seasonal fresh fruits are used in many of the desserts. We especially like the poached prunes in red wine with cinnamon and the *sablés* with almonds and fresh apricots.

Rhône Valley wines are chef André's passion, but the wine list also has many interesting Bordeaux.

This little, hidden gem is certainly located in an inconvenient area, far off the beaten track, but it is well worth seeking out, for it is the kind of place Parisian gourmets keep to themselves.

RECOMMENDED DISHES

Fricassée de Girolles Feuilleté, Parmesan. Mushrooms stewed in a white cream sauce, presented in a puff pastry sprinkled with Parmesan cheese.

Terrine de Canard, Noisette, Cerfeuil. Duck liver pâté with hazelnuts and chervil.

Pélardon en Cocotte à la Crème et au Thym. Goat cheese in a round casserole with cream sauce herbed with thyme.

Fricassée d'Asperges Sauvages et Févettes. Vegetarian stew of wild asparagus and broad beans.

Côte de Veau de Lait, aux Girolles. Tender veal cutlet with chanterelle mushrooms.

Lièvre à la Royale. Boned hare braised with red wine, shallots, and onions and stuffed with foie gras and truffles.

Entrecôte Bordelaise à la Moelle. Grilled beef rib steak with *cèpes* (mushrooms) garnished with poached bone marrow.

Fondant d'Agneau de Lait, aux Olives de Nice. Baby lamb croquette with black olives.

Poisson du Moment. Fish, fresh from the market, prepared as you like it.

Compote de Poire, Pomme, Anis Étoilé. Stewed pears and apples with a pinch of star anise.

Croustillant au Praliné Glacé et Abricots Marinés. Caramel and toasted nut crunch topped with ice cream and stewed apricots.

Excellent selection of little-known Bordeaux.

MENU DU MARCHÉ | 148 francs.

Velly

M. ALAIN BRIGANT

52, rue Lamartine, 75009 (at rue Milton, just up from Place Kossuth) | Notre-Dame-de-Lorette

☎ 01-48-78-60-05 | Fax 01-48-78-60-05

Ø Saturday lunch and Sunday; three weeks in August

$ | VISA MasterCard

👥👥 | ☼

Each morning Alain Brigant, young, classically trained chef, shops at the food markets for the six to eight meat and fish dishes that will be featured on his daily slate menu. His culinary skills, honed in the restaurants of the Bristol, the Manoir de Paris, and Chez Fauchon, can be observed, as he works out of an open kitchen of gleaming stainless steel and copper.

The minuscule dining room, entered through a red

lacquered front, is pleasingly decorated with cream-colored walls and tiles accented by red bricks, a few wine-colored banquettes, and tables covered with white cloths overlaid with wine-colored paper. English is spoken, and the service is friendly and prompt. The clientele is almost exclusively French except for a few savvy visitors who frequent the nearby Drouant auction house. Although the choice on any day depends on the market, fillet of duck breast in cider vinegar and veal kidney in a *confit* of port are often available, and there are always two or three choices of fresh fish.

With only 25 places available, reservations are essential. A recently constructed upstairs dining room promises to add a few more tables.

RECOMMENDED DISHES

Salade d'Andouille Poêlée. Panfried pork tripe sausage, sliced, in a salad.

Croustillant aux Pommes et Pont-l'Évèque. Crunchy cake made of potato and flavorful Normandy cheese.

Rognon Confit au Porto. Preserved veal kidney cooked with port wine and embellished with wild mushrooms.

Pied de Porc Braisé à la Sauge. Braised pig's trotter herbed with sage.

Agneau de Sept Heures, à Manger à la Cuillère. Slow-cooked seven-hour lamb so tender that it can be eaten with a spoon.

Minute de Bar aux Girolles. Quickly cooked sea bass with highly prized orange-colored mushrooms.

Fricassée de Saint-Jacques et Galette d'Oreille de Cochon. Slow-stewed scallops in white sauce with a potato and pig's ear cake.

Palet au Chocolat. Chocolate petit four.

Soupe de Pamplemousse à l'Orgeat. Thick, chunky grapefruit soup with chopped almonds and sugar syrup.

✎ Cahors, Morgon, Vacqueyras, Menetou-Salon, Chablis.
MENU-CARTE | Lunch 145 francs, dinner 170 francs.

10^E ARRONDISSEMENT

LE BOULEDOGUE BISTROT

LA GRILLE

CHEZ MICHEL

LE PARMENTIER

LE RÉVEIL DU X^E

GARE DU NORD–
GARE DE L'EST

PLACES OF INTEREST

Canal St-Martin

Gare du Nord, Gare de l'Est

Musée de l'Affiche et de la Publicité

Place de la République
(3e, 10e, 11e)

Porte St-Denis

Porte St-Martin

Rue de Paradis

Le Bouledogue Bistrot

M. GUILLAUME BELLOT

56, rue de Lancry, 75010 (at Canal St-Martin off boulevard de Magenta. Cross street, rue Jean Poulmarch) |
🚊 Jacques-Bonsergent
☎ 01-42-08-38-81
∅ Saturday lunch and Sunday; August
$ $ | 💳 💳 💳
🍲

Formerly known as Au Gigot Fin, this atmospheric 1920s bistro just steps from the Canal St-Martin has been taken over by a young chef who has scaled down the menu but wisely retained the classic *gigot du Limousin* (roast lamb) for which the restaurant is famous.

We have always admired the authentic appointments that give this little place a special charm. It has a polished wooden bar, warm paneling beneath cream-colored walls, and a beautiful metal spiral staircase, decorated with a grape motif, leading up to the bathrooms.

Guillaume Bellot prepares a very traditional offering of bistro classics, drawing from such diverse regions as Burgundy, the southwest, and Provence. You might start with pan-roasted foie gras with caramelized onions and grapes, a specialty; Burgundian snails; or smoked Norwegian salmon—followed by a veal chop with wild mushrooms, marinated baked sea bream, duck confit, or the tender oven-roasted leg of lamb with whole garlic cloves, served with large white haricot beans Provençal style. The charlotte with two chocolates and the profiteroles are the recommended desserts. There is a nice choice of wine from the Beaujolais and the Côtes du Rhône.

RECOMMENDED DISHES

Foie Gras Poêlé, Oignons et Raisins Caramélisé. Panfried foie gras with caramelized onions and grapes.

Six Escargots de Bourgogne. Plump Burgundian vineyard snails served in their shells with garlic butter.

Terrine de Lièvre à l'Armagnac. Hare pâté prepared with Armagnac brandy and served in an earthenware terrine.

Gigot du Limousin Piqué à l'Ail, Haricots Blancs. Roast leg of lamb studded with garlic and accompanied by broad white beans.

Marbré de Poisson Mariné, Menthe et Basilic. Striped sea bream marinated with fresh mint and basil.

Confit de Canard de Barbarie. Grilled preserved Barbary free-range duck.

Côte de Veau aux Morilles. Grilled veal chop with morel mushrooms.

Coeur de Rumsteak au Roquefort. Thick heart of rumpsteak in a Roquefort (blue cheese) sauce.

Profiteroles Maison. Small hollow pastry balls made with *choux* paste and covered with hot chocolate sauce.

Charlotte au Deux Chocolats. Molded custard cream like a chocolate mousse, lined with sponge fingers.

Côtes de Blaye (Chante Alouette), Brouilly (Château La Chaize), Aloxe-Corton (Domaine Maillard), Côte de Gascogne (Domaine de la Jalousie).

MENUS | Lunch 80 francs, dinner 100 francs.

La Grille

M. Yves Cullerre
Mme. Geneviève Cullerre
Chef: Yves Cullerre

80, rue du Faubourg-Poissonnière, 75010 (at the intersection of rue de Montholon and rue des Messageries) |
🚌 Poissonnière
☎ 01-47-70-89-73
∅ Saturday and Sunday; two weeks in August
$ $ $ | 💳 🆅🅸🆂🅰 💳
♨ ♨ ♨

We always seem to order the same meal at La Grille: Yves Cullerre's creation *turbot grillé au beurre blanc*. His renowned sauce is made not only with freshest Nantais butter but also with shallots, wine vinegar, fish stock, seasoning, and—most important of all—his skill at whipping the mixture into a froth of tangy perfection. This exquisite sauce accompanies specially selected turbot (served for two) shipped directly from Brittany and a mouthwatering cake of potatoes. In the fall the same sauce is served on plump sea scallops. If you choose herring with warm potato salad, the fresh mackerel marinated in white wine, or a seafood terrine to start, you might like to try the *beef bourguignon*—another exceptional dish. Mme. Cullerre will welcome you into a cozy, theatrically adorned room with antique laces, embroideries, old hats, and assorted mementos. This is one of those rare places that will not last forever.

RECOMMENDED DISHES

Terrine au Canard aux Noisettes. Duck liver and hazelnut pâté served in an earthenware terrine.

Maquereaux Frais "Vin Blanc." Whole fresh mackerel poached in white wine.

Turbot Grillé au Beurre Blanc. Grilled turbot served with a white wine butter sauce accompanied by a potato loaf cooked with bacon (for two).

Brochette de Saint-Jacques au Beurre Blanc. Skewered sea scallops with a white wine butter sauce (available during the fall).

Tête de Veau, Gribiche. Hot calf's head served with a spicy mustard-mayonnaise sauce.

Boeuf Bourguignon à l'Ancienne. Beef stewed in red wine with mushrooms, onions, and bacon.

Andouillette de Pays, à la Moutarde. Grilled pork sausage in mustard sauce.

Filet de Boeuf au Poivre Vert. Grilled tenderloin of beef in a green peppercorn sauce.

Oeufs au Lait. Egg custard flan, baked in the oven.

Dame Blanche. Vanilla ice cream with Chantilly cream and hot chocolate sauce.

Bordeaux (Château Taris), Chinon, Menetou-Salon (Chez Clément).

Chez Michel

M. THIERRY BRETON

10, rue Belzunce, 75010 (behind St-Vincent-de-Paul church off boulevard de Magenta) | Gare du Nord or Poissonnière

☎ 01-44-53-06-20 | Fax 01-44-53-61-31

Ø Sunday and Monday; middle of July through middle of August

$ $ | VISA MasterCard

♟ ♟ ♟

One would never guess that within the rustic walls of Thierry Breton's little inn some of the most inspired and truly original cooking is taking place. Chez Michel is located near the Gare du Nord, opposite the church of St-Vincent-de-Paul. Breton, who trained in the kitchens of the Ritz, Tour d'Argent, and the Crillon, is setting records of his own.

One can forgive the good-natured but amateurish service as densely flavored terrines appear. Breton's specialty is a *terrine d'andouille* served with pancakes, fresh butter, *cornichons,* and grainy mustard. Sea scallops might be accompanied by endives braised in orange juice or combined with anchovies in a light tomato sauce. Delicate goat cheese and artichoke ravioli or thinly layered lasagna appear in a garlicky pesto sauce. Thin slices of *boudin noir* are perfectly matched with a puree of potatoes. There is no limit to Breton's imaginative and audacious use of ingredients. In season there is a special lobster menu, and in the fall a separate game menu includes partridge with *cèpes* (mushrooms) and grouse stuffed with foie gras. *Paris-Brest* is a pastry ring with coffee butter and hazelnuts; and *kuing amann* (a traditional Breton yeast cake) is warm and buttery with apples and served with cider sherbet.

If you are not able to reserve at Chez Michel, you might try Breton's inexpensive smaller bistro, Chez Casimir, which is just down the street (6, rue de Belzunce, 01-48-78-28-80).

RECOMMENDED DISHES

Terrine d'Andouille Galette et Beurre Salé au Guérande. Pork sausage terrine with peppercorns accompanied by shortbread biscuits made with slightly salted butter.

Kig Ha Farz de Joues de Cochon et Lard Grillé Paysan. Pot-au-feu of pig's cheeks and grilled pork fat.

Brouillade d'Oeuf d'Oie dans sa Coque Crémeux de Langoustine Mouillettes. Scrambled goose egg presented in the shell with crawfish sauce and bread strips for dipping.

Poitrine de Colvert au Fruits et sa Cuisse Confite en Salade.
Mallard duck in two services: first the breast with berries, then the preserved legs in a salad.

Saint-Jacques Rôties en Coquilles, Endives Braisées à l'Orange.
Roast scallops presented on the shell with braised endives in orange sauce.

Palombe Rôtie sur l'Os aux Cèpes, Jus de la Bête. Roast wild pigeon with bone marrow mixed with *cèpes* (mushrooms) and beet juice.

Tête de Veau Croustillante aux Huîtres, Tagliatelles de Blé Noir. Caramelized calf's head with oysters and buckwheat noodles.

Fricassée de Veau Fermière Cocos de Paimpol à l'Estragon. Creamed veal stew with haricot beans spiced with tarragon.

Paris-Brest. Choux pastry ring filled with coffee butter cream and toasted hazelnuts.

Kuing Amann du Pays Servi Tiède. Large, rich yeast cake with cooked apples.

A short *carte* of mostly moderate-price wines. Superb cider from Breton's father's orchard in Normandy.

MENU-CARTE | 180 francs.

Le Parmentier

M. CÉLINE COSTIL

12, rue Arthur-Groussier, 75010 (between avenue Parmentier and rue St-Maur) | � Goncourt

☎ 01-42-40-71-75

Ø Saturday lunch and Sunday; August

$ | VISA

☞☞ | ☼

idden away in a somber, difficult-to-find street near the St-Louis hospital is the azure-blue mosaic entrance of this inexpensive, cheerful neighborhood bistro. The decor is a little bare, almost austere, but pretty flowers and tables covered with white cloths lend an air of sophistication, the perfect complement to the subtle and refined menu prepared by the owner-chef, Céline Costil. Ravioli with creamed eggplant, rillettes of salmon with lime-green lentil salad, and a homemade veal terrine with pistachios are among the enticing appetizers. To follow, the fillet of beef in a creamy pepper sauce and a flavorful chicken curry are two popular choices. Fish dishes might include a risotto with squid and *dorade* (sea bream) with a confit of fennel and lime. *Hachis Parmentier* is a specialty. This is a lightened version of a bistro classic (shepherd's pie) invented in the eighteenth century by Auguste Parmentier to convince a snobbish French public that potatoes were both edible and delicious. Everyone raves about the apple crumble, and there is a nice *crème brûlée* sprinkled with ginger.

The dinner menu at 150 francs includes wine and coffee served with delicious petits fours. For those with smaller appetites, all the choices on the slate menu may be ordered à la carte.

RECOMMENDED DISHES

Terrine au Veau. Rustic veal and pistachio pâté served in an earthenware terrine.

Rillettes de Saumon au Citron Vert. Chopped salmon bits cooked to a paste, flavored with lime juice, and accompanied by toast.

Saumon Poché, Courgettes Vapeur. Poached salmon with steamed zucchini.

Daube de Boeuf à la Provençale. Slow-cooked Provençale beef stew with red wine and black olives.

Hachis Parmentier. Outstanding version of shepherd's pie, minced meat and mashed potatoes baked in the oven.

Morue Poêlée, Purée de Pomme de Terre à l'Huile d'Olive.
Panfried fresh cod with mashed potatoes and olive oil.

Filet de Boeuf, Sauce au Poivre. Grilled beefsteak coated
with a crushed peppercorn sauce.

Rognons de Veau à la Moutarde. Veal kidney in mustard
sauce.

Fondant au Chocolat. Bonbon-like pastry with a glazed
chocolate icing.

Crêpes à l'Orange. Very thin pancakes with orange filling.

🥄 Nice but small selection of varied wines including
some moderate-price Bordeaux.

MENUS | Lunch 80 francs, dinner 128 francs or 150 francs.

Le Réveil du Xᵉ

M. DANIEL VIDALENC
MME. CATHY VIDALENC
CHEF: CATHY VIDALENC

35, rue du Château-d'Eau, 75010 (off rue du Faubourg-
St-Martin, down the street from the district town hall)
| 🚎 Château-d'Eau or République

☎ 01-42-41-77-59 | Fax 01-42-41-77-59

Ø Sunday; two weeks in August

$ | VISA MasterCard 💳

☕ | 🍷

One might easily pass by this slightly run-down
corner zinc bar and bistro in a working-class
neighborhood, but a real awakening (*réveil*) awaits
you if you opt to enter. Here Cathy and Daniel Vidalenc, a
charming young couple from the Auvergne region, offer
a vast assortment of special wines from the Beaujolais

region and some of the best authentic Auvergnat cuisine to be found in Paris.

Cathy has brought with her many of the hearty recipes from the mountains of central France and prepares down-home, earthy food to the delight of a large following of regular customers. The offerings include a heartwarming *potée,* a thick stew of meat and vegetables; a mouthwatering *pounti,* another one-dish meal, consisting of chopped pork, Swiss chard, onions, and prunes; *truffade,* a potato pancake of onions, bacon, and *tomme* cheese; and on the first Tuesday of the winter months, an intense *aligot,* a rich dish of potatoes, garlic, and *tomme* cheese, deceptively rustic. Perfectly aged Cantal cheese and a glass of fruity Beaujolais are a fine way to end the meal.

RECOMMENDED DISHES

Charcuteries. Sausages, terrines, and smoked Auvergne ham.

Tripoux. Tripe stuffed with minced pork, veal, and garlic, braised for hours over low heat.

Potée. Thick stew of pork and vegetables cooked in stock in an earthenware pot.

Pounti. Auvergne dish composed of chopped pork, Swiss chard, onions, and prunes baked in a casserole.

Truffade. Pancake made with shredded potato and *tomme* cheese. Accompanied by either a veal chop or a sausage.

Aligot. Fresh garlic and Cantal cheese combined with mashed potatoes.

Confit de Canard aux Pommes Sarladaises. Grilled preserved duck with sliced garlic potatoes.

Pied de Porc Farci aux Lentilles. Grilled pig's trotters heavily herbed and accompanied by small green lentils from Puy.

Clafoutis aux Cerises. Unpitted black cherry batter tart.

Tarte au Citron. Freshly made lemon tart.

➤ Nice selection of country wines, many available by the glass. Brouilly, Morgon, Chiroubles.

11ᵉ ARRONDISSEMENT

LES AMOGNES

ASTIER

AUBERGE PYRÉNÉES CÉVENNES

AU C'AMELOT

CARTET

CHARDENOUX

DAME JEANNE

LES JUMEAUX

LE PASSAGE

LE REPAIRE DE CARTOUCHE

À SOUSCEYRAC

LE VILLARET

RÉPUBLIQUE–NATION

PLACES OF INTEREST

Cirque d'Hiver

Église de Ste-Marguerite

Hôtel Tubeuf

Le Marché
(place d'Aligre)

Place de la Bastille
(Opéra de la Bastille)

Place de la République

Rue du Faubourg-St-Antoine

Rue de Lappe

Rue de la Roquette

Les Amognes

M. THIERRY COUÉ

243, rue du Faubourg-St-Antoine, 75011
   (off rue de Reuilly) | 🚇 Faidherbe-Chaligny
   or Reuilly-Diderot
☎ 01-43-72-73-05 | Fax 01-43-28-77-23
Ø Saturday lunch, Sunday and Monday lunch; first three
   weeks in August
$ $ $ | VISA MasterCard
♟♟♟

Thierry Coué, a Burgundian, is one of the best young chefs working in Paris today. As chef de cuisine at Alain Senderens's Michelin three-star restaurant L'Archestrate, he learned to concoct elaborate epicurean dishes but soon decided to strike out on his own, becoming one of the first celebrated chefs to open a bistro offering imaginative food at unbeatable prices.

The atmosphere and the setting recall a small country inn. In the sparkling white-paneled interior, the ceiling, with its painted wood beams, provides a stark contrast to the dark floors, stone wall, and bright splashes of modern art. The superb 180-franc menu is changed four times a year, but two of Coué's signature dishes are almost always available. One is an entrée: *tarte fraîche aux sardines,* a tart filled with marinated sardines. The other is a dessert: *crêpe fourrée de compote d'aubergines à la cardamome,* a delightful crepe of sweet stewed eggplant spiced with cardamom.

The cuisine is elaborate and very modern, with superlative touches in the use of vegetables. Typical of Coué's culinary talent is the ravioli, which he stuffs with various meats—rabbit, veal, or oxtail—and uses in soups or serves by themselves with cream sauces or vegetables; sausages wrapped in phyllo dough; or fish and shellfish matched with vegetables in unusual ways, such as a mussel soup with lentils or scallops with confit of tomato and *cèpes* (mushrooms). His very personal selection of marvelous little wines shows the same kind of imagination and good value as the food.

RECOMMENDED DISHES

Boudin Tiède, Marmelade d'Oignons au Cassis, Coing Poêlé. Lukewarm pudding sausage topped with stewed onions and quince paste.

Terrine de Foie Gras de Canard au Naturel. Pure fattened duck liver served in a terrine.

Tarte Fraîche aux Sardines Marinées. Marinated sardines in a cold open tart.

Rôti de Tête de Porc et Haricots Écrasés Cinglés d'une Vinai-grette Tiède. Roast pig's head and crushed beans mixed with a semisweet warm vinaigrette.

Ris de Veau Poêlé Minute. Quickly pan-roasted calf's sweetbreads.

Aile de Raie Rôtie aux Câpres et aux Bigorneaux. Roast skate wing in caper sauce with periwinkle snails.

Côte de Boeuf, Truffade Auvergnate. Roast rib of beef served with an Auvergne potato cake of Cantal cheese, bacon, and garlic.

Magret de Canard, Sauce Carottes, Poivreaux aux Miel et Soja. Fattened duck breast in carrot sauce accompanied by pepper stuffed with soybean sprouts infused with honey.

Compotée de Fruits de Saison, Bugnes Lyonnaises. Compote of stewed fruit in a sugar-dusted fritter.

Crêpe Fourrée de Compote d'Aubergines à la Cardamome. Sweet stewed eggplant spiced with cardamom served in a thin pancake.

Nice selection of about 50 *crus;* particularly fine Rhône Valley wines and the top Arbois wines of Pierre Overnoy.

MENU-CARTE | 180 francs.

Astier

M. Jean-Luc Clerc
M. Bertrand Vergnaud

44, rue Jean-Pierre-Timbaud, 75011 (off avenue de la
   République) | 🚃 Parmentier or Oberkampf
☎ 01-43-57-16-35
Ø Saturday and Sunday; August
$ | VISA MasterCard
☞

F
rom its beginning in the 1960s, this bustling, unpretentious bistro has been filled day and night with
well-heeled regulars and knowledgeable tourists
who come for the spectacular 145-franc, four-course
menu-carte (120 francs at lunch). Rows of small tables
covered with paper cloths are so closely packed together
that customers are squeezed elbow to elbow, making service a bit strained, but the congenial staff manages to keep
everyone happy.

The menu offers a huge selection of at least ten different choices for each of the courses. There are heaping
plates of herring, foie gras, country terrines, sausages,
salmon with tarragon, lamb with flageolets, veal stew, rabbit in mustard sauce with tagliatelle, chicken in cream
sauce with foie gras, duckling, fillets of beef, and baskets
of *pommes frites*—enough to satisfy the most ravenous
appetite. Astier also offers an excellent selection of about
20 cheeses, an impressive array of desserts, and a surprisingly comprehensive wine list featuring some of the best
names, a real treat for a modest price.

The decor is nonexistent, and the room is noisy and
smoky, with a constant flow of customers heading up the
narrow staircase to the first floor; but people come for the
food, the jovial company, and the conversation.

RECOMMENDED DISHES

Mousseline de Saumon au Beurre Blanc. Salmon mousse in a white wine butter sauce.

Soupe de Rouget au Safran. Thick, hearty fish soup made with red mullet seasoned with saffron.

Salade de Gésiers de Canard Confits. Salad of preserved chicken gizzards.

Fricassée de Joue de Porc aux Chanterelles. Pig's cheek stew with chanterelle mushrooms (*girolles*).

Navarin d'Agneau à l'Ancienne, avec Flageolets. Lamb stew with turnips, carrots, and onions and garnished with flageolet beans.

Lapin à la Moutarde aux Pâtes Fraîches. Rabbit in mustard sauce served with fresh pasta.

Brochette d'Onglet de Boeuf Grillé. Skewered beef flank, marinated and grilled.

Brandade de Morue. Creamed salt cod.

Sole de Ligne Meunière. Line-caught fillet of sole floured and panfried in butter with lemon juice and parsley added.

Clafoutis aux Mirabelles. Traditional batter tart made with small golden-yellow plums.

Gâteau au Chocolat avec sa Crème au Café. Rich chocolate cake layered with coffee cream.

Exceptionally well-priced and varied wine list.

MENUS-CARTES | Lunch 120 francs, dinner 145 francs.

Auberge Pyrénées Cévennes

M. Daniel Constantin
Mme. Françoise Constantin
Chef: Daniel Constantin

106, rue de la Folie-Méricourt, 75011 (off rue de la
    Fontaine au Roi across from Canal St-Martin) |
    🚌 République
☎ 01-43-57-33-78
Ø Saturday lunch; Sunday; July 14 through August 15
$$$ | 💳 VISA 💳
🍲🍲🍲

*A*fter being closed for a year following the death of its
longtime owner, Philippe Serbource, the Auberge
was taken over by a talented young couple from
Burgundy, and within a year it was awarded the Lillet Prize
as best traditional bistro of the year (1999) by the noted
critic Claude Lebey.

Wisely, the Constantins have maintained the tradition
of generous portions of regional classics in the unchanged
atmosphere of a rustic country inn. Copper pots, hanging
hams and garlic, deer heads, rough-hewn beams, mosaic
tile floors, and an impressive zinc bar make for lovely sur-
roundings.

The emphasis is on the rich cream and butter, sausage,
and pork dishes of the Lyonnais, with a significant nod to
the southwest with dishes like fresh duck foie gras, Ba-
yonne ham, Basque *pipérade,* preserved goose, and *cassoulet*
prepared with *confits de l'auberge.*

Regular customers who appreciate fine traditional
cooking have never deserted this place. Newcomers will
discover that the characteristic foods of the Lyonnais and
the southwest are always luscious.

RECOMMENDED DISHES

Cochonnailles de l'Auberge. Assorted sausages and terrines.

Salade de Lentilles du Puy, Vinaigrette. Salad of the small green lentils of Puy, vinaigrette dressing.

Petit Salé. Lightly salted pork tenderloin.

Salade Gourmande au Foie Gras. Fresh duck foie gras in a salad.

Cassoulet aux Confits de l'Auberge. Languedoc stew of white beans, pork, preserved goose and duck, sausages, garlic, and bread crumbs.

Foie de Veau Poêlé à la Lyonnaise. Panfried young calf's liver, sliced onions braised in butter with vinegar and chopped parsley added.

Andouillette de Maison Bobosse à la Moutarde. Grilled pork and veal tripe sausage in mustard sauce.

Pieds de Porc Pané, Sauce Ravigotte. Breaded pig's trotters in a hot spicy sauce of white wine and butter mixed with capers, tarragon, gherkins, and chopped hard-boiled eggs.

Quenelle de Brochet, Sauce Nantua. Pike dumplings in a béchamel sauce flavored with crayfish and tomato puree.

Crème Brûlée Cassonade. Rich cream-based custard topped with unrefined brown sugar, caramelized under the grill.

Nougat Glacé au Coulis de Framboise. Nougat ice cream with a puree of fresh raspberries.

Coteaux du Lyonnais, Côtes du Rhône, Bourgogne-Aligoté.

MENU | 154 francs.

Au C'Amelot

M. DIDIER VARNIER

50, rue Amelot, 75011 (off rue St-Sabin) |
🚃 Chemin-Vert
☎ 01-43-55-54-04 | Fax 01-43-14-77-05
Ø Sunday and Monday; August
$ | VISA MasterCard
🍲🍲

Didier Varnier, another talented chef and protégé of Christian Constant, took over this nondescript, narrow café a few years ago and now offers a bargain-priced five-course *menu unique* (no choice except for dessert) of traditional yet highly flavored gourmet dishes and a modest list of well-chosen wine.

The corridor dining room speaks of the original café, with its wooden wainscoting, beige banquettes, and hanging ceiling fans. Wall shelves are cluttered with an eclectic mix of old bottles, china, pottery, cooking implements, and forgettable pictures.

Every day chef Varnier changes his 170-franc blackboard menu according to the market and the season, but it always begins with a soup, crusty country bread, a pâté of the day, and a plate of thin-sliced sausages. A fish dish follows the entrée; then there is a meat or fowl course with all the trimmings. There is a small but excellent cheese selection from Alleosse and finally a choice from among six desserts, with coffee included. As everything is delicious, no one complains about not having a choice.

RECOMMENDED DISHES

Crème aux Crabes et Vermicelles. Cream of crab soup with fine vermicelli.

Beignet de Tête de Veau Braisée aux Épices. Diced calf's head fritter braised with spices.

Pigeon Rôti Aigre-Doux Taboulé de Fruits Secs. Roast pigeon in a sweet-and-sour sauce with a Lebanese salad of crushed wheat and dried fruits.

Dos de Lieu Jaune Croustillant Rémoulade de Céleri aux Câpres. Crispy fillet of yellow pollack garnished with a celery and caper mayonnaise sauce.

Canard au Miel. Duck roasted with honey.

Tartare de Daurade avec Rémoulade de Fenouil. Chopped sea bream in a spicy mayonnaise sauce with fennel.

Épaule d'Agneau de Lozère Rôtie Couscous de Fruits Secs. Roast shoulder of baby lamb with a couscous of dried fruits.

Lapin au Romarin. Roast rabbit with rosemary.

Riz au Lait aux Clémentines Caramélisées. Rice pudding with caramelized seedless orange sections.

Feuilleté aux Pêches. Flaky pastry stuffed with peaches.

Pinot noir (Joseph Binner), Gamay (Marionnet).

MENU-CARTE | Dinner 170 francs.

Cartet

M. RAYMOND NOUAILLE
MME. MARIE-THÉRÈSE NOUAILLE
CHEF: RAYMOND NOUAILLE

62, rue de Malte, 75011 (off place de la République at rue du Faubourg du Temple) | ▆▆▆ République

☎ 01-48-05-17-65

Ø Saturday and Sunday; August

$$$ | ⬒ NONE

ᗕᗕ

*A*n intimate, homey atmosphere is found in this very fine old-fashioned bistro, which carries on the culinary secrets of Mme. Marie-Antoinette Cartet. Founded in 1936, Cartet has had only one change in ownership, and it remains the top Lyonnais *bouchon* (bistro) in Paris. Here you will find the recipes of yesteryear, flaw- lessly executed.

Located in a charmless street hidden behind the place de la République, this miniscule restaurant with its humble exterior continues to serve absolutely traditional food and wine to knowledgeable customers who ask nothing more than perfection. The dining room, when full, holds only 20 people, and the unpretentious decor has not been updated in years. Dark wood-paneled walls are set off by a few old-fashioned mirrors and a scattering of lithographs. A handsome etched-glass central chandelier bathes the room in soft light reflected from the yellow ceiling and gives the green velour upholstery an old-world warmth. A small service bar in the rear holds oversize terrines of the classic desserts that are always on hand.

One should arrive with a hearty appetite to appreciate the abundant portions of meaty terrines, warm Lyonnais sau- sages, creamed pike dumplings, a perfect *boeuf à la ficelle,* and for the more adventurous *tripe à la Lyonnaise* and sheep's trot- ters in cream sauce with onions and mushrooms. The fine Beaujolais wines and the warm welcome of Mme. Nouaille are two more reasons to visit this treasure.

RECOMMENDED DISHES

Choix de Charcuteries Maison. Four terrines of exceptional quality. Help yourself.
Jambon Persillé. Parsleyed ham in white wine aspic.
Croûte aux Morilles. Pastry case filled with morel mush- rooms.
Maquereaux Marinés au Vin Blanc. Mackerel fillets poached in white wine.

Pieds de Mouton, Sauce Poulette. Sheep's trotters in a white cream sauce flavored with lemon.

Quenelles de Brochet. Light pike dumplings formed into small ovals, poached in stock, and served with a béchamel sauce flavored with crayfish and tomato puree.

Boeuf à la Ficelle. Boiled beef, tied up and cooked in an aromatic broth, served with root vegetables.

Gras-Double Lyonnaise Flambé. Tripe sautéed with onions and parsley, then flamed upon presentation.

Saucisson Chaud de Lyon, Gratin Dauphinois. Large poached Lyonnais sausage accompanied by outstanding potatoes sliced and simmered in cream, sprinkled with cheese, and baked au gratin.

Brandade de Morue. Creamed salt cod.

Lotte, Sauce Nantua. Monkfish, prepared in a sauce with crayfish tails, cream, and butter.

Gigot d'Agneau aux Herbes de Provence. Roast leg of lamb infused with herbs.

Choix de Pâtisseries Maison. Choice of lemon tart, chocolate mousse, fritters, cream puff pastry, and floating island.

White wines of Bugey, Morgon, Chiroubles, and Coteaux du Lyonnais.

Chardenoux

M. MICHEL CORNUBET

1, rue Jules-Vallès, 75011 (at rue Chanzy and rue Jean-Macé) | Charonne or Faidherbe-Chaligny

01-43-71-49-52 | Fax 01-45-62-04-07

Ø Saturday lunch and Sunday; August

$ $ | VISA MasterCard

Chardenoux caters to a sophisticated clientele, who are delighted with the excellence of the new ownership and menu. Michel Cornubet has wisely not painted or polished the original fixtures in this charming old bistro, now listed as a historic monument. An unrestored marble entrance leads into a room divided by etched-glass and wood panels where original murals, molded ceiling, mirrors, tulip lamps, and a marvelous zinc bar made with 17 different marbles take one back to the turn of the last century. The cuisine includes delectable dishes such as a Roquefort and endive salad, shrimp on a bed of radicchio drizzled with chestnut oil, line-caught sea bass, monkfish with saffron, tender veal kidneys in a tangy mustard sauce, and a daube of beef cheeks prepared *à la provençale*. A great selection of wines includes more than fifty bottles of red and thirty bottles of dry white.

RECOMMENDED DISHES

Oeufs en Meurette. Eggs poached in red wine with pieces of bacon and tiny onions.

Terrine de Lapin Maison. Rabbit pâté served in an earthenware terrine.

Salade d'Endives au Roquefort et aux Noix. Endive salad with Roquefort cheese and walnuts in a vinaigrette dressing.

Côte de Veau Fermier aux Morilles. Grilled veal chop with morel mushrooms.

Daube de Joues de Boeuf. Beef cheeks slowly stewed in red wine and stock with vegetables and herbs.

Blanquette de Veau. Veal stew in a white sauce thickened with egg yolks and cream.

Gigot d'Agneau. Roast leg of lamb flavored with thyme. Seven-hour leg of lamb available on Saturday.

Onglet Poêlé aux Champignons. Panfried skirt steak with mushrooms.

Omelette à la Norvégienne. Baked Alaska: ice cream on sponge cake coated with meringue and flamed at the table. (Order in advance.)

Gratin de Framboises. Raspberry dessert baked in the oven and crusted on top.

🥄   Great selection of over 80 *crus,* very varied and quite reasonable for the quality.

Dame Jeanne

M. FRANCIS LÉVÈQUE
M. GÉRARD BELLOUARD
CHEF: FRANCIS LÉVÈQUE

60, rue de Charonne, 75011 (at the corner of passage de la Main d'Or) | 🚋 Ledru-Rollin
☎ 01-47-00-37-40 | Fax 01-47-00-37-45
Ø Saturday and Sunday; three weeks in August
$$ | VISA MasterCard
♟

I n 1997 chef Francis Lévèque left Apicius, a restaurant with two Michelin stars, and he and his partner Gérard Bellouard opened this congenial modern bistro where a good-value seasonal menu brims with flavor and sophistication.

Not far from the Bastille, the arched glass picture windows and doorway welcome you into the sunny ocher-and-red interior of Dame Jeanne. Another archway separates the two refined dining areas filled with potted plants and dried floral arrangements. Wine-colored napkins and mini eggplant and artichoke salt and pepper shakers (a theme carried out on the menu) brighten the comfortable tables, which are covered with white cloths. The menu-carte presents two formulas: one at 148 francs, which offers an appetizer and main course or a main course and dessert; and a 178-franc menu, which includes all three courses. Not a hint of tradition is seen in the subtle and beautifully presented dishes. For those avoiding meat, a three-course seasonal menu of fruits, vegetables, and pasta is available. There is no choice, but the selection is always light and appetizing, with things like a salad of baby vegetables in balsamic vinaigrette, tagliatelle with a ratatouille of Provençal vegetables, and for dessert sliced pears in orange sauce with licorice-flavored ice cream.

There are some very good Bordeaux, but look for the *carte* of discoveries—10 wines, all priced at 90 francs per bottle, all well chosen and perfectly delicious.

RECOMMENDED DISHES

Croustillant de Pieds de Porc, Chèvre Rôti. Crunchy pig's feet topped with roasted goat cheese.

Effeuillé de Raie au Vinaigre Balsamique, Chou Croquant. Skate sliced paper-thin and dressed with balsamic vinegar and crisp cabbage.

Magret de Canard Grillé Panade Olive et Ciboulette. Grilled fattened duck breast, panada stuffing of olives and onions.

Joue de Boeuf Confite au Vin avec Purée de Pois Cassés. Preserved beef cheeks cooked in wine with a puree of split peas.

Poitrine de Veau Farcie aux Herbes, Pommes Purée. Breast of veal stuffed with herbs, served with mashed potatoes.

Cabillaud Rôti Jus au Basilic Miettes de Pommes de Terre Écrasées. Roasted fresh cod with sweet basil and crushed potatoes.

Pièce de Boeuf Grillée Gros Sel Sauce Foyot. Grilled top rump of beef with sea salt, glazed and accompanied by a béarnaise sauce.

Demi-Carré d'Agneau Rôti, Pâtes à la Mimolette. Half rack of lamb roasted with pasta and a mild-flavored cow's milk cheese.

Gâteau Chocolat et son Sorbet Cacao. Chocolate cake with cocoa-flavored sorbet.

Brandade de Pamplemousse, Cacao Amer. Crushed grape-fruit dessert with bitter chocolate.

✎ Very affordable wines from the discoveries list. Côtes d'Auvergne et de Duras, Cheverny.

MENUS-CARTES | 148 francs and 178 francs.

Les Jumeaux

M. KARL VANDEVELDE

M. ÉRICK VANDEVELDE

CHEF: KARL VANDEVELDE

73, rue Amelot, 75011 (off rue St-Sabin) |

🚃 Chemin-Vert or St-Sébastien-Froissart

☎ 01-43-14-27-00

Ø Saturday lunch and Sunday; three weeks in August

$$ | [VISA] [MasterCard]

♟♟ | ☼

Karl and Érick Vandevelde, identical twin brothers, have recently opened this handsome, modern bistro as a joint venture where Karl's talent as a chef is revealed in refined, inventive preparations.

Well-spaced tables are surrounded by high-back chairs upholstered in elegant red, gold, and green stripes—a color theme carried throughout the room, and a nice contrast to the basic background of beige and brown. Deco-style wall fixtures and chrome ceiling spotlights highlight whimsical modern paintings and sculptures.

There are all sorts of intriguing dishes. Foie gras in an open tart filled with a puree of onions and preserved lemons should not be missed, and tender veal kidneys accompanied by a sauté of beets and sausages are a blend of perfect tastes. In the fall luscious seasonal scallops are served on a split-pea puree and accented by grapefruit-infused butter. There is a small but well-chosen selection of wines, which includes the elegant Chinon of Charles Joquet, a slightly petulant Vouvray blanc, and Lalande-de-Pomerol from the tiny vineyard of Châteaux la Croix St-André.

RECOMMENDED DISHES

Galette de Foie Gras Chaud aux Oignons et Citrons Confits. Flat round cake consisting of duck foie gras and preserved onions and lemons.

Terrine de Lapin au Persil, Crème de Moutarde. Rabbit pâté with chopped parsley and a mustard cream sauce.

Huîtres Chaudes Gratinées Provençale. Oysters, tomatoes, garlic, and olives cooked in a casserole, crusted on top.

Coquilles Saint-Jacques à la Purée de Pois Cassés, Jus de Pamplemousse Rose. Caramelized scallops on a split-pea puree accompanied by grapefruit-flavored butter.

Rognons de Veau à la Betterave et au Cumin. Whole veal kidneys in natural juices with a light stew of beet roots and cumin seeds.

Jarret de Porc Braisé à la Bière. Pork knuckle braised in beer.

Souris d'Agneau Caramelisée, Pruneaux, Figues, et Raisins. Caramelized flavorful lamb shank cooked with prunes, figs, and grapes.

Cabillaud Rôti sur Peau Purée de Pommes de Terre Condiments à l'Huile d'Olive. Fresh cod roasted with the skin, accompanied by seasoned mashed potatoes drizzled with olive oil.

Crème Brûlée à la Vanille. Creamed vanilla flan with a caramelized topping.

Gâteau aux Amandes, Poêlée Ananas. Almond cake with panfried pineapple rings.

Chinon (Charles Joquet), Lalande-de-Pomerol (Château La Croix St-André), Vouvray blanc.

MENUS-CARTES | Lunch 150 francs, dinner 185 francs.

Le Passage

MME. SOIZIK DE LORGERIL
M. GÉRARD PANTANACCE
CHEF: FRÉDÉRIC BOYER

18, passage de la Bonne Graine, 75011 (in an alley
between avenue Ledru-Rollin and rue du Faubourg
St-Antoine) | 🚇 Ledru-Rollin or Bastille
☎ 01-47-00-73-30 | Fax 01-47-00-14-00
∅ Saturday lunch and Sunday; August
$ $ | ▮▮ VISA MasterCard
☞ | 🍷

Hidden away in a narrow eighteenth-century passage once used to store and sell grain, Le Passage
today attracts a trendy upscale clientele. The rustic interior with overhead beams, green banquettes, and a
fine zinc bar makes you feel right at home. If you have
ever had an urge to try *andouillettes* (pork tripe sausages),
this is the place to do it. There is a separate menu featuring
eight of the best AAAAA* "boutique" varieties made in
France. Each selection is pan-roasted and served either
with a mustard sauce or with a cream and bacon garnish
and a generous side dish of gratin potatoes. In contrast to
this down-home bistro favorite, there is a large, highly
sophisticated menu, which includes stuffed zucchini blos-
soms, sorrel soup, pasta with smoked salmon, *chèvre* (goat
cheese) and spinach crepes, squid and bean sprout salad,
and risotto. Cheese is ripened on the premises, and there
are thirty desserts to choose from.

---

*AAAAA The *Association Amicale des Amateurs d'Authentique An-
douillettes* (The Amicable Association of Appreciators of Authentic
Pork Tripe Sausages). See footnote on page 114.

The impressive nine-page wine list includes selections from all over the world, but those from the Rhône Valley are probably the most interesting.

Four years ago, a chic annex, the Café du Passage (12, rue de Charonne, 01-49-29-97-64) was opened. This cozy clublike place, just around the corner, has a nice selection of wine, single-malt scotch, and Calvados. There is also a limited but select *carte* of foie gras, a hot dish of the day, salads, cheese, and desserts served until 2 A.M.

RECOMMENDED DISHES

Mini-Parmentier de Joues de Cochon. Small portion of shepherd's pie made with pig's cheeks and mashed potatoes.

Ouefs Brouillés au Parmesan en Coque de Courgette. Scrambled eggs with Parmesan cheese served in a hollowed-out zucchini.

Carpaccio de Magret de Canard à l'Huile de Noisette. Very thin slices of cured duck breast in hazelnut oil.

Filet de Mérou Braisé aux Petits Légumes au Pistou. Braised filet of grouper and baby vegetables flavored with pesto sauce.

Andouillettes. Choice of eight different varieties, panroasted and accompanied by *gratin dauphinois*.

Daube de Boeuf à la Sauge. Slow-cooked beef stew flavored with sage.

Steak Tartare. Raw lean minced beef seasoned with chopped onions, capers, anchovies, and parsley, accompanied by outstanding *pommes frites*.

Onglet de Boeuf aux Échalotes Confites. Grilled flank steak with a sauce of preserved shallots.

Crème Brûlée. Rich cream-based custard topped with brown sugar and caramelized under the grill.

Petit Pot Crème Vanille et ses Madeleines. Individual cup of vanilla cream accompanied by shell-shaped tea cakes.

✎ Vast in scope and quality, especially strong in Rhône Valley wines. Many wines available by the glass.

Le Repaire de Cartouche

M. RODOLPHE PAQUIN

99, rue Amelot / 8, boulevard des Filles-du-Calvaire,
   75011 | 🚋 St-Sébastien-Froissart
☎ 01-47-00-25-86 | Fax 01-43-38-85-91
Ø Sunday and Monday; July 15 through August 15
$$ | 💳 VISA 💳

🍲 🍲 🍲

Rodolphe Paquin is one of the most influential young chefs in Paris, owing to his uncanny ability to combine unusual ingredients into traditional French classics with an adventurous and earthy flair.

After several successful years as chef of the restaurant Le Saint-Amarante, Paquin arrived to make this old two-level inn his own. If you enter on boulevard des Filles-du-Calvaire, you climb several steps up to the main dining room and are greeted by dark wood paneling, small glass-paned windows, stucco walls decorated with frescoes of rustic scenes, well-spaced tables, and provincial chairs. The decor recalls an eighteenth-century inn, but the cooking is distinctly modern, filled with bursts of flavor. You will be treated to a bread that is one of the best in Paris—a country loaf studded with seeds. It is a perfect accompaniment to starters such as eel and leek terrine, foie gras garnished with thin slices of *cèpes* (mushrooms) and celeric, or wild mushrooms stuffed with ham and artichokes. A tempting roast fillet of skate served with carrots is infused with blood-red orange juice; and sea bass with endives is caramelized with lemon. During hunting season wild game is added to the menu. Wild duck, a magnificent grouse, a *pot-au-feu* of wood pigeon, and luscious sea scallops are among the specialties. For the meat course, savory veal chops and *entrecôte* with bone marrow are basic, but for the more adventurous there are intriguing dishes made with beef cheeks, tongue, and muzzle.

When M. Paquin is not in the kitchen, he likes to spend time chatting with customers; this makes for a friendly, comfortable atmosphere.

RECOMMENDED DISHES

Gratin de Champignons Farcis aux Artichauts et Jambon. Mushrooms stuffed with artichokes and ham, then cooked au gratin.

Crème de Langoustines avec un Cappuccino à la Vanille. Cream of prawns with a frothy vanilla topping.

Tête de Cochon Croustillante. Pig's head, crunchy.

Pavé de Raie Rôti Jus à l'Orange Sanguine et Étuvée de Carottes. Thick piece of skate, roasted, sprinkled with blood orange juice, and garnished with carrots.

Poitrine de Canette Rôtie Rosée Artichauts Sautés à Cru. Roast duck breast cooked rare, with sautéed artichokes.

Côte de Veau Rissolée au Vinaigre de Cerise Topinambours. Veal chop browned in hot oil and cherry vinegar, garnished with Jerusalem artichokes.

Gibiers. Outstanding game dishes available in the fall, such as grouse, wood pigeon, venison, hare, and duck.

Entrecôte de Boeuf Poêlée, Moelle et Échalotes. Pan-roasted rib steak in a sauce with bone marrow and shallots.

Gratin d'Agrumes au Muscat. Citrus fruit marinated in sweet red wine, then cooked au gratin.

Petit Pot de Crème à la Chicorée, Madeleines. Individual cup of vanilla cream flavored with chicory and accompanied by small tea cakes.

Morgon (Guy Breton), Touraine (Puzelat), Côtes du Rhône (Gramenon), Hermitage (J.-L. Grippat).

À Sousceyrac

M. GABRIEL ASFAUX

M. LUC ASFAUX

M. PATRICK ASFAUX

35, rue Faidherbe, 75011 (between rue de Charonne and
   rue Chanzy) | 🚃 Faidherbe-Chaligny or Charonne
☎ 01-43-71-65-30 | Fax 01-40-09-79-75
Ø Saturday lunch and Sunday; August
$ $ $ | 💳 VISA 💳 💳

🍷🍷🍷

À Sousceyrac is always an inviting place to dine, and it
is particularly appealing during the game season,
when *lièvre à la royale*—a sumptuous wild hare preparation that is this bistro's most famous specialty—is on the
menu. But one need not wait for the game season to enjoy
the marvelous duck and goose pâtés, made from fresh livers delivered directly from the Landes; or the *cassoulet,* a
hearty stew laden with *soissons* (white haricot beans) and
generous helpings of duck confit, lamb sausages, and preserved pork; or the thick slices of duck breast, liver, and
kidneys in a velvety cream sauce swimming with wild
mushrooms. Braised *ris de veau* (calf sweetbreads) with
morel mushrooms is also a specialty, as is the *pannequet
de filet de boeuf et canard,* a crepe filled with beef and
duck and served with *gratin dauphinois.* Another specialty
is the Bresse chicken with foie gras (*volaille de Bresse des
gastronomes*). There is a menu at 185 francs, which begins
with a terrine of foie gras and offers a changing selection
from the à la carte dishes as well as seasonal specialties.
The wine list is impressive, with some 200 selections, but
the wine that goes best with this food is a pitcher of the
black wine of Cahors.

Sousceyrac is a small village in the Quercy region; it was the home of Adolphe and Ida Asfaux, who opened this lovely old bistro in 1923. Their grandsons Luc and Patrick continue the tradition of fine Gascon cooking and maintain the attractive dining rooms, the exquisite zinc bar, and the collection of country pottery with loving care.

RECOMMENDED DISHES

Terrine de Foie Gras Frais d'Oie ou Canard. Homemade foie gras of goose or duck liver from the Landes.

Salade de Sot-l'y'Laisse et Lentilles du Puy. Salad of chicken "oysters" and Puy lentils dressed in vinaigrette sauce.

Pieds de Porc, Désossé, Grillé Saint-Antoine. Deboned pig's trotters, breaded and grilled.

Volaille de Bresse des Gastronomes. Free-range Bresse chicken garnished with glazed chestnuts, truffles, morel mushrooms and kidneys.

Lièvre à la Royale. Extremely rich dish, available only on weekends during the game season. Boned hare stuffed with foie gras and truffles and braised in red wine and brandy.

Cassoulet Comme à Sousceyrac. Languedoc stew with mutton, preserved duck and goose, sausage, and broad white beans.

Ris de Veau Entier aux Pleurotes. Braised sweetbreads with oyster mushrooms or morels.

Pannequet de Filet de Boeuf et Canard. Folded crepe stuffed with tenderloin of beef and duck breast.

Pièce de Boeuf de Salers, Pommes Pont Neuf. Grilled slab of Salers beef served with classic *pommes frites.*

Baba au Rhum. Yeast cake made with raisins and bathed in rum, baked and served in a mold.

🥄 Cahors (by the pitcher), Sancerre, Saint-Véran, Bandol rouge, Saumur-Champigny, Bourgogne (Côtes d'Auxerre).

MENU | 185 francs.

Le Villaret

M. OLIVIER GASLAIN
M. JOËL HOMEL
CHEF: OLIVIER GASLAIN

13, rue Ternaux, 75011 (off rue Oberkampf) |
🚋 Parmentier
☎ 01-43-57-89-76
Ø Saturday lunch and Sunday; August
$$ | VISA   MasterCard
♟♟

L ocated in a quiet neighborhood only a short dis-
tance from the hectic place de la République, this
tiny 12-table bistro is packed with spirited young
people who come for the refined cuisine of chef Olivier
Gaslain.

Michel Picquart transformed this half-timbered space
from a small bar into a bustling bistro a few years ago, then
retired, leaving Joël Homel, who was responsible for the
dining room, and chef Gaslain in charge. They have man-
aged to continue the great success of Le Villaret with a
winning formula, a daily slate menu of dishes derived
from the best market produce and astonishingly low in
price, considering the freshness of the ingredients and the
quality of the preparations. Depending upon what is avail-
able that day, appetiziers might be scallops with thyme, a
fricassee of *cèpes* (mushrooms) with garlic, or a hare and
mushroom soup. Main courses could include medallions
of monkfish in a crab sauce, *rouget* with a puree of celery
and creamed spinach, calf's liver in Banyuls vinegar,
braised nuggets of oxtail and foie gras, or minced beef
cheeks and mashed potatoes served with a lamb's lettuce
salad splashed with a tangy vinaigrette. During the game
season a nicely seared venison steak is accompanied by

trompettes des morts (mushrooms), and there is always a sirloin steak with shallots on hand, but it is only served *bleu*, meaning very rare. Two favorite desserts are the *clafoutis*, often made with mangoes and coconut milk; and *pain perdu* (French toast) with warm clementines.

The room is a bit somber, with the air of an intimate club. As you might expect, reservations are obligatory.

RECOMMENDED DISHES

Crémeux de Cèpes au Foie Gras. Mushrooms in cream sauce with foie gras.

Salade de Bulots et Pommes Ratte. Snails in a white wine sauce with yellow-potato salad.

Terrine de Foies de Volaille aux Fruit Secs, Confiture d'Oignons. Chicken liver pâté with dried fruit and onion confit.

Entrecôte de Veau Fermier aux Asperges et Morilles. Veal rib steak with fresh asparagus and morel mushrooms.

Filets de Rouget à la Purée de Céleri avec Crème d'Épinard à l'Oseille. Fillets of red mullet with creamed spinach flavored with sorrel.

Hachis Parmentier, Joue de Boeuf avec Salade de Mâche. Shepherd's pie of suckling pig's cheeks and mashed potatoes, baked in a casserole, accompanied by a lamb's lettuce salad and vinaigrette dressing.

Blanquette de Poulet Fermier aux Trompettes des Mort. Free-range roast chicken in white sauce with wild mushrooms.

Médaillons de Lotte à la Crème d'Étrilles. Monkfish medallions in a cream sauce of tiny crabs.

Riz au Lait et ses Rissoles de Poire Caramélisées. Rice pudding dessert with caramelized, browned pears.

Clafoutis Tiède de Mangue et Lait de Coco. Warm batter tart with mango and coconut milk.

Small but exceptionally well selected and moderately priced. Côtes du Ventoux, Chinon.

MENUS | Lunch 120 francs and 150 francs.

12ᵉ ARRONDISSEMENT

AUBERGE LE QUINCY

À LA BICHE AU BOIS

JEAN-PIERRE FRELET

LE SQUARE TROUSSEAU

GARE DE LYON–
DAUMESNIL–
REUILLY-DIDEROT

PLACES OF INTEREST

Place de la Bastille

Place de la Nation

Gare de Lyon
(Restaurant Le Train Bleu)

Bois de Vincennes
(Château de Vincennes,
Parc Zoologique, Parc Floral)

Musée National des Arts Africains
et Océaniens

Cimetière de Picpus

Place d'Aligre
(flea market)

Auberge le Quincy

M. MICHEL BOSSHARD (BOBOSSE)

28, avenue Ledru-Rollin, 75012 (between rue de Bercy
    and rue de Lyon) | 🚋 Gare de Lyon
☎ 01-46-28-46-76 | Fax 01-46-28-46-76
∅ Saturday, Sunday, and Monday; August 15 through
    September 15
$$$ | ▭ NONE
🍲🍲

T he convivial owners, M. and Mme. Bosshard, con-
tinue to serve sparkling wine, wonderful country
ham, sausages, and provincial specialties from the
Berry and Ardèche regions in their little country farm-
house set in the middle of Paris. Red-and-white-checked
café curtains are hung at the windows of an oak-and-glass-
enclosed terrace decorated with hand-painted pictures of
farm animals. Inside, a pretty tile floor, provincial tables
and chairs, and bunches of fresh and dried flowers add to
the cheerful country atmosphere.

Michel Bosshard, nicknamed "Bobosse," divides his
time between the kitchen and the dining room, emerging
to suggest one of his copious specialties, such as *caillette
ardèchoise,* a warm minced pork and vegetable sausage on
a bed of mesclun salad; or *terrine fermière,* a cognac-laced
liver terrine with cabbage and garlic salad. This might be
followed by *queue de boeuf,* braised oxtail served with a
puree of celeric; or roast quail garnished with mush-
rooms; or rabbit sautéed with white wine and shallots.
There are several good desserts. An outstanding offering is
La Vieille Prune de Bobosse, a glass of prune de Souillac,
which is heated and flamed to perfection.

RECOMMENDED DISHES

Caillette Ardèchoise. Country sausage of chopped pork liver, spinach, parsley, and herbs, rolled and baked.

Foie Gras Frais Maison. Fresh duck liver foie gras.

Assiette de Jambon Hors d'Age. Plate of smoked country hams from the Ardèche.

Douze Escargots de Bourgogne. Cooked vineyard snails in garlic butter with minced shallots.

Lapereau aux Échalotes et Vin Blanc. Rabbit sautéed in white wine with shallots.

Cassoulet au Confit d'Oie. White bean casserole with sausages, pork, lamb, and preserved goose.

Boudin aux Pommes. Large blood sausage with fried apples.

Pieds et Paquets. Mutton tripe and sheep's trotters rolled in small parcels, stewed and simmered in broth with veal skin, onions, carrots, celery, and tomatoes.

Côte de Veau aux Morilles, Sauce Crème. Grilled veal chop with morel mushrooms in a cream sauce.

Pot-au-feu. Classic dish of boiled beef and root vegetables, preceded by an intense bouillon made from the *tendron de veau* strips, jellied oxtail, and the *tranche* (silverside) *de boeuf.*

Panier de Crottins de Chavignol et le Mélange Maison. Wicker basket of perfectly aged goat cheeses.

Brouilly, Cornas, Quincy, Sancerre, vin de l'Ardèche.

À la Biche au Bois

M. Gérard Méttler
Mme. Monique Méttler
Chef: Gérard Méttler

45, avenue Ledru-Rollin, 75012 (off rue de Lyon) |
Gare de Lyon or Bastille
☎ 01-43-43-34-38
Ø Saturday and Sunday; July 14 through August 15
$$ |

Since 1989, Monique and Gérard Méttler have scurried between kitchen and table preparing and serving delicious terrines fresh from the oven, marvelous fois gras, excellent game, and flavorful dishes from the southwest. At their bistro, located near the Gare de Lyon, a little hedge-enclosed terrace and a bright green-and-yellow awning welcome you into a long corridor-like dining room artfully decorated with floor-to-ceiling mirrors along one side. Benches, booths, and about 20 tables are crowded into a small front room and a larger room in the rear; between the two dining rooms is a small service area. A Louis XIV-style clock, artificial flowers, color prints, and paintings of the woods in autumn add to the old-fashioned clutter.

Almost everyone begins the meal with a Lorraine, the house aperitif, made with red wine and blackberry and black currant liqueur. If you save this place for the game season, you will be offered a wonderfully rich wild boar stew with chestnut and celeriac purees; wild duck with cherries, currants, and blackberries; and woodcock or pheasant in its own casserole. Domestic meats are treated with the same richness as game. For example, *coq au vin* arrives in the dish it was cooked in, filled with mushrooms and potatoes; and beef is served in a creamy sauce of *cèpes* mushrooms. Desserts are uninteresting except for *l'opéra biche,* a chocolate cake. The best wine buys are those offered as wines of the month.

RECOMMENDED DISHES

Foie Gras de Canard "Maison" au Torchon. Duck foie gras covered in cloth and steeped in brine, a house specialty.

Salade Périgourdine. Mixed salad with tomatoes, truffles, and a slice of foie gras.

Coq au Vin. Cockerel slow-cooked in red wine with onions, garlic, mushrooms, and bacon. Served in the deep pot in which it was cooked.

Filets de Biche Grand Veneur. Roast venison served with black pepper sauce and red currant jelly.

Canard Sauvage aux Fruits des Bois. Game duck roasted with wild berries.

Estouffade de Sanglier. Wild boar stew, slowly cooked with red wine, carrots, and onions.

Filet de Boeuf Poêlé au Poivre, Frites. Tenderloin of beef pan-roasted in pepper sauce, with a heaping platter of first-rate *pommes frites;* seconds are encouraged.

Saumon au Champignons des Bois. Grilled fillet of salmon with wild mushrooms.

Gâteau Opéra Biche. Rich custard-filled black chocolate cake.

Crème Caramel Maison. Vanilla-flavored custard surrounded with soft caramel, served in a big bowl; seconds are encouraged.

Côtes de Castillon and other good-value country wines.

MENUS | 128 francs and 185 francs.

Jean-Pierre Frelet

M. JEAN-PIERRE FRELET

25, rue Montgallet 75012 (off rue de Reuilly) |
🚋 Montgallet
☎ 01-43-43-76-65
∅ Saturday lunch and Sunday; August
$ $ | [VISA] [MasterCard]
♟♟♟ | ☼

O ne of the most innovative of the new establishments, this elegant little bistro is located a brisk
ten-minute walk from the place de la Nation.
You might pass right by the unadorned glass exterior were
it not for the bright-blue awning and little sign with the
name. Once inside the small rectangular interior, which
seats exactly 22, one is entranced by the uncluttered, sophisticated decor. Blue suede banquettes, small tables neatly
covered with white cloths, and wicker barrel chairs with
matching blue suede cushions line either side of the room.
A slightly arched white ceiling with track lights and cream-
colored walls are a nice balance to the starkness of the
wooden floor. Simple architectural drawings sparsely
hung above the banquettes are the only decorations. A
small service bar and kitchen are in the rear.

The elegance of the room is a perfect background for
the cuisine prepared by the owner and chef, Jean-Pierre
Frelet. A small but flawless menu, full of appealing contemporary dishes, is prepared according to the season.
Originality rules here. One might find lobster bisque with
asparagus tips, scallops in cider butter, lamb with artichokes flavored with basil, pan-roasted deer with blueber-
ries in a game sauce, and a *panache* of fresh fish garnished
with spinach and raisins. Frelet, who is known for attention to detail, bakes several kinds of whole-grain bread

and presents seasonal salads, fresh fruit desserts accompanied by pastry cream, *sabayon,* or homemade ice cream—and outstanding coffee, some say the best in Paris.

RECOMMENDED DISHES

Salade Tiède de Lentilles au Chou avec Saucisse de Morteau et Foie Gras Poêlé. Warm lentil salad with smoke-cured sausage and panfried fattened duck liver.

Tartines de Rouget et Encornet, Poivrons Doux Marinés. Homemade bread spread with red mullet and squid accompanied by marinated sweet bell peppers.

Terrine de Lièvre au Foie Gras et Céleri Confit. Homemade pâté of rabbit and duck foie gras coupled with a celery root confit.

Blinis de Saumon et Langoustine, Beurre Citron Vert. Little golden savory pancakes topped with salmon and prawns drizzled with fresh lime juice.

Poêlée de Gigot d'Agneau, Artichauts et Basilic. Panfried leg of lamb in cream sauce with artichokes and basil.

Pièce de Boeuf, Sauce Foie Gras, Gâteau de Pommes de Terre. Grilled rump steak in foie gras sauce accompanied by a fried potato loaf seasoned with bacon.

Poêlée de Biche aux Airelles, Sauce Venaison. Panfried venison fillet with cranberries, in a thickened game sauce of cream and butter seasoned with red pepper.

Goujonnette de Sole au Curry. Slices of fried fillet of sole seasoned with curry.

Mousseaux Moelleux au Chocolat. Soft rich chocolate cake with molten bittersweet chocolate.

Clafoutis de "Madame Dédé." Old family recipe of Limousin: batter tart with black cherries.

Small *carte* of mostly country wines; Quincy, Garnay, Sauvignon.

MENUS | Lunch 105 francs, dinner 150 francs.

Le Square Trousseau

M. Philippe Damas
Chef: David Spinga

1, rue Antoine-Vollon, 75012 (off rue du Faubourg
   St-Antoine) | 🚃 Ledru-Rollin
☎ 01-43-43-06-00 | Fax 01-43-43-00-66
∅ Open every day, all year
$$ | 💳 VISA MasterCard

🍲

Overlooking a pretty square of the same name,
this rather chic belle epoque bistro is busy day
and night. High molded ceilings, sweeping arch-
ways, huge mirrors, glass chandeliers, ocher walls, and an
antique bar create an atmosphere of extravagance in
which well-heeled people from the worlds of fashion, film,
and media like to hang out.

There is no gastronomic showmanship here, but the
owner, Philippe Damas, is committed to quality, and his
à la carte menu—which changes every month—reflects
the season's finest offerings. A daily lunch menu at 120
francs, chalked on a blackboard, usually includes a fish of
the day. Chef David Spinga is new and makes a fine duck
foie gras in Vouvray wine, *petits-gris* snails with ratatouille
flavored with thyme, a juicy fillet of beef, chicken in
cream sauce, and his most popular dish, *gigot de sept heures*,
leg of lamb that is meltingly tender. There is a fine range
of wines, which are also for sale at a recently opened bou-
tique annex where charcuterie, cheese, and other gourmet
foodstuffs are also found.

Try to combine a visit to the animated flea market
(Marché d'Aligre) with a stop here for the fixed-price Sun-
day brunch (90 francs). It includes fresh-squeezed orange
juice, scrambled eggs with bacon, and deep-fried potatoes.

RECOMMENDED DISHES

Croustillant de Petits-Gris aux Pleurotes. Tiny gray snails and oyster mushrooms in a pastry case with cream sauce.

Foie Gras de Canard Mi-Cuit au Vouvray Demi-Sec. Fresh duck liver half-cooked with Vouvray wine.

Velouté de Potiron au Jambon Cru et Croutons Dorés. Creamed pumpkin with country ham and toasted bread cubes.

Fricassée de Ris de Veau au Gingembre et Pignons de Pin. Veal sweetbreads stewed in white sauce with ginger and pine seeds.

Hachis Parmentier à la Joue de Cochon. Minced pig's cheeks and mashed potatoes baked in the oven—like a shepherd's pie.

Gigot de Sept Heures. Leg of lamb braised (for seven hours) until it is falling off the bone, served with zucchini.

Petit Jarret de Porc Caramélisé aux Pousses de Lentilles Fondantes. Pork knuckle caramelized in the oven, accompanied by lentil croquettes with bacon.

Coeur de Filet de Boeuf à la Moelle. Small tender prime cut of beef tenderloin garnished with poached bone marrow.

Tuiles Caramélisées à l'Orange. Delicate almond cookies, caramelized and flavored with orange sauce.

Crème Vanille Brûlée à la Cassonade. Vanilla custard flan topped with brown sugar and caramelized under the grill.

Côtes du Rhône (Domaine Gramenon), Morgon (Marcel Lapierre), Chinon (Clos de Roches), Sancerre (P. Prieur).

MENUS | 100, 120, 135 francs.

13ᵉ ARRONDISSEMENT

L'ANACRÉON

L'AVANT-GOÛT

CHEZ PAUL

LE PETIT MARGUERY

LE TERROIR

VIRGULE

PLACE D'ITALIE

PLACES OF INTEREST

Bièvre
(small river flowing into the Seine)

Butte-aux-Cailles

Cité Floréale
(artists' colony)

Cité Verte

Gare d'Austerlitz

Manufacture des Gobelins

Les Olympiades

Place d'Italie

Quartier Chinois

L'Anacréon

M. ANDRÉ LE LETTY

53, boulevard St-Marcel, 75013 (off rue le Brun) |
🚋 Les Gobelins
☎ 01-43-31-71-18 | Fax 01-43-31-94-94
Ø Sunday and Monday; August
$ $ | 🔲 *VISA* 🔲
♟♟

We don't think André Le Letty ever regretted leaving the fast track of prestigious cooking at the famous gastronomic temple Tour d'Argent to open his simple, unstylish bistro, decorated with a permanent exhibition of black-and-white photos of Paris in the 1940s and 1950s by Robert Doisneau.

The restaurant is located on a quiet street not far from the place d'Italie and draws a loyal following of yuppies who are thrilled to have such refined cooking in such an unremarkable, unstylish neighborhood. Le Letty successfully combines country produce with imaginative modern touches to create a hearty cuisine full of lusty tastes and flavors. His signature appetizer, *terrine de lapin au foie gras et legumes,* is an extremely tasty rabbit terrine with foie gras and vegetables; another popular appetizer is scrambled eggs with tomatoes and peppers. The menu-carte at 180 francs always begins with an *amuse-gueule* calculated to wake up the taste buds. At our most recent meal, we were served a little bowl of smooth pumpkin soup enhanced by flavorful sausage bits. We chose as a main course *rognons de veau à la moutarde et éminé de choux,* a marvel of robust tastes combining veal kidneys in an unusual mustard sauce with slivers of cabbage. A Loire Valley Chinon, Les Roches, was a perfect complement to our meal.

RECOMMENDED DISHES

Terrine de Lapin au Foie Gras et Légumes. Rabbit terrine
with foie gras and vegetables.

Feuilleté d'Escargots à la Crème d'Ortie. Snails and nettle in
cream sauce filled in a flaky pastry.

Carré d'Agneau Rôti au Jus de Curry. Roast rack of lamb in
natural juices flavored with curry.

Paleron de Boeuf aux Carottes. Braised shoulder of beef
with carrots.

Magret de Canard Rôti à l'Orange. Roast duck breast in
orange sauce.

Rognons de Veau à la Moutarde et Émincé de Choux. Grilled
veal kidneys in mustard sauce with cabbage slivers.

Cabillaud à la Vapeur Pommes Purées. Steam-cooked fresh
cod and mashed potatoes.

Thon au Beurre de Poivron Rouge. Fillet of tuna with red
pepper butter.

Clafoutis aux Pruneaux. Traditional batter tart with prunes
and Armagnac ice cream.

Blanc-Manger à la Rhubarbe. Chilled almond milk pudding
with rhubarb.

Morgon (Marcel Lapierre), Chinon (Les Roches),
Beaujolais blanc (Château Meylet). Extensive selection
of natural wines.

MENUS-CARTES | Lunch 120 francs, dinner 180 francs.

L'Avant-Goût

M. CHRISTOPHE BEAUFRONT

26, rue Bobillot, 75013 (off place d'Italie) |
🚎 Place d'Italie
☎ 01-53-80-24-00 | Fax 01-53-80-00-77
Ø Sunday and Monday; three weeks in August
$ $ | VISA MasterCard
♟♟♟

*A*n appealing atmosphere, unbelievably reasonable prices, and wonderful food make this bistro one of the most popular in Paris. Christophe Beaufront has an extraordinary knack of conceiving dishes that will appeal to both the knowledgeable gourmet and the down-to-earth customer. His regional country recipes are treated with a sophistication you might expect from a three-star restaurant. This is not surprising, since he was a young protégé of Guy Savoy and also trained with the famous chef Michel Guérard. The menu-carte at 150 francs is inscribed on an *ardoise* (slate) and changes about every two weeks. In the late fall and winter, Christophe's signature dish is available: *pot-au-feu de cochon,* a marvel of the rustic and the refined. It comes in two parts—first a spicy bouillon, followed by a platter of root vegetables and various delicious cuts of pork. At other times of the year you are likely to find *boudin noir* with a chutney of apples, a vichyssoise of fava beans with shrimp, beef cheeks with a caviar of mushrooms, or farm-raised chicken with potatoes and olives. Delicious gratin potatoes are usually on hand.

Success has its price, and the café-style dining room—which has yellow walls, an enclosed terrace, and red leather seats and banquettes—can be excessively noisy as harried waiters try to keep up with the crush. Reservations at any time are at a premium.

RECOMMENDED DISHES

Soupe Mousseuse de Lentilles et Petits-Gris. Puree of lentil
soup with tiny gray snails.

Tarama de Saumon Fumé et Piquilos. Appetizer of fresh
cream, lemon juice, smoked salmon, and small sweet
red peppers.

Râble de Lapin aux Olives. Roast saddle of rabbit with
olives.

Gigot Rôti, Flageolets. Roast leg of lamb with small green
kidney beans.

Chou Farci de Caille Confite aux Légumes. Rolled cabbage
stuffed with preserved quail with fresh vegetables.

Onglet de Veau, Aulx Confits, Gratin Dauphinois. Veal skirt
steak dressed with whole preserved garlic and accompanied by sliced potatoes, baked in cream and crusted
on top.

Pot-au-Feu de Cochon aux Épices. Pork stewed with vegetables and spices, stock served first (specialty of the
house).

Filet de Mulet, Pâtes Fraîches à l'Encre et Huile d'Olive. Fillet
of gray mullet on fresh pasta mixed with squid ink and
olive oil.

Chaud-Froid Moelleux au Chocolat, Glace Vanille. Glazed
chocolate dessert with vanilla ice cream.

Flognard de Rhubarbe aux Fruits Rouges. Limousin batter
pie with rhubarb and fresh berries.

Pleasant fresh fruity wines bought direct from
maker-owned vineyards.

MENUS-CARTES | Lunch 63 francs, dinner 150 francs,
dégustation (tasting) menu 190 francs.

Chez Paul

M. Paul De Saivre
Chef: José Barrios

22, rue de la Butte aux Cailles, 75013 (off rue Bobillot) |
🚊 Place d'Italie or Corvisart
☎ 01-45-89-22-11 | Fax 01-45-80-26-53
Ø Open every day, all year
$ $ | 💳 VISA MasterCard
☞

T he Butte aux Cailles neighborhood remains one of the most original and atmospheric of its kind in Paris. The unrestored buildings house many small shops that include used bookstores, bric-a-brac shops, artisans' places, and quirky little bars and bistros. Chez Paul stands out as the high-quality restaurant of the street by virtue of its pleasantly decorated low-key setting and first-class Lyonnaise cuisine. The atmosphere is that of a *bouchon* (bistro), with deep yellow walls and red banquettes; and a particularly calm and charming terrace is open in the summer. M. Paul, the patron, is omnipresent and lends an air of *joie de vivre* and good humor as he plans your meal.

The extensive menu is supplemented by a few blackboard offerings. We chose a delicious glass of chilled Jurançon wine from the list of old-fashioned aperitifs to contrast with the coarse salt and bone marrow spread on toast that started our meal. For the main course, the roast suckling piglet with homemade mashed potatoes was excellent as was the perfectly cooked *pot-au-feu,* a beef stew with root vegetables doused with a dense, flavorful bouillon.

On Sunday a lovely brunch is served from twelve to four.

RECOMMENDED DISHES

Tartines d'Os à Moelle. Bone marrow spread on toasted thick-sliced homemade bread.

Assiette de Cochonnailles Chaudes. Assortment of *charcuterie*—warm sausages and other pork products.

Terrine de Queue de Boeuf. Oxtail pâté presented in an earthenware terrine.

Rôti d'Agneau avec ses Mojettes. Roast lamb served in a clay pot with mojette beans in tomato sauce.

Cochon de Lait Rôti à la Sauge. Roast suckling pig with sage.

Boudin Noir au Four Pommes Purée. Roasted blood sausage with exceptional homemade mashed potatoes.

Pot-au-Feu et ses Légumes. Boiled beef and vegetables in a rich broth.

Tablier de Sapeur. Lyonnaise-style tripe, dipped in egg and bread crumbs and grilled.

Marquise au Chocolat et son Coulis à la Pistache. Chilled, creamy chocolate mousse with a pistachio puree.

Crème Brûlée. Cream custard topped with brown sugar and burned under the grill to form a hard crust.

Lyonnais wine by the "pot" bottle. Mâcon-Villages (Les Jumelles), Brouilly.

Le Petit Marguery

M. Alain Cousin
M. Jacques Cousin
M. Michel Cousin
Chefs: Jacques Cousin and Michel Cousin

9, boulevard de Port Royal, 75013 (off avenue des
   Gobelins) | ▆▆▆▆ Les Gobelins

☎ 01-43-31-58-59

Ø Sunday and Monday; August

$$$$ | ▆▆ ▆▆ ▆▆ ▆

🍲🍲

The Cousin brothers, Jacques and Michel in the
kitchen and Alain in the dining room, run one of
the great classic bistros, renowned for serious traditional food prepared with verve and unaccustomed
sophistication. Two stylish dining rooms in the style of the
1930s are decorated with old-fashioned sconces, matching
chandeliers, terra-cotta walls, hand-painted frescoes, and
accents of red, pink, and blue.

The extensive handwritten menu poses a challenge for
the uninitiated, but everything here is so enticing that any
choice will be delicious. Game season is a particular
delight, with superb renditions of the famous hare, foie
gras, and truffle dish *lièvre à la royale;* venison in a game
sauce flavored with raisins and pine nuts; wild duck with
cabbage and foie gras; and *poêlé* of seasonal mushrooms.
For starters there are chunky terrines of pheasant and
rabbit studded with foie gras, wild boar, and the popular puree of grouse with juniper berries. Fish specialties
are carefully prepared and served in combinations that
enhance their natural flavors: turbot with lobster sauce,
fresh cod with crayfish puree, and scallops with *cèpes*
(mushrooms). There are tender cuts of beef and veal,

homemade *andouillette* braised in *Aligoté,* and milk-fed lamb from the Pyrenees. You can conclude a meal with a luscious Grand Marnier soufflé or a fabulous chocolate cake topped by a frothy mocha *sabayon.* A distinguished *carte* of Burgundies is available if your budget permits.

RECOMMENDED DISHES

Saumon Mariné à Suèdoise. Cured salmon fillet Swedish-style in a jelly of pureed fruit.

Maquereaux Marinés au Poivre Vert. Mackerel marinated in white wine with green peppercorns.

Foie Gras de Canard. Fresh duck foie gras.

Terrines. Exceptional terrines including wild duck, pheasant, hare, wild boar, and chicken livers.

Spécialités de Chasse. Large selection of outstanding game dishes available seasonally.

Pintadeau Fermier aux Champignons des Bois. Young farm-fresh guinea fowl, roasted with wild mushrooms.

Andouillette Fabrication Maison. Grilled homemade pork sausage.

Petit Salé de Canard à la Poitevine. Duck cured in salt brine, then poached and served in the style of Poitou with lentils.

Lièvre à la Royale. Boned hare stuffed with foie gras and truffles, braised in red wine and brandy.

Raie Rôtie au Gingembre et à la Menthe Fraîche. Roast skate with ginger and fresh mint.

Soufflé au Grand Marnier. Light, puffy whipped egg dessert flavored with Grand Marnier.

Burgundies, Loire, Touraine.

MENUS | Lunch 165 francs, dinner 215 francs, game menu 450 francs.

Le Terroir

M. Michel Chavanon
Chef: Philippe Pierre

11, boulevard Arago, 75013 (off avenue des Gobelins) |
🚋 Les Gobelins
☎ 01-47-07-36-99 | Fax 01-42-72-52-20
∅ Saturday lunch and Sunday; three weeks in August
$ $ | VISA
☞

One is always greeted warmly by the *patron,* Michel Chavanon, who earned his bistro stripes at Chez Pierrot in Les Halles. He beckons you to his little bar, where you may relax with an aperitif or a glass of fruity Chénas (the house specialty) served with bowls of olives and radishes, and a platter of dried sausages and other pork products. The dining room, where clients sit in ample armchairs in an atmosphere of a country auberge, is alive with conversation (mostly French).

The cuisine, handled by chef Philippe Pierre, is served in copious portions and is solidly traditional. Most people come here for the well-chosen and properly aged meats, which include a hearty *pièce de boeuf* for two, a fillet of beef tenderloin in pepper sauce, a *faux-filet* (sirloin steak), and a particularly tasty *entrecôte* (rib steak) served with meltingly delicious buttered potatoes.

The two cheese platters are a must. The first is an assortment from M. Chavanon's native Auvergne region that includes Saint-Nectaire, *tomme du Cantal,* and a stunning Roquefort. The second is an assortment of marvelous *chèvres* (goat cheeses), farm-made and offered in various degrees of ripeness.

This is a bistro that you will always return to, as it is totally reliable and satisfying.

RECOMMENDED DISHES

Filets de Hareng à l'Huile. Large bowl of herring fillets with warm potatoes in oil and vinegar.

Maquereaux au Vin Blanc. Fillets of mackerel in white wine.

Tête de Veau Mijotée aux Herbes. Calf's head simmered with herbs.

Salade au Chèvre Chaud. Hot goat cheese salad.

Lapin à la Moutarde. Rabbit in mustard sauce.

Entrecôte avec des Pommes de Terre au Beurre. Rib steak with buttered potatoes.

Rognons de Veau Cuisinés en Cocotte. Veal kidneys cooked and served in a casserole.

Gibiers. Wild boar, hare, and young partridge (available in the game season).

Millefeuille aux Fruits Rouges. Cream-filled flaky pastry topped with berries.

Plateau de Fromages. Outstanding regional cheese platters.

Chénas, Brouilly, Mâcon-Villages.

Virgule

M. Dao-Heng
M. Denis Legroux
Chef: Dao-Heng

9, rue Véronèse, 75013 | Place d'Italie or Les Gobelins

☎ 01-43-37-01-14

Ø Sunday lunch and Monday lunch; August 10 through 20

$ | 💳 💳

♟♟ | ☼

I t was a pleasure to discover this monument to gastronomy in such an unlikely locale. This kind of artistry in the kitchen has not gone unnoticed, and Virgule has begun to attract a cosmopolitan clientele of both Parisians and tourists. There is no pretension about this little restaurant, decorated with pretty green plants, mirrored walls, and paper napkins neatly rolled into wineglasses on simple tables.

After spending a few years in the kitchens of Chez Lenôtre and Jules Verne, chef Dao-Heng and his charming wife decided to open their own place. There are two formulas: a limited menu at 105 francs and a more expensive menu at 145 francs (including either cheese or dessert and coffee) selected from the à la carte list, which offers the full range of chef Dao's talent. He is a master at sauces, each a subtle mixture to perfume the dish for which it is intended. There is no special emphasis on seafood, but the fish are superb. Sea bass is grilled and flamed in pastis; salmon is paired with a light, creamy *pistou;* monkfish is served with a cream horseradish; and tuna is marinated in coconut milk, then grilled and served with a tangy lemon sauce. Meats are not neglected; they include a tender *entrecôte* with marrow, turkey breast in a zesty orange-flavored garnish, and fillet of duck sauced with luscious pears. Chocolate lovers will be delighted with such desserts as profiteroles in chocolate sauce flavored with whiskey, and chocolate cake topped with a rich coffee cream.

RECOMMENDED DISHES

Terrine de Foie de Lapin au Porto. Pâté of rabbit livers made with port wine and presented in an earthenware terrine.

Salade de Pétoncles au Soja. Sautéed baby scallops creamed with soybeans and walnuts.

Carpaccio de Foie Gras de Canard Maison. Very thin slices of slightly cooked duck liver served with condiments.

Bigarade de Canard Braisé. Braised duck with thickened juices flavored with orange, lemon, and Grand Marnier.

Brochette de Gigot au Carvi. Cubed leg of lamb and vegetables flavored with caraway seeds, grilled and presented on a skewer.

Cochon de Lait Braisé aux Épices. Suckling pig braised with spices.

Entrecôte Poêlée à la Moelle "Comme à Soulac." Panfried beef rib steak garnished with poached bone marrow as prepared in Soulac.

Filet de Sandre au Coulis de Framboise. Fried fillet of pike perch with a puree of raspberries.

Omelette Norvégienne. Baked Alaska: ice cream on sponge cake coated with meringue and flamed.

Gâteau au Chocolat Léger Maison Sauce Café. Light chocolate cake with mocha sauce.

Southwest wines; Madiran is a standout.

MENUS | 105 francs and 145 francs.

14ᵉ ARRONDISSEMENT

LA RÉGALADE

AU VIN DES RUES

MAINE–MONTPARNASSE

PLACES OF INTEREST

Boulevard du Montparnasse
(The cafés Coupole, Dôme, Sélect, Rotonde)

Catacombes
(tours leave from 1, place Denfert Rochereau)

Cimetière du Montparnasse

Cité Universitaire

Parc de Montsouris, Observatoire

Place Denfert Rochereau
(Lion of Belfort by Bartholdi)

Puces de la Porte de Vanves
(flea market)

Rue Daguerre
(open-air market)

Les Villas
(Léone, Camélias)

La Régalade

M. YVES CAMDEBORDE

49, avenue Jean-Moulin, 75014 (off boulevard Brune at
   place de la Porte de Châtillon) | ▦▦ Alésia
☎ 01-45-45-68-58 | Fax 01-45-40-96-74
∅ Saturday lunch; Sunday; and Monday; middle of July
   through middle of August
$ $ | VISA ⬤
🍲🍲🍲

The success continues for this low-key Provençal-
style bistro located in the quiet Alésia residential
area not far from the Porte d'Orléans. The starkly
simple dining room is set off by a few photos and has as a
centerpiece a tempting display of crusty country breads.
Since its debut in 1992, the restaurant has been packed
with gourmets who endure the frenetic atmosphere and
elbow-to-elbow seating to experience the hottest table in
Paris next to Taillevent. In an effort to accommodate more
customers, M. Camdeborde has added a third dinner seating at about 10:30, but bookings still take about three
weeks.

Young Yves Camdeborde, yet another lieutenant of
Christian Constant at the Crillon, has the talent of a master and a light, inventive touch. The simplest of ingredients are turned into elaborate presentations with exciting
nuances of taste, color, and smell.

When you are seated, by Claudine Camdeborde, a generous terrine of homemade pâté is put at your disposal.
Go easy, because the three-course 195-franc menu-carte,
with 30 choices, offers a wide selection of mouthwatering
dishes ending with fabulous desserts. For starters a huge

basket of *cochonailles du Béarn* supplied by the chef's father is brought to the table with a cutting board and knife, and it is up to you to curb your indulgence. Two other winners are the panfried goose liver slices on spice bread and the Provençal-style vegetable fritters (*beignets*) quickly deep-fried and brought to the table piping hot.

The main course most popular with regulars is the spicy blood sausage covered with a layer of mashed potatoes and topped with béarnaise sauce (*Parmentier de boudin noir béarnais*). In the winter game dishes are a specialty; the *gibier du jour* is often wood pigeon (*palombe*), young partridge (*perdreau*) or wild boar (*marcassin*). The skillfully executed desserts are topped by an individual *soufflé chaud au Grand Marnier* or little *pots de crème à la vanille* served with "cat's tongues," small finger cookies.

The wine list includes little-known southwest *vin de pays* at giveaway prices, but also some fine Armagnacs.

RECOMMENDED DISHES

Pot-au-Feu de Foie de Canard en Gelée aux Fruits Secs. Duck foie gras in aspic and dried fruits.

Pétoncles en Coquille, Beurre Demi-Sel Persillé. Tiny bay scallops served in a scallop shell with slightly salted butter sauce sprinkled with parsley.

Cassoulet. An authentic cassoulet in the style of Toulouse can be ordered in winter 72 hours in advance.

Hachis Parmentier de Boudin Noir Béarnais. Blood sausage rendition of shepherd's pie.

Petit Salé de Pigeon, Galette d'Oreille de Cochon, Tranche de Lard. Lightly salt-cured pigeon with a pig's ear pancake and a slice of bacon.

Pièce de Boeuf Cuisinée aux Anchois Grenailles Girolles. Thick piece of beef cooked with an anchovy puree and wild yellow mushrooms.

Viennoise de Rognons de Veau Confiture d'Oignons. Veal kidneys coated in bread crumbs and served in onion confit.

Saint-Pierre Rôti Vinaigrette de Girolles. Roast John Dory with an oil and vinegar dressing on wild chanterelle mushrooms.

Fromage de Brebis de la Vallée d'Osso et sa Confiture de Cerises Noires. Gascogne sheep's milk cheese in black cherry preserves.

Soufflé Chaud au Grand Marnier. Hot orange liqueur soufflé, a specialty from the Crillon.

Pot de Crème Vanille, Langues de Chat. Creamy cold vanilla dessert in an individual cup with finger cookies.

A number of inexpensive little country wines (*vins de pays*) from the southwest are available.

MENU-CARTE | 195 francs at lunch or dinner.

Au Vin des Rues

M. Didier Gallard
Mme. Niky Gallard

21, rue Boulard, 75014 (off rue Daguerre) |
Denfert Rochereau
☎ 01-43-22-19-78 | Fax 01-43-22-19-78
Ø Sunday and Monday; August
$ $ | VISA

W e wondered why the fabled wine bistro proprietor Jean Chanrion's disposition has been markedly improved of late. The answer is simple—he has sold his wonderful little place to an ambitious young couple who have the capability to carry on in precisely the same outstanding manner. The fact is that although the bistro has been turned over for some time, on a recent Wednesday evening Chanrion was still behind the bar and out front, assisting Didier Gallard and really enjoying the role.

Au Vin des Rues is a unique place. It hasn't changed much since it opened as an old Auvergnat café; it is still serving top-notch Lyonnais dishes and the best Beaujolais wines in a completely unpretentious atmosphere. Sadly, this kind of bistro is rapidly becoming a thing of the past and soon may be seen only in a Doisneau photo. We are grateful that M. and Mme. Gallard have taken over and are continuing the famous daily specials served each day at lunch. Dinner is available only on Wednesdays, Fridays, and Saturdays, and a reservation is required. Expect to find rich and generous fare such as braised *andouillettes, petit salé, boeuf à la ficelle, blanquette de veau,* and *brandade de morue.* Portions can easily be split for two. Desserts are homemade and delicious.

RECOMMENDED DISHES

Salade de Lentilles aux Cochonailles. Lentil salad accompanied by *charcuterie*—meats, sausages, and pâtés.

Terrine de Langue. Ox tongue terrine.

Filets de Hareng Pommes Vapeur. Herring fillets cured in oil and served with steamed potatoes.

Cervelas à la Moutarde. Short, thick pork sausages in mustard sauce.

Lapin Morvandelle. Rabbit in a piquant cream sauce with white wine, vinegar, juniper berries, shallots, and cream.

Poulet au Vinaigre. Bresse chicken cooked with shallots, tomatoes, white wine, vinegar, and cream.

Brandade de Morue aux Câpres et Croûtons. Salt cod and garlic puree with pickled capers and toasted bread cubes.

Pigeon Rôti aux Morilles et Chanterelles. Roast pigeon with wild mushrooms.

Clafoutis aux Mirabelles. Traditional batter tart with small
   yellow plums.
Pruneaux au Vin. Prunes stewed in Beaujolais.

🍾 All the *crus* of Beaujolais and Côtes du Rhône.

15ᵉ ARRONDISSEMENT

LE BISTRO D'HUBERT

LES COTEAUX

LE GASTROQUET

L'OS À MOELLE

LE PÈRE CLAUDE

CHEZ PIERRE

RESTAURANT DU MARCHÉ

LE TROQUET

PORTE DE VERSAILLES

PLACES OF INTEREST

Gare Montparnasse

Héliport de Paris

Institut Pasteur

Musée Antoine Bourdelle

Musée Postal

Palais des Sports,
Parc des Expositions

Parc Georges Brassens

La Ruche
("The Beehive,"
an artists' colony
built by Eiffel)

Square St-Lambert

Statue de la Liberté

Tour Montparnasse

Village Suisse
(antiques market)

Le Bistro d'Hubert

M. Hubert
Mlle. Maryline Hubert
Chef: M. Hubert

41, boulevard Pasteur, 75015 (off rue du Docteur Roux) |
🚊 Pasteur
☎ 01-47-34-15-50 | Fax 01-45-67-03-09
Ø Open every day, all year
$ $ $ | [cards]
👨‍🍳👨‍🍳

T his is a real charmer, a dream of a "Martha Stew-
art" country kitchen, sunny, colorful, and inviting.
The large light-filled room with polished stone
floors is outfitted with white-lacquered rush-covered
country chairs and matching tables colorfully set with
blue, yellow, and white checkered "dish towel" napkins
and cloths. Floor-to-ceiling glass-enclosed cupboards are
filled with displays of chic pantry items, and the walls are
decorated with open shelves of wine bottles, old cas-
seroles, jars of preserves, bottles of olive oil, and hanging strings of drying red peppers and sausages. At the
entrance you are greeted by a magnificent bouquet of
fresh flowers and a country armoire in which to hang your
coat.

This place is the concept of a former *fromagère*
M. Hubert, who oversees the kitchen while his daughter
Maryline looks after the dining room. Chef Hubert divides
his retro chic 210-franc menu-carte into two categories, traditional and "discovery," which can be mixed or matched.
On the traditional side you can choose from such dishes
as country sausages, farm-fresh fowl, and roasted monkfish; on the other side you might choose a more fanciful

standing veal rump with black mushrooms and Jerusalem artichokes in herb butter or little beef-cheek patties with foie gras and tomato confit in a curry cream sauce.

It is a real pleasure to find so endearing a place with such very good food and delightful surroundings in a location so far from the center of town.

RECOMMENDED DISHES

Galette de Pieds de Porc en Crépinette aux Pleurotes. Pig's foot sausage pancake with oyster mushrooms.

Pimientos del Piquillo Farcis au Jambon à la Txanduro. Red peppers stuffed with smoked ham.

Nougat de Joues de Boeuf au Foie Gras. Ox cheeks with duck foie gras.

Carré d'Agneau Rôti au Thym Bouquetière de Légumes. Roast rack of lamb with thyme and a garnish of vegetables.

Quasi de Veau aux Champignons Noirs et Topinambours au Beurre d'Herbes. Standing veal rump with black mushrooms and Jerusalem artichokes in herb butter.

Boudin Campagnard Landais sur Brioche, Pommes Écrasées. Country sausage in a bun served with crushed potatoes.

Travers de Porc Caramélisé à la Bohémienne. Caramelized pork ribs on a stew of rice, tomatoes, onions, and sweet peppers.

Pavé de Thon Poêlé et Laqué au Caramel Balsamique sur Verdurette. Pan-roasted tuna steak sprayed with syrup and dressed with a vinaigrette sauce with chopped hardboiled eggs.

Chocolat Amer aux Griottines. Dark, bittersweet chocolate combined with morello cherries.

Petites Crêpes Chaudes "Joëlle" à la Crème. Hot pancakes with cream sauce.

Château Fougas, Côtes de Bourg, Château Tourans, St-Émilion Château Chenaie (les Douves), Faugères.

MENUS-CARTES | Lunch 160 francs, dinner 210 francs.

Les Coteaux

M. Bernard Olry

26, boulevard Garibaldi, 75015 (off avenue de Ségur) |
🚋 Cambronne or Ségur
☎ 01-47-34-83-48 | Fax 01-45-88-89-08
Ø Saturday, Sunday; and Monday evening; August
$ | VISA
🥄 | 🍷

I
t is hard to believe that there still exists in Paris a
totally authentic Lyonnais wine bistro that features
tasty Lyonnais cuisine, fruity Beaujolais, and astound-
ingly moderate prices. Bernard Olry has fashioned his
little place, located in a modest neighborhood with ele-
vated trains passing overhead, after the very successful
wine bar of Jean Chanrion (Au Vins des Rues, 14e). Chanrion has recently retired.

The restaurant has a faithful clientele of substantial
business habitués who arrive for the traditional French
two-hour lunch or a simple leisurely dinner. The atmosphere is without pretention; the two rooms are cluttered
with wine bottles, and the little tables are covered in red-
and-white checkered oilcloth protected by paper. Several
different menus are chalked on blackboards, with the
Lyonnais specialties of the house indicated as *plats de terroir*. There are no-nonsense plates of marinated herring,
smoked salmon, assorted salads, country ham and sausages,
snails, stuffed cabbage, tripe, grilled pig's ears, cod casserole, grilled chicken, and pike dumplings.

Every *cru* of Beaujolais is represented, personally
selected by Olry and shipped directly from the vineyard.
These wines may be had by the glass, pitcher, or bottle.

RECOMMENDED DISHES

Foie Gras de Canard Entier Maison. Whole cooked duck liver.

Oeufs en Meurette. Poached eggs in red-wine sauce.

Cassolette de Bourgogne. A dozen Burgundian snails in garlic butter.

Andouillette au Mâcon-Villages et à la Moutarde de Charroux. Grilled smoked sausage, cooked in wine and served in a mustard sauce.

Tablier de Sapeur. Panfried ox tripe.

Gratin de Tripes à la Lyonnaise. Tripe (baked in the oven in a serving dish), with a toasted surface.

Daube de Boeuf Beaujolaise. Slow-stewed beef in Beaujolais wine.

Tête de Veau, Sauce Gribiche. Calf's head meat poached in a white wine with a creamy vinaigrette.

Quenelles de Brochet, Sauce Nantua. Pike dumplings in a crayfish puree.

Pruneaux ou Poires au Vin. Poached prunes or pears in red wine.

Beaujolais, Burgundy, Côtes du Rhône.

MENUS | Lunch 90 francs, dinner 140 francs.

Le Gastroquet

M. Dany Bulot
Mme. Madeleine Bulot
Chef: Dany Bulot

10, rue Desnouettes, 75015 (at place Henri Rollet, corner
of rue du Clos Feuquières | 🚋 Porte de Versailles
or Convention
☎ 01-48-28-60-91 | Fax 01-45-33-23-70
Ø Saturday and Sunday; August
$ $ $ | 💳 VISA MasterCard
🥘🥘

For more than a decade the *patron*-chef Dany Bulot
was in charge of the kitchen at Benoît (4e). His reputation for robust, artfully prepared country cooking has earned him a large following from all over the city.
His signature dish à la Benoît is always on the menu: *soupe
de moules paysanne,* a deep tureen of soup filled with mussels that makes a delicious starter. Seconds are encouraged. M. Bulot and his gracious wife Madeleine are always
present to greet each guest personally, and before returning to the kitchen Dany patiently describes the specials
of the day. The menu changes daily, but some of the
dishes that appear frequently are warm foie gras, roast
guinea fowl, *aiguillettes* of duck breast with bilberries, the
house *cassoulet* with preserved goose, and fresh cod served
Mediterranean-style with a garlicky aïoli.

Beyond a facade of French windows with delicate lace
curtains is a little terra-cotta tiled reception area and bar
leading into a lovely turquoise-carpeted dining room with
wine-colored velour banquettes, peach walls with large
mirrors, and comfortably spaced tables. Although this
bistro is usually closed on weekends, it will stay open

when there are major shows in the Parc des Expositions at the nearby Porte de Versailles.

RECOMMENDED DISHES

Soupe de Moules Paysanne. Large tureen of mussel soup.

Maquereaux en Nage aux Herbes. Mackerel fillet poached in white wine and aromatic stock, served cold.

Foie Gras Chaud aux Lentilles. Warm duck foie gras in a lentil salad.

Cassoulet Maison à la Graisse d'Oie. Languedoc stew with white beans, cooked in goose fat.

Pintadeau Fermier aux Pointes d'Asperges. Roasted farm raised young guinea fowl and asparagus tips.

Tête et Langue de Veau, Sauce Ravigote. Calf's head meat and tongue in a spicy vinaigrette with mustard, cornichons, and capers.

Parmentier de Jarret à la Lyonnaise. Veal knuckle and potato casserole.

Filet de Rouget sur Tartine de Tapenade. Fillet of red mullet on toasted bread spread with a mix of anchovies and black olives.

Crème Brûlée Pommes et Calvados. Caramelized flan with apples soaked in cider brandy.

Millefeuille au Praune. Flaky cream puff pastry coated with almond kernels, a variation on pralines.

Well-chosen list with many high-quality wines at reasonable prices.

MENUS | Lunch 125 francs, dinner 155 francs.

L'Os à Moelle

M. Thierry Faucher

3, rue Vasco da Gama, 75015 (at rue de Lourmel) |
  🚋 Lourmel
☎ 01-95-57-27-27 | Fax 01-95-57-27-27
Ø Sunday and Monday; August
$$ | VISA MasterCard
♟♟♟

Don't even think of coming here without a reserva-
tion, as this cramped little corner bistro is always
fully booked days in advance. Misguided walk-ins
are instructed to try across the street, where master chef
Thierry Faucher has recently opened a *cave*-bistro annex
(Cave de l'Os à Moelle, 15e, 01-45-57-28-28). With a mere
15 seats clustered around a communal table, this little
gourmet wine bar annex has also become so popular that
seats are at a premium.

Faucher opened his bistro after working for several years
under Christian Constant. He offers an outstanding six-
course meal (three courses at lunch) with no choice except
for dessert. The wines come from the *cave* across the street
and are well selected for quality and price. A recent meal we
enjoyed consisted of the following six dishes: a creamy but
light vegetable and bacon soup; foie gras coated with spices
on a bed of Swiss chard; panfried fresh cod in a lobster and
wild mushroom cream sauce; roasted fillet of venison in
a celery mousse with pine nuts; a farm cheese salad of
Camembert, endives, and chives; and finally a dessert
selected from six very gourmet choices. A set meal of this
quality at 190 francs is certainly one of the great bargains,
and one can overlook the cramped seating, the rushed serv-
ice, and the no-frills decor. This is certainly a place not to be

missed and should be included among one's top dining choices in Paris.

RECOMMENDED DISHES

Foie Gras Pané au Pain d'Épice et Salade de Betteraves. Foie gras breaded with spice cake on a beet salad.

Poêlée de Courgettes à la Fleur de Thym et Beurre au Cumin. Fried zucchini with sprigs of thyme and caraway butter.

Demi-Caille Rôtie en Salade. Half roast quail on dressed salad greens.

Pigeon Rôti à l'Embeurrée de Choux. Roast squab with buttery cooked cabbage.

Agneau de Lozère et Purée Écrasée. Roast Lozère lamb with crushed potatoes.

Paleron de Boeuf Braisé à la Moelle, Petits Légumes Liés au Jus. Braised shoulder of beef with bone marrow and new vegetables.

Rascasse Confite à l'Olive Poivrons Doux et Crémeux de Homard à la Coriandre. Scorpion fish cooked with a confit of olives and sweet bell peppers in a lobster cream sauce flavored with coriander.

Raie à l'Échalote et à la Civette. Skate cooked with shallots and chives.

Quenelles de Chocolat, Sauce Safranée. Chocolate dumplings in a sauce flavored with saffron.

Ananas Confit aux Épices, Sorbet Fromage Blanc. Candied pineapple with spices and cream cheese sherbet.

🥄 Inexpensive wines from all regions, from 65 to 180 francs.

MENUS | Lunch 170 francs, dinner 190 francs.

Le Père Claude

M. Claude Perraudin

51, avenue de la Motte-Picquet, 75015 (off avenue de
   Suffren) | 🚌 La Motte-Picquet
☎ 01-47-34-03-05 | Fax 01-40-56-97-84
Ø Open every day, all year
$$ | 💳 VISA MasterCard
🍲

hat sets this bistro apart from all the others is the
personality of its owner, Claude Perraudin,
known to his friends as "Father Claude." This
modest man has extraordinary cooking skills honed in
the three-star kitchens of Bocuse, Gúerard, and Troisgros
and by most accounts is the finest rotisserie chef in Paris.
His repertoire of carefully roasted meats includes leg of
lamb, spareribs, sirloin steak, duck, chicken, game, and on
Wednesdays suckling pig.

M. Claude is always present in his animated dining
room chatting with his numerous friends. Under colorful
hedonistic frescoes, they sit at communal tables discussing
politics and the state of French cuisine. Over a bottle or two
of top-quality Beaujolais, the discussions can reach quite a
pitch, but the cheerful, noisy atmosphere and the venue of
good fellowship make up the unique charm of this place.

RECOMMENDED DISHES

Les Trois Terrines du Père Claude. Three house terrines:
   beef cheeks, rabbit, and calf's head.
Salade Folle. Salad of lobster, smoked salmon, and home-
   made duck foie gras.
Boudin du Père Duval, Pommes Reinettes. Blood sausage from
   the House of Duval, grilled with slices of yellow apple.

Souris d'Agneau Mijotée au Romarin. Simmered lamb
shank stew flavored with rosemary.

Canette aux Oignons, Pommes Purées. Duckling grilled with
onions and accompanied by mashed potatoes (Tuesday).

Coq au Vin de Beaujolais. Cockerel stewed in Beaujolais
wine.

Assiette du Père Claude Rôties à la Broche. A mixed grill of
spareribs, lamb, veal, chicken, and kidneys cooked on a
rotisserie and served with scalloped potatoes.

Cochon de Lait Pommes Maxime. Split roasted suckling pig
with chunky *pommes frites* (Wednesday).

Grenouilles Fraîches Sautées au Beurre et Fines Herbes. Fresh
frogs' legs sautéed in herb butter.

Fricassée de Lotte aux Pâtes Fraîches Provençales. Monkfish
stew in a white sauce flavored with Mediterranean
spices and served on fresh pasta.

Délice du Père Claude. Vanilla ice cream, red berries, and
caramel sauce.

Nice choice of wines under 150 francs; "Selection of
the Month" should be considered.

MENUS │ Lunch 120 francs, dinner 170 and 250 francs.

Chez Pierre

M. DIDIER BOURRAT

117, rue de Vaugirard, 75015 (at the start of avenue du
Maine where it runs into boulevard du Montparnasse)
│ ▆▆▆▆ Falguière

☎ 01-47-34-96-12

Ø Saturday lunch and Sunday; middle of July through
middle of August

$ $ │ ▆▆ VISA MasterCard

Didier Bourrat has successfully taken over this Burgundian bistro from a family who ran it for three generations, and to his credit he has maintained the friendly spirit, unpretentious surroundings, and absolutely traditional repertoire of Burgundian dishes. The setting is old-fashioned, plain and modest in appearance, with brass coatracks, globe lights, and etched-glass panels separating the bar from the dining room, which is lined with banquettes set against yellowing walls imprinted to look like tin.

It is difficult to single out special dishes as outstanding, the general level of the food being so excellent. The regional *oeufs en meurette* and parsleyed ham can be followed by *andouillettes* AAAAA,* cooked in Chablis, *coq au vin,* or a superb *boeuf bourguignon.* The à la carte list is a combination of regional dishes and more updated fare with specialties such as foie gras with tagliatelle, leeks, or lentils in vinaigrette; calf's liver sautéed in honey and served on a bed of spinach; and, in game season, rabbit stew, roast pheasant, and wild duck. There are also tempting, rich desserts. An impressive list of Burgundy wines includes moderately priced *crus* from Irancy.

RECOMMENDED DISHES

Foie Gras de Canard Maison. Homemade duck foie gras.

Oeufs en Meurette. Poached eggs in red wine sauce with onions and pieces of bacon.

Six Escargots de Bourgogne. Burgundian vineyard snails presented in their shells with snail butter.

Jambon Persillé. Chunks of cooked ham molded in parsleyed aspic jelly.

Confit de Canard, Pommes Sarladaises. Preserved duck grilled and served with baked sliced potatoes and truffles.

*AAAAA The *Association Amicale des Amateurs d'Authentique Andouillettes* (The Amicable Association of Appreciators of Authentic Pork Tripe Sausages). See footnote on page 114.

Coq au Vin. Cockerel stewed in red wine with button mushrooms and tiny onions.

Boeuf Bourguignon aux Pâtes Fraîches. Beef stewed in red wine with bacon, small onions, and mushrooms, accompanied by fresh noodles.

Gibiers.   Game dishes include roast pheasant, wild duck, and rabbit stew (in season).

Andouillette "AAAAA" (Duval) à la Chablisienne. Top-quality House of Duval pork sausage grilled in Chablis wine.

Crème Caramel Maison. Caramel-flavored custard dessert.

🥄 Irancy and other northern Burgundy wines of the Yonne Valley around Chablis.

MENUS | Lunch 90 and 120 francs, dinner 185 francs.

Restaurant du Marché

M. BRUNO FAVA

MME. BÉATRICE FAVA

CHEF: BRUNO FAVA

59, rue de Dantzig, 75015 (off boulevard Lefèbvre) |
🚎 Porte de Versailles or Convention
☎ 01-48-28-31-55 | Fax 01-48-28-18-31
Ø Saturday lunch and Sunday; July 15 through August 15
$$$ | 🔳 VISA MasterCard 🅞
🍲🍲🍲

*A*fter many successful years a change of ownership has brought an experienced Basque chef and his charming wife to run this well-established southwestern regional bistro. They hardly changed a thing in the lovely old 1930s dining room graced by lace table covers, a multicolored tile floor, little oval mirrors, old banquettes, and a pretty wooden bar adorned with fresh flowers.

This is a great place to sample the duck and goose specialties of the region. Ever present are *mi-cuit* foie gras, warm foie gras with figs, duck confit, and Gascon *cassoulet.* Each meal should conclude with one of the vintage Armagnacs, priced from 65 to 280 francs per glass. By sticking to the excellent menu-carte at 168 francs, you do not run the risk of a big tab, but then you would miss chef Fava's sensational Roquefort sauce on a juicy fillet of beef and the rarely encountered classic dish *tournedos Rossini,* a tenderloin with foie gras and truffles priced at 245 francs. Whatever direction your meal takes, you should try to save room for a wonderful Basque specialty—*ardi gasna et sa confiture de cerises,* a strong sheep's milk pressed cheese served with homemade cherry preserves.

The Favas are proud of their artfully put together little boutique offering authentic products from the Béarn and Basque regions—perfect gifts to take home to family and friends.

RECOMMENDED DISHES

Asperges Blanches des Landes aux Truffes. White asparagus with truffles.

Jambon "Gbérico." Plate of sliced country ham.

Escalope de Foie Gras Chaud aux Figues. Slice of fresh foie gras served hot with fresh figs.

Poêlée de Morilles au Jus de Truffes. Panful of morel mushrooms cooked in truffle oil.

Magret de Canard et son Foie Gras Poêlée. Fillet of fattened duck grilled with foie gras.

Daube de Boeuf. Braised beef stew with vegetables.

Confit de Canard de Landes. Duck cooked and preserved in its own fat.

Agneau de Lait des Pyrénées. Milk-fed lamb with seasonal vegetables.

Lièvre à la Royale. Braised, boned hare stuffed with foie gras and truffles (in season).

Pimentos del Piquillo Farcis à la Morue. Peppers stuffed with creamed salt cod.

Cassoulet Gascon. White bean stew with mutton, preserved duck, goose, and sausage.

Glace aux Pruneaux à l'Armagnac. Prune ice cream with Armagnac brandy.

Millefeuille Croustillante au Caramel. Flaky pastry filled with cream and topped by caramel icing.

🥄 Buzet, Bordeaux, and other southwest regional wines. Extensive selection of old Armagnacs.

MENU-CARTE | 168 francs lunch or dinner.

Le Troquet

M. CHRISTIAN ETCHEBEST

21, rue François-Bonvin, 75015 (off rue Miollis about two blocks from boulevard Garibaldi) |

🚋 Cambronne or Sevres-Lecourbe Volontaires

☎ 01-45-66-89-00 | Fax 01-45-66-89-83

Ø Sunday and Monday; three weeks in August

$$ | VISA MasterCard

🍲🍲 | ☼

Another talented young alumnus of Christian Constant has completed his stint at the Crillon and set up shop in his uncle's slightly faded neighborhood café-like bistro. This place is certainly off the beaten track, with an inconvenient metro stop, but the effort is well worth the reward. Chef Christian Etchebest has conceived a superlative *dégustation* formula at 170 francs which brings the tastes and flavors of his native Pyrenees to the table.

We enjoyed recently a beautifully prepared and presented meal here. The no-choice five-course evening menu was a subtle harmony of textures and tastes. We began with a peasant soup with chorizo sausages and onions followed by panfried *chipirons* (squid) in parsley and garlic, stuffed saddle of rabbit with mashed potatoes, Pyrenees sheep's cheese in a confit of black cherries, and for dessert caramelized pineapple on *pain perdu* in custard sauce. A regional Béarn red wine at 95 francs was a delightful accompaniment to the meal.

Great success is predicted for this place, so try to get here while you can.

RECOMMENDED DISHES

Tartelette à l'Oignon Confit. Open tart of candied onions.

Quenelles de Chèvre Frais au Piment d'Espelette. Goat cheese dumplings with hot chili peppers.

Foie Gras de Canard Confit Poivre et Sel Quenelle de Figue Séchée. Homemade duck foie gras seasoned with salt and pepper, accompanied by dumplings filled with dried figs.

Aiguillettes de Canard Poêlées et Escalopine de Foie Gras. Thin slices of panfried duck breast with foie gras.

Onglet de Boeuf aux Échalotes. Panfried flank steak smothered in cooked shallots.

Caille Rôtie au Poêlon, Jus Perté aux Olives. Quail roasted in a covered saucepan with natural juices and olives.

Tranche de Foie de Veau au Vinaigre de Xérès Concassée de Tomates. Slice of calf's liver sauteed with sherry vinegar and crushed tomatoes.

Selle d'Agneau Rôtie aux Senteurs Méridionales. Roast saddle of lamb with Mediterranean flavors.

Succès au Chocolat. A rich chocolate pastry flavored with candied fruit, cut into small squares and served as a petit four.

Crémeux de Riz au Lait aux Fruits Secs. Creamy rice pudding with dried fruit.

Fine southwest wines; Béarn, Madiran, Irouléguy.

MENUS | Lunch (3 dishes) 140 francs, dinner (5 dishes) 170 francs.

16ᵉ ARRONDISSEMENT

A & M LE BISTROT

LE PETIT BOILEAU

AUTEUIL–PASSY–
LA MUETTE–TROCADÉRO

PLACES OF INTEREST

*Bois de Boulogne (Longchamp and Auteuil
racetracks; Jardin d'Acclimatation children's park;
Jardin Fleuriste d'Auteuil gardens, hothouses,
and arboretum; Jardin Fleuriste de la Ville de Paris)*

Musée d'Art Moderne

Musée de la Mode du Costume

Musée des Arts et Traditions Populaires

Musée Balzac

Musée Guimet

*Palais de Chaillot (Musées de la Marine,
de l'Homme, des Monuments Français,
du Cinéma Henri Langlois)*

Place du Trocadéro (gardens and aquarium)

A & M Le Bistrot

M. Jean-Pierre Vigato
M. François Grandjean
Chef: Benoit Chagny

136, boulevard Murat, 75016 (at rue du Général Niox) |
🚇 Porte de St-Cloud
☎ 01-45-27-39-60 | Fax 01-45-27-69-71
Ø Saturday lunch, Sunday; two weeks in August
$ $ | 💳 VISA 💳
♟

B ehind the lamppost at the corner of boulevard Murat and rue du Général Niox is the green awning of the A & M Le Bistrot. Potted plants and flowers line the outside under the wood-framed windows. Step up into a large space, comfortable but devoid of charm, with the bar in front and a modern dining room, mauve and white, that holds 20 spacious tables surrounded by leather-backed chairs. Fresh flowers in tall glass vases add color, with accents of blue in the dishes of sea salt on the tables. Another ten tables are in the bar area. Black-and-white vertical-striped shades cover the windows.

This is the first bistro annex of two master chefs, Jean-Pierre Vigato (of Apicius fame) and his brother-in-law François Grandjean (of Marius). The food is imaginative and well prepared by Benoît Chagny, who formally worked as station chef at Apicius. He has added some interesting preparations to a classic menu, such as warm red mullet presented with an uncooked combination of tomatoes, olives, mint, and basil; roasted cod with artichokes stuffed with mushrooms, ham, and coriander; and his signature dish, *hachis Parmentier,* a copious shepherd's pie made with finely chopped beef cheeks and oxtail. The mashed potatoes served with truffle sauce are another specialty. The wine carte is unusually large and offers some inexpensive choices, listed as regional *vins rouges* including a Chénas (Domaine des Ducs) Corbières, *vieille vigne* (Château Lastours), and a Mediterranean Fitou—a wine not often found in Paris.

Encouraged by the success of their first bistro annex, the partners have recently opened a second place with the same name in the 17e arrondissement (105, rue de Prony, 01-44-40-05-88).

RECOMMENDED DISHES

Rémoulade de Céleri aux Copeaux de Foie Gras Cru. Celery root in a mustard mayonnaise sauce served with a spiral-shaped pastry filled with foie gras.

Oeufs Brouillés Crémeux aux Langoustines. Creamed scrambled eggs with crayfish tails.

Terrine de Campagne, Salade de Pignons de Pin, Tartine Grillée. Country pâté on a salad of pine nuts served on a thick slice of bread.

Hachis Parmentier de Joue de Boeuf et de Queue de Boeuf. Shepherd's pie of beef cheeks and oxtail cooked in a gratin dish with mashed potatoes. Signature dish.

Thon Mi-Cuit Sauce en Aigre-Doux Balsamique Fraîcheur de Mâche Tiède. Semicooked tuna steak in a sweet-and-sour sauce on a wilted salad dressed with balsamic vinegar.

Foie de Veau Épais Grosses Échalotes Fondantes. Thick slice of calf's liver with shallots and potatoes.

Cabillaud Pané au Poivre Mignonnette, Lingots Verts Écrasés à la Ménagère. Cod breaded with coarse pepper accompanied by mashed white beans.

Pigeon Rôti Entier, Mange-Touts au Beurre, Jus de Carcasse. Whole roast squab with buttered snap beans in natural juices.

Entremets Chaud au Chocolat Amer Glace Pistache. Bittersweet hot chocolate dessert with pistachio ice cream.

Figues Rôties Entières, Piquées du Bois de Cannelle. Roasted whole figs spiced with cinnamon.

Extensive wine list of high-priced Burgundies and Bordeaux. Stick to the regional country wines for price.

MENU | 170 francs.

Le Petit Boileau

M. Claude Chazalon
Mme. Chrystal Chazalon
Chef: Claude Chazalon

98, rue Boileau, 75016 | 🚋 Exelmans or Porte de St-Cloud

☎ 01-42-88-59-05

Ø Saturday and Sunday; August

$ | VISA MasterCard

🍲🍲 | ☀

In a rather chic area of the 16^e arrondissement, Claude Chazalon has recently created a true neighborhood bistro where the atmosphere is relaxed, the prices are moderate, and the food is absolutely delicious. Petit Boileau has already earned a reputation for fine food and wine and attracts an upscale clientele who appreciate the lively ambience, attractive surroundings, and copious cuisine prepared with the finest products and recipes from the Ardèche and Aubrac regions of central France. Chazalon, a native of the Lozère, maintains a close relationship with relatives in the area from whom he gets his meats and the coteaux de l'Ardèche wine vinified by a cousin. Wine, in fact, is the theme of the modern decor, with colorful posters, prints, and an etched-glass divider between the bar and dining area. There are about 30 *couverts* (place settings) with a long *table d'hôte* in the rear surrounded by pictures of grapes, vineyards, and wine-crate plaques.

There is a small *carte* that offers three entrées and three *plats* plus the changing daily specials, which might include veal or roast pork with lentils from Le Puy, stuffed cabbage, or *saucisse* from Lozère with potatoes. Marinated herring and the extraordinary chicken liver terrine are the starters most regulars enjoy, followed by *entrecôte* or *faux-filet* from Aubrac with gratin potatoes or lamb from Lozère. A meal can conclude with the wonderful goat cheeses and Camemberts from the Chazalons' own *cave*.

RECOMMENDED DISHES

Hareng Frais Mariné. Marinated herring fillets served with potato salad in oil.

Charcuteries de l'Ardèche (Cochonnailles). Assortment of pork sausages and pâté from the Ardèche region.

Terrine aux Foies de Volaille. Chicken liver pâté made in and served from an earthenware terrine.

Navarin d'Agneau Printanier. Lamb stew with spring vegetables.

Faux-Filet Saignant de l'Aubrac, Gratin Dauphinois. Sirloin steak served rare accompanied by sliced potatoes baked with cream and browned on top.

Rôti de Porc Froid aux Lentilles du Puy. Roast pork served lukewarm with green lentils from Le Puy.

Brochette de Poulet Fermier au Citron. Skewered farm chicken with vegetables and lemon.

Andouillette "AAAAA"* au Chablis. Grilled pork tripe sausage in Chablis wine and accompanied by mashed potatoes.

Plateau de Fromages au Lait Cru. Perfectly aged farm cheeses from the owners' region.

Pruneaux au Vin et à l'Orange. Prunes in red wine flavored with orange.

---

*AAAAA The *Association Amicale des Amateurs d'Authentique Andouillettes* (The Amicable Association of Appreciators of Authentic Pork Tripe Sausages). See footnote on page 114.

Coteaux de l'Ardèche (J. Paul Chazalon), St-Joseph (Dard et Ribo), Morgon (Lapierre), Chablis (G. Robin), St-Émilion (Château Meylet).

MENUS | 89 and 125 francs.

17e ARRONDISSEMENT

BAPTISTE

LE BISTROT D'À CÔTÉ FLAUBERT

LE BISTROT DE L'ÉTOILE "NIEL"

CAFÉ D'ANGEL

CAVES PÉTRISSANS

LA CÔTE DE BOEUF

LE TROYON

BATIGNOLLES–TERNES

Baptiste

M. Jean-Baptiste Gay

M. Denis Croset

Chef: Denis Croset

51, rue Jouffroy-d'Abbans, 75017 (off boulevard
Malesherbes at place du Nicaragua) |
🚋 Wagram or Malesherbes

☎ 01-42-27-20-18 | Fax 1-42-27-20-18

∅ Saturday lunch and Sunday; August

$ $ | ■ VISA MasterCard

♟♟ | ☼

The atmosphere is unpretentious and friendly and
the prices are reasonable at this bistro, newly
opened (in September 1999) in an out-of-the-way
neighborhood near Parc de Monceau. Chef Denis Croset
and his partner Jean-Baptiste Gay have cleaned and polished the large wall mirrors and colorful art deco tile floor
and added brightly upholstered banquettes, chairs, and
crisp linens to update the simple 1930s decor of an old
neighborhood restaurant.

Chef Croset has drawn up an appealing contemporary
menu-carte at 180 francs, which depends on the market
and season, as he likes to enhance his preparations with
fresh aromatic herbs and seasonal vegetables. He sprinkles
dill on the rabbit terrine, serves basil with the Serrano
ham, composes a salad tossed with fresh greens and herbs,
and serves a warm vegetable gazpacho with shrimp and
thyme. Tender stalks of asparagus and tiny green beans
accompany the lamb and veal; duck is served with fresh
spinach; sea bream is served with a *pipérade* of vegetables;
and a grilled veal chop is surrounded by a tender vegetable
confit. There is a selection of five or six desserts, including

a luscious dish of little crepes filled with apples and raisins, which must be ordered at the beginning of the meal.
The wine list is not very large, but you can drink a *petit*
Chablis with the fish and, for a red, a Corbières or one of
the Beaujolais.

RECOMMENDED DISHES

Tartare d'Huîtres à la Crème de Beaufort. Minced oysters in
   a Gruyère cheese sauce.
Salade Pastorale aux Herbes Fraîches. Tossed green salad
   and fresh herbs dressed with a vinaigrette.
*Terrine de Lapereaux à l'Aneth, Compote de Fruits Secs à
   l'Aigre-Doux.* Rabbit terrine flavored with dill, compote
   of dried sweet-and-sour fruits.
Foie Gras Frais Maison, Cuit au Torchon. House duck liver
   cooked lightly in brine, tied up in a cloth.
*Agneau en Brunoise de Légumes Aromatisée, Galette de
   Pommes de Terre.* Grilled lamb and seasoned vegetables
   served with a fried potato cake.
Entrecôte au Jus Spätzle Maison. Rib steak with natural
   juices accompanied by the house specialty, tiny fried
   noodle dumplings, spaetzle.
*Daurade Rôtie au Fumet de Tomates, Macaronis et Basilic
   Tuile au Parmesan.* Sea bream roasted with tomatoes in
   fish stock, accompanied by pasta and Parmesan cheese,
   with a little mound of biscuits flavored with basil.
*Magret de Canard, Jus au Citron Vert, Tombée d'Épinards
   Frais.* Fattened duck breast dressed with lime juice and
   accompanied by fresh spinach.
Petites Crêpes aux Pommes Fruits et Raisins. Little apple-
   and raisin-filled pancakes (order at beginning of meal).

Brouilly, Fleurie, Saumur-Champigny, Coteaux du
Languedoc.

MENUS │ 148 francs or 180 francs.

Le Bistrot d'à Côté Flaubert

M. MICHEL ROSTANG
CHEF: PIERRE NEGREVERGNE

10, rue Gustave-Flaubert, 75017 (off rue Rennequin) |
🚋 Ternes
☎ 01-42-67-05-81 | Fax 01-47-63-82-75
Ø Open every day, all year
$ $ $ | 💳 VISA MasterCard 💳
🍲

The several fashionable bistro annexes of Michel Rostang have been going strong for a number of years, all serving very high-quality, inventive, but reasonably priced bistro fare. The first "Bistro Next Door" is colorfully installed in an early 1900s grocery store, where the original shelves, tin ceiling, and tile floor provide a backdrop for a collection of bric-a-brac, flea market antiques, and old Michelin guides. A dozen or so marble-top tables fill the inside while several more crowd the sidewalk out front.

There are no elaborate preparations, but each establishment encourages its chef to be creative. Here, the menu is prepared with such things as artichokes, cold cucumber soup, Serrano ham, ravioli, lobster, squid, polenta, salt cod, tuna steak, *souris* of lamb, and tender veal chops. The wine list includes such suggested choices as a white Côtes du Lubéron and a red and rosé Côtes du Ventoux.

Michel Rostang now counts four spin-offs, each called Bistrot d'à Côté except for the one on St-Germain, which was recently turned into a seafood bistro and called Le Bistrot Côte Mer (16, boulevard St-Germain, 75005, 01-43-54-59-10).

Flaubert, 10, rue Gustave-Flaubert, 75017, 01-42-67-05-81.
Villiers, 16, avenue de Villiers, 75017, 01-47-63-25-61.
Neuilly, 4, rue Boutard, Neuilly 92200, 01-47-45-34-55.

RECOMMENDED DISHES

Vinaigrette Tiède de Homard et Ravioles du Romans au Basilic. Lobster ravioli with basil in a vinaigrette dressing.

Terrine de Foies de Volailles aux Pistaches et aux Raisins. Chicken liver pâté with pistachio nuts and grapes.

Pieds de Porc aux Lentilles. Pig's trotters with lentils.

Rognon de Veau Clouté à la Réglisse. Grilled veal kidney studded with licorice.

Volaille de Bresse Rôtie, Pommes Purée, et sa Salade de Cuisses. Roast Bresse chicken in two services, first with mashed potatoes, then the thighs in a salad.

Dos d'Agneau aux Échalotes Confites, Gratin Dauphinois. Roast saddle of lamb with preserved shallots, outstanding sliced potatoes baked in cream and crusted on top.

Noix de Saint-Jacques d'Erquy Poêlées et leur Polenta Crèmeuse aux Herbes. Panfried scallops in a creamed polenta with herbs.

Faux-Filet de Boeuf de Race Poêlé "Beurre Maître d'Hôtel." Panfried sirloin steak with a warm butter sauce of lemon juice, salt, pepper, and parsley accompanied by green string beans.

Pots de Crème au Chocolat à l'Ancienne. Classic chocolate custard dessert served in individual cups.

Fondant au Chocolat "Extra Bitter" et sa Glace Vanille. Bitter chocolate dessert with vanilla ice cream.

Extremely varied and well-priced cellar. House wine is "la Fillette d'a Côté," Côtes du Ventoux.

MENUS │ Lunch 150 francs, dinner 198 francs.

Le Bistrot de l'Étoile "Niel"

M. GUY SAVOY

M. BRUNO GENSDARMES

CHEF: BRUNO GENSDARMES

75, avenue Niel, 75017 (off rue Rennequin) |
🚎 Pereire or Ternes
☎ 01-42-27-88-44 | Fax 01-42-27-32-12
∅ Closed Saturday lunch and Sunday
$ $ | 💳 VISA 💳 💳
♗

G uy Savoy's minichain of three Bistrots de l'Étoile are clustered around the Arc de Triomphe and were among the first spin-off annexes established by a famous chef. Wisely, Savoy creates each of his bistros in collaboration with a creative chef. The one on avenue Niel is run by the experienced Bruno Gensdarmes and is the one we return to most often. The place is decorated in fine taste with film posters and pictures of film stars discreetly placed on the walls. Because of the small space, a *table d'hôte* is installed for single diners and others who don't mind eating with strangers. The terrace expands the seating by about 35 and is a pure delight in the summer months.

Chef Gensdarmes offers a fixed-price lunch consisting of classic renditions of bistro fare that always includes a *plat du jour* (Monday, *pot-au-feu;* Tuesday, *rognons de veau;* Wednesday, *raie aux câpres;* etc.). In the evening a more expensive, totally à la carte menu offers more inventive dishes and usually includes a seafood risotto, which is a specialty of the chef.

Similar in quality are the two other bistros: Bistrot de l'Étoile "Troyon," 13, rue Troyon 75017, 01-42-67-25-95;

and Bistrot de l'Étoile "Lauriston," 19, rue Lauriston 75016, 01-40-67-11-16.

RECOMMENDED DISHES

Terrine de Lapereau en Bouillabaisse Froide. Rabbit terrine in cold broth accompanied by a saffron-accented potato salad.

Soupe au Pistou et Gambas à la Sarriette. Savory Provençal bean and vegetable soup with jumbo shrimp added to the broth.

Millefeuille de Radis Noir et Saumon Fumé. A flaky pastry filled with black radish shavings and smoked salmon.

Supions et Légumes de Provence Grillés à la Plancha. Grilled Provençal vegetables and squid on a cutting board.

Thon Mariné Grillé au Piment d'Espelette, Marmelade de Courgettes. Grilled marinated tuna steak with chili peppers and stewed zucchini.

Entrecôte du Nebraska Purée de Pommes de Terre à l'Ail Confit. Beef rib steak served with mashed potatoes and crystallized garlic.

Carré d'Agneau Rôti en Chapelure d'Herbes, Polenta Crèmeuse Jus aux Olivettes. Roast lamb chops in herb bread crumbs accompanied by a polenta with plum tomatoes.

Cabillaud, Anchois sous la Peau et Niçoise de Légumes. Fresh cod and anchovies with their skins accompanied by a mix of Provençal vegetables.

Salade de Fraises au Miel de Lavande, Sorbet au Thé-Citron. Strawberry salad with honey and tea-and-lemon sherbet.

"Chaud-Froid" Vanille-Chocolat. Homemade vanilla ice cream covered in hot chocolate.

Bordeaux rouge (Guy Savoy), Bordeaux blanc (Guy Savoy).

MENUS | 145 francs and 170 francs for lunch only.

Café d'Angel

M. Jean-Marc Gorsy
Mme. Mireille Valette
Chef: Jean-Marc Gorsy

16, rue Brey, 75017 (off avenue de Wagram near Arc de
Triomphe) | 🚋 Charles de Gaulle-Étoile or
Ternes
☎ 01-47-54-03-33 | Fax 01-47-54-03-33
Ø Saturday and Sunday; three weeks in August
$$ | VISA
♟♟

I n the shadow of the Arc de Triomphe on an ani-
mated bourgeois street, this cheerful bistro has a large
following. The combination of carefully thought out
modern preparations and reasonable prices attracts a
steady stream of curious gourmets seeking a new eating
experience, and chef Jean-Marc Gorsy has the imagination
and skill to give it to them.

The stylish modern decor is highlighted by terrazzo tile
floors and white wall tiles, the only remnants of the old
charcuterie. Chef Gorsy, late of Jules Verne and Haberlin's
Auberge d'Ill (which has three Michelin stars) offers many
delicious and varied choices on his market-driven black-
board menu. Crepes with raw tuna, smoked salmon, and
crab in a potato *croûte,* roast sturgeon or haddock with cab-
bage, rabbit with rosemary and a terrine or *girolles* (mush-
rooms), swordfish with asparagus and sea urchin caviar, a
classic hanger steak with potatoes, and venison with wheat
risotto and chestnuts are some of the tempting pleasures to
be found here. Desserts are equally seductive; they include
an orange-flavored *millefeuille* served with a Grand Marnier
crème anglaise, crème brûlée with chocolate, and a warm

rhubarb *clafoutis*. There is a small list of unpretentious wines, and as the menu changes every two or three weeks, there is always something new and interesting to eat and drink.

RECOMMENDED DISHES

Aumônière de Thon Cru aux Herbes. A thin crepe "purse" filled with herbed raw tuna.

Croustillant de Pieds de Porc et Saint-Jacques Poêlées. Deboned crunchy pig's trotter cake accompanied by panfried scallops.

Araignée et Saumon Fumé en Croûte de Pommes de Terre. Crabmeat and smoked salmon encased in pastry with potatoes.

Civet de Biche avec son Risotto de Blé aux Châtaignes. Venison stewed in red wine with a side dish of wheat risotto flavored with chestnuts.

Fricassée de Rognons de Veau aux Champignons, Galette de Pommes de Terre et Céleri. Stew of veal kidneys and mushrooms served with a potato and celery cake.

Onglet de Boeuf aux Échalotes, Millefeuille de Pommes de Terre. Panfried hanger steak with shallots accompanied by a flaky pastry filled with potato.

Dos d'Esturgeon Rôti Mijoté au Chou Vert Jus de Poule aux Herbes. Roast back of sturgeon simmered in chicken broth with green cabbage.

Espadon aux Asperges et Corail d'Oursin. Grilled swordfish steak with asparagus and sea urchin roe.

Gâteau Tiède au Chocolat et Framboises. Warm chocolate tart with fresh raspberries.

Clafoutis Tiède à la Vanille et Rhubarbe Rôtie. Warm batter tart with roasted rhubarb and whipped cream.

Selection of unpretentious little wines. Gamay de Touraine.

MENUS | Lunch 90 and 105 francs, dinner 180 francs.

Caves Pétrissans

Mme. Marie-Christine Allemoz

M. Jean-Marie Allemoz

30, bis, avenue Niel, 75017 (off place Aimé Maillard) |
🚋 Charles de Gaulle-Étoile or Ternes

☎ 01-42-27-52-03 | Fax 01-40-54-87-56

∅ Saturday and Sunday; first three weeks in August

$$ | 💳 VISA MasterCard

🍲🍲 | 🍷

A truly unique place, Caves Pétrissans will delight and excite even the most jaded "been there, done that" traveler. The moment you see the corner entrance, framed in wood, and the well-preserved belle epoque building with graceful wrought-iron window rails and elegant cornices, you are led to expect something out of the ordinary. As you enter the tile-floor foyer lined with shelves holding hundreds of bottles of excellent vintages, the impression is one of a fine old *cave* rather than a restaurant. There is a sense of history here, as well there should be. Martin Pétrissans, the great-grandfather of the current owner, Marie-Christine Allemoz, opened this place more than one hundred years ago as a wine shop. Mme. Allemoz continues that tradition; her husband Jean-Marie is in charge of the bistro.

Walk by the bar into an inviting clublike atmosphere with oak furnishings, leather banquettes and chairs, a black-and-white tile floor, and tables covered with snowy white linen. This is a place to appreciate traditional bistro food, which is executed with only the finest products. Try the homemade terrine with onion confit, the spicy celery root salad, or the anchovies from Collioure to start. The veal tenderloin is reputed to be one of the best in Paris, and the *faux-filet* from Salers, an area known for exceptional beef, is tender and juicy. If you feel in a more adventurous mood, the *tête de veau* is exceptional; it is served here with enormous pieces of tongue and brains in a pungent *sauce ravigote*. The daily specials are a comforting fixture, with Monday bringing veal stew, Tuesday roast duck, Wednesday roast pork, Thursday *hachis Parmentier,* and Friday fish, depending on the day's market. The wine selection, not surprisingly, is quite large, with many *grands crus* as well as numerous country wines, all available at the shop.

RECOMMENDED DISHES

Terrine Maison et sa Confiture d'Oignons. Homemade terrines, always accompanied by onion *confit.*

Oeufs Durs Mayonnaise. Hard-boiled eggs with mayonnaise.

Steak Tartare. Raw, seasoned ground beef garnished with chopped onions, capers, and parsley, accompanied by pommes frites.

Filet de Cabillaud Poêlé Huilade aux Herbes Aromatiques. Panfried cod, oiled and sprinkled with herbs.

Tendron de Veau à la Campagnarde. Braised veal served country-style with vegetables.

Faux-Filet de Salers. Top-quality sirloin steak.

Andouillette de Philippe Ravel. Grilled tripe sausage from the House of Philippe Ravel.

Île Flottante au Caramel et à la Nougatine. Floating island dessert, meringue floating in custard cream topped with caramel sauce.

Crème Brûlée à la Cassonade. Cream-based custard flan topped by soft brown sugar and caramelized under the grill.

Very good selection of reasonably priced wines, all of which may be purchased in the shop. Bordeaux are a strong point.

MENU | 170 francs.

La Côte de Boeuf

M. Jean-Dominique Bessière

4, rue Saussier-Leroy, 75017 (off rue Poncelet,
   two blocks from avenue des Ternes) |
   🚃 Ternes
☎ 01-42-27-73-50
∅ Saturday lunch and Sunday; August
$ $ $ | ▪️ 💳 💳 💳
☞

The congenial owner, Jean-Dominique Bessière, pre-
sides over his convivial bistro with an engaging
manner. "Our meats are a dance for the man-
dibles," he exclaims with a gleam in his eye.

The interior is oriented toward Provence, decked out
with pictures of steers, braids of hanging garlic and peppers, dried flowers, gleaming copper pots, and tables gaily
draped with red cloths overlaid with white linen. A grace-
ful balustrade ascends to a second floor.

The cooking and the menu are straightforward, with
uncomplicated starters such as Baltic herring in cream,
shellfish bisque, shrimp cocktail, duck foie gras, and snails
prepared à la "papa" Bessière. As the name of this bistro
suggests, beef is the specialty, with succulent cuts of entrecôte, rump steak, and onglet done to a turn and served with
a favorite accompaniment. These delights keep the regulars happy, but great care is taken also to prepare a fresh
fish of the day, tender lamb with thyme, and rabbit in mustard sauce. The favored wines are also traditional, with
many hearty reds suggested to stand up to the meats. The
proximity to the food markets on rue Poncelet make this
place a double delight for the epicure.

RECOMMENDED DISHES

Bisque de Crustacés. Thick shellfish soup with white wine, cognac, and fresh cream.

Champignons à la Provençale. Sautéed wild mushrooms with tomatoes, garlic, and onions.

Les Six Escargots au Potée "Bessière." Six Burgundian snails cooked and served in an earthenware pot.

Entrecôte Marchand de Vin. Grilled rib beefsteak with a red wine and shallot sauce.

Carré d'Agneau Rôti au Thym. Roast rack of lamb with thyme.

Côte de Boeuf. Roast ribs of beef (for two).

Osso Buco de Lotte. Monkfish braised in white wine with garlic, onions, and tomatoes.

Pavé dans le Coeur de Rumsteak, au Poivre ou au Roquefort. Thick piece of prime grilled steak served with either a pepper or a Roquefort sauce.

Mousse au Chocolat. Whipped cream and meringue folded into melted chocolate with a touch of rum added.

Baba au Rhum. A yeast cake made with raisins and moistened with rum, baked in a mold.

Extensive *carte* of Bordeaux wines and more than thirty *eaux-de-vie.*

MENU | Lunch 123 francs.

Le Troyon

M. JEAN-MARC NOTELET

4, rue Troyon, 75017 (off avenue de Wagram) |
🚋 Charles de Gaulle-Étoile
☎ 01-40-68-99-40 | Fax 01-40-68-99-57
Ø Saturday lunch and Sunday; August
$$ | 💳 VISA MasterCard
♟♟♟

The service is warm and attentive at this pleasant bistro, located just off the place d'Étoile, and the owner-chef, Jean-Marc Notelet, is a force to be reckoned with. His training was with chefs Marc Meneau and Gerald Boyer (each of whom earned three Michelin stars), and it is said that Olivier Roellinger, the master of cooking with spices, is his spiritual father. After eating here one can't help feeling that someday M. Notelet will be encountered in a loftier setting, with stars attached to his name.

Brown banquettes, yellow walls, finely set tables, bentwood chairs, and a wonderful aroma of exotic herbs and spices greet you as you enter the slightly austere, carpeted room decorated with seasonal bouquets. Candles are lit in the evening, lending a subtle warmth to the room.

Originally from the north, Notelet honors his native region with touches gathered from his Flemish background, but most of all he enjoys experimenting with unusual flavors, using herbs and spices to enhance classic produce. Herring is scented with thyme, bay, and juniper; mackerel is crusted and roasted with a five-peppercorn mix; sweet potatoes are made into salad; spinach is cooked with lemon peel; roast chicken is made with walnut butter or cocoa beans; duckling is made with Malaga wine; rabbit is braised with prunes; spareribs are caramelized with wild honey, coriander, and citrus zest; and strawberries are flavored with hibiscus. Mushrooms and vegetables are among the specialties. In fact, for three days in October a menu of mushroom preparations is featured. The *carte* changes daily and between lunch and dinner. Any meal may be concluded with one of the fine ports from a superb wine list.

RECOMMENDED DISHES

Harengs Frais Marinés au Genièvre, Pommes Grenailles. Marinated herring fillets with juniper berries served with a potato salad.

Fondant de Cailles (de Normandie) Tiède, Jus au Vieux Porto. Small quail croquette served warm with natural juices spiked with vintage port.

Foie Frais de Canard et Compote de Figues. Delicately cooked fresh fattened duck liver served with stewed figs.

Artichaut Frais Tiède, et Vinaigre Balsamique. Ultrafresh artichoke served warm with a balsamic vinegar dressing.

Gibiers. In the fall many outstanding game dishes appear on the menu; venison and game birds are coupled with wild mushrooms.

Veau de Lait en Cocotte au Cerfeuil. Young milk-fed veal cooked and served in a lidded earthenware pot and flavored with chervil.

Poitrine de Pigeonneau Rôtie au Poivre Farce à Gratin et Jus Frais au Cacao. Roast squab breast with pepper stuffing in natural juices flavored with cocoa powder.

Lapereau Braisé aux Pruneaux, Purée de Carottes. Braised young rabbit with prunes accompanied by a carrot puree.

Moelleux Chocolat, Glace Pistache du Piémont. Soft chocolate dessert served with pistachio ice cream.

Small but exceptionally well chosen list of diversified wines.

MENU | 198 francs.

18ᵉ ARRONDISSEMENT

L'ÉTRIER BISTROT

MARIE-LOUISE

MONTMARTRE–CLICHY

PLACES OF INTEREST

Basilique du Sacré-Coeur

Cimetière St-Vincent

Espace Montmartre Dali

Marché aux Puces
(Porte de Clignancourt)

Moulin de la Galette

Moulin Rouge, Lapin Agile

Musée d'Art Juif
(Jewish Art Museum)

Musée du Vieux Montmartre

Place du Tertre

La Vigne
(Vineyard)

L'Étrier Bistrot

M. Thierry Facheaux
M. Jean-Philippe Colin
Chef: Thierry Facheaux

154, rue Lamarck, 75018 (off avenue de St-Ouen) |
🚌 Guy Môquet
☎ 01-42-29-14-01
Ø Sunday and Monday; last three weeks of August
$$ | VISA
♟♟ | ☼

A complimentary glass of wine from the Landes and a plate of roasted peanuts welcome you to this pretty little bistro nicely situated away from the touristy part of Montmartre.

White marble floors are a lovely balance to the tastefully warm colors of the walls, seats, and framed pictures, and though every corner of the small room is filled, high ceilings, huge floor-to-ceiling windows, and tall columns hung with large rustic lanterns give an illusion of spaciousness.

Jean-Philippe Colin and chef Thierry Facheaux, no strangers to the restaurant business, have made a great success, offering a changing blackboard menu based on what is fresh at the market. The daily *carte* always includes fillet of beef either made in a red, white, and black peppercorn sauce and smothered in shallots or served with duck foie gras. One might begin the meal with a *tatin* of endives in sage butter or an *estouffade* of bordelaise snails followed by a *cassolette* of fresh fish in snail butter or chicken fricasseed with mushrooms served with rice pilaf. As for dessert, pears prepared with a caramel sauce anglaise, a fruit salad of mangoes and oranges, a lemon tart, and a *gourmandise* of house pastry are all remarkably delicious.

A faithful clientele from the quarter keeps the place busy, but recently a few tourists who have discovered that this is one of the few spots in the area where one can eat very well inexpensively have begun vying for seats.

RECOMMENDED DISHES

Mijotée d'Escargots en Fondu d'Endives. Simmered snails garnished with melted-down endives.

Croustillant d'Aubergines au Chorizo Grillé. Crunchy eggplant with a grilled spicy chorizo sausage.

Pavé de Morue Fraîche au Foie Gras. Thick slice of grilled cod covered in a sauce with duck foie gras.

Filet de Boeuf au Foie Gras de Canard Poêlé, Pommes Craquantes. Prime cut of tenderloin in a foie gras sauce, served with potato cakes.

Fricassée de Volaille Forestière, Riz Pilaf. Creamed chicken stew with mushrooms on a bed of browned spiced rice.

Rognons de Veau Rôti, Sauce Noble Cru. Pan-roasted veal kidney in a red wine sauce.

Rôti de Boeuf à l'Échalote Confite. Roast beef covered in shallot sauce with potato cakes.

Cassolette de Poissons Beurre de Pistou, Petits Légumes. Mediterranean fish in a small casserole, cooked with fresh basil, garlic, and new vegetables.

Charlotte de Bananes, Caramel. Baked banana charlotte topped with caramel sauce.

Gâteau de Pommes au Caramel, Sauce Anglaise. Apple cake with caramel and custard cream.

Buzet (Château des Tournelles), Coteaux du Languedoc (Domaine du Tariquet Blanc), Graves (Château de Malle), Crozes-Hermitage (Domaine des Entrefaux).

MENUS | Lunch 92 francs or 140 francs, dinner 180 francs.

Marie-Louise

M. JOHANN LeCLERC

52, rue Championnet, 75018 (off place Albert Kahn) |
   🚇 Simplon or Porte de Clignancourt
☎ 01-46-06-86-55
Ø Sunday and Monday; first three weeks of August
$$$ | VISA MasterCard

🥘🥘

O ver the last decade the neighborhood has be-
come a bustling ethnic enclave, but this tran-
quil, pleasant bistro has remained remarkably
unchanged. It is a showcase for the highest level of bour-
geois cuisine with a steady repertoire of bistro classics.

When you enter this old restaurant, you are struck by
the display of gleaming brass and copper saucepans hang-
ing from the walls, the authentic 1950s bar, and the well-
spaced tables set with crystal and covered with white
linen. Fresh flowers are always in abundance.

The original owners have retired after 37 years, and the
new regime has had the good sense not to change a thing.
You will still find the wonderful pâté starter of *tête de cochon;*
the famous *poularde de Marie-Louise,* chicken with tomato
and tarragon in a white wine sauce with chicken livers; the
mijoté de rognons de veau au madère, veal kidneys simmered in
Madeira sauce; and the renowned *boeuf à la ficelle.*

Why not combine a trip to the antique flea markets
around Clignancourt with a lunch or dinner at this revered
antique?

RECOMMENDED DISHES

Salade Maison. Mélange of wild mushrooms, sliced ham,
and greens in a creamy vinaigrette.

Pâté de Tête de Cochon. Terrine of suckling pig's head.

Harengs à l'Huile. Herring fillets in oil, served with a salad of sliced potatoes.

Côte de Veau Grand-Mère. Veal chop with onions, mushrooms, bacon, and potatoes.

Poularde Marie-Louise. Chicken cooked in a white wine sauce with tomatoes, tarragon, and chicken livers.

Boeuf à la Ficelle, Pommes Rissolées. Poached fillet of beef with fried potatoes (for two).

Coq au Vin. Cockerel cooked slowly in red wine with onions, garlic, mushrooms, and chunks of bacon.

Langue de Boeuf Ménagère. Boiled ox tongue simply garnished with onions, carrots, and potatoes.

Clafoutis aux Cerises. Deep-dish batter tart with black cherries.

Crème Caramel. Vanilla-flavored custard flan baked in a caramel-lined mold.

🌰 Excellent Loire Valley wines, Chinon, Saint-Nicolas-de-Bourgueil, Muscadet.

MENU | Lunch 130 francs.

19ᵉ ARRONDISSEMENT

LA CAVE GOURMANDE

BUTTES-CHAUMONT

PLACES OF INTEREST

Bassin de la Villette

Canal d l'Ourcq, Canal St-Denis

Cité de la Musique

Cité des Sciences et de l'Industrie

Parc de la Villette
(Inventorium)

Parc des Buttes-Chaumont

Pont de Crimée
(last surviving drawbridge in Paris)

La Cave Gourmande

M. Eric Fréchon
Mme. Sylvie Fréchon
Chef: Lilian Oukouloff

10, rue du Général-Brunet, 75019 (a short walk from
   Parc des Buttes-Chaumont) | 🚋 Botzaris
☎ 01-40-40-03-30 | Fax 01-40-40-03-30
Ø Saturday and Sunday; August
$$ | VISA MasterCard
👨‍🍳👨‍🍳

The owner and former chef, Eric Fréchon, has left
his enormously popular Buttes-Chaumont bistro
in the capable hands of Mme. Sylvie Fréchon and
chef Lilian Oukouloff (who was second in the kitchen)
and moved on to the grand kitchens of the Hôtel Bristol.
The continued success of this rustic-chic restaurant,
renamed La Cave Gourmande, is ensured by a very small
but superb 170-franc menu-carte, which changes daily.

La Cave Gourmande is located in an out-of-the-way
section of northeastern Paris, so one doesn't just drop in
for a quick bite; but a dedicated clientele ventures here for
the appetizing dishes—ravioli of duck foie gras in a mush-
room cream sauce, poached oysters in bouillon, roast
pigeon with cabbage, glazed pork with creamy lentils, ten-
der pieces of guinea fowl, fresh cod with brown butter and
a puree of watercress, and for dessert poached pears in
chocolate sauce with vanilla ice cream and prunes poached
in red wine and served with orange sorbet.

Part of the restaurant has been transformed into a
gourmet food and wine shop, so any wine chosen for the
meal is *prix-cave,* meaning that it is sold by the bottle at the
retail price.

RECOMMENDED DISHES

Huîtres Pochées dans un Bouillon aux Fanes de Radis. Poached oysters in a broth of radish leaves.

Brandade d'Oeufs au Jus d'Oseille. Creamed eggs with sorrel juice.

Ravioles de Foie Gras de Canard, Jus de Morilles à la Crème. Ravioli stuffed with foie gras and flavored with a mushroom juice cream sauce.

Royale au Lard Fumé, Crème de Lentilles et Petits Croûtons. Smoked pork and creamed lentil salad garnished with flavored croutons.

Canette Rôtie aux Épices, Cuisse Confite, Écrasé de Pomme de Terre Ratte. Roast duckling infused with spices served with preserved duck leg and crushed yellow potatoes.

Pintade aux Noix. Grilled guinea fowl in a walnut cream sauce.

Cabillaud Rôti Persillé, Piment Farci de Brandade à l'Huile Vierge. Roast cod in aspic and peppers stuffed with salt cod made with cold-pressed olive oil.

Foie de Veau Poêlé à la Moutarde Torrifiée, Compotée d'Oignons Rouges au Vinaigre de Framboise. Panfried calf's liver in mustard sauce accompanied by stewed red onions in raspberry vinegar.

Fondant au Chocolat Praliné Noisette. Soft bittersweet chocolate cake with caramelized almonds and ground almonds.

Sablé aux Fraises. Shortbread soaked in strawberry syrup and covered with fresh strawberries.

🖋 Bottles are selected in the *cave,* then served at table. The selection has depth, is well diversified, and is fairly priced.

MENU | 170 francs.

20ᵉ ARRONDISSEMENT

LES ALLOBROGES

LE BARATIN

LA BOULANGERIE

LE ZÉPHYR

MÉNILMONTANT

PLACES OF INTEREST

Carrefour de Belleville

Cimetière de Belleville

Cimetière du Père Lachaise

Église de St-Germain-de-Charonne

Villa de l'Ermitage

Villa Faucheur

Les Allobroges

M. OLIVIER PATEYRON
MME. ANNETTE PATEYRON
CHEF: OLIVIER PATEYRON

71, rue des Grands-Champs, 75020 (off rue des Pyrénées) |
🚌 Maraîchers or Buzenval
☎ 01-43-73-40-00
Ø Sunday and Monday; three weeks in August
$$ | ███   VISA   ▩
♟♟

A breezy, upscale Parisian clientele wends its way to
the wilds of the 20e arrondissement, lured by the
menu of fresh, original dishes prepared by the
owner-chef, Olivier Pateyron.

Soft lights and pretty prints of animals, fruit, and veg-
etables lend a countrified elegance to two small rooms
decorated in pastel colors. The atmosphere is rather for-
mal, as chef Pateyron and his wife, Annette, pay atten-
tion to the smallest details. Their refinements include a
double *amuse-gueule* of raw carrots with a spicy dip, fol-
lowed by a delicious bowl of lobster soup and lovely home-
made rolls, some stuffed with *lardons* and others sprinkled
with herbs.

The menu at 99 francs is based on one *plat du jour* with
a choice of *entrée*, cheese, and dessert and is certainly a
bargain; but the more extensive menu at 181 francs
includes most of the house specialties. Two of chef Patey-
ron's favorites are the braised leg of lamb with roasted
garlic served with a puree of split peas (*souris d'agneau*)
and a dessert of bread pudding accented with *fromage blanc
sorbet.*

This little gem is worth the trip, but be warned—the
service is slow. Be prepared to spend the evening.

RECOMMENDED DISHES

Foie Gras de Canard Cuit en Terrine. Homemade duck foie gras cooked in an earthenware terrine.

Petites Langoustines Rôties à Point à la Ratatouille. Roast shrimp accompanied by a Provençal stew of eggplant, tomatoes, onions, peppers, and garlic in oil.

Terrine de Foies de Volaille. Potted chicken livers with candied onions.

Tomates Confites à l'Huile d'Olives Vertes, Salade Amère. Preserved tomatoes with olive oil and mashed green olives on a bed of bitter greens.

Poulet de Bresse Rôti, Gâteau de Pommes de Terre. Roasted free-range Bresse chicken accompanied by a savory potato cake (order in advance).

Souris d'Agneau Braisée et Ail Confit en Chemise. Braised lamb shank with candied garlic cloves and mashed split peas.

Filet de Canette Rôti, Pommes de Terre Écrasées à l'Huile d'Olive. Roast fillet of duckling with crushed potatoes in olive oil.

Ragoût de Joue de Porc, Petite Morille et Grenaille de Noirmoutier. Light stew of pig's cheeks accompanied by potatoes mixed with morel mushrooms.

Gros Oignons Farcis d'Andouille Fumée et Civette, Caramel de Cidre. Large onions stuffed with smoked pork tripe sausage flavored with chives and topped with caramelized apple cider.

Marquise au Chocolat. Chilled cake of chocolate mousse and custard cream.

Small list with several good buys: Bandol rouge (Domaine de Terrebrone), Collioure, Quincy (Domaine Maison Blanche).

MENUS | 99 francs and 181 francs.

Le Baratin

M. Olivier Camus
Mme. Raquel Carena Camus
Chef: Raquel Carena Camus

3, rue Jouye-Rouve, 75020 (off rue de Belleville) |
🚃 Pyrénées or Belleville
☎ 01-43-49-39-70
Ø Sunday and Monday; first week in January
$ | VISA MasterCard
⌐ | 🍷

There is no pretension about this little bistro in the heart of Belleville, where the wine enthusiast Olivier Camus offers one of the most original and least expensive wine lists in Paris.

Two no-frills rooms with pale walls, wooden tables and chairs, black-and-white photographs, maps of the wine regions, and a big bar with a few stools provide the background for a colorful clientele—people who come not only for the unusual wines and company but for the astonishingly good slate menu concocted by Raquel Carena, Camus's wife. Her cooking is consistently good with slight Latino-Italian overtones and is of the caliber one would expect to find in more stylish surroundings. She especially likes to create homey ragouts, daubes, and stews, but she is equally deft at seafood. *Escabèche* (cold marinade sauce) flavors many of her dishes, and her ceviche is a tantalizing mixture of fresh fish, lime juice, red onions, chili pepper, and coriander. She prepares a different risotto every day; and in winter, hearty soups and game appear.

Meanwhile, behind the bar, Olivier regales his customers with a diverse *carte* of more than 200 wines, always listing a dozen or so by the glass.

If you have the time to trek out to this place, we promise you an unusual and satisfying experience.

RECOMMENDED DISHES

Artichauts Barigoule. Artichokes stuffed with chopped mushrooms and ham, then cooked in an airtight pan.

Escabèche de Fenouil à l'Orange. Fried marinated sardines served cold with orange-flavored fennel.

Supions aux Piments Doux. Deep-fried squid with sweet red peppers.

Daube de Joues de Cochon et Pied. Slow-cooked Provençal stew of pig's cheeks and trotters in red wine, onions, and herb stock, flavored with orange peel.

Onglet de Veau au Vinaigre Balsamique. Grilled veal flank in balsamic vinegar.

Espadon Poêlé, Petits Légumes. Panfried swordfish steak with new vegetables.

Pot-au-Feu. Beef and root vegetables cooked slowly in seasoned stock.

Saint-Jacques à la Réglisse. Panfried scallops flavored with licorice.

Charlotte aux Épices et aux Poires. Creamy fruit dessert prepared in a mold with spices and pears.

Crumble aux Pommes et Figues. Apple crumble with fresh figs.

One of the top lists in Paris of affordable and interesting wines, many available by the glass.

MENU | Lunch 73 francs.

La Boulangerie

M. Mohamed Mehenni
Chef: Pascal Louise

15, rue des Panoyaux, 75020 (off rue des Amandiers) |
🚋 Ménilmontant
☎ 01-43-58-45-45 | Fax 01-43-58-45-46
Ø Saturday lunch
$ | VISA MasterCard
ʊ ʊ | ☼

Housed in a lovely old bakery a ten-minute walk from the Père Lachaise cemetery, this attractive bistro opened in 1998 and has already earned a reputation as one of the best and least expensive places in the city.

The handsome mosaic floor—a vestige of the past—and frescoes and bas-reliefs by local Ménilmontant artists depicting breadmaking create a charming background for the wooden chairs and the tables covered with paper. When the downstairs room becomes full, there is another upstairs.

The ambience is youthful, and in the evenings this bistro is filled with a spirited, trendy local crowd. Everything is fixed price; a three-course meal costs 112 francs. The cuisine is traditional with a few creative flourishes such as rillettes of mackerel (considered a specialty), poached eggs on a bed of spinach, and tiny green du Puy lentils sprinkled with crunchy chicken bits. Poached haddock and grilled salmon are served in a nice *beurre blanc* sauce; pork knuckle is accompanied by tangy braised cabbage; and the rump steak in red wine sauce is tender and tempting. Desserts include a crusty pear crumble and *crème brûlée* infused with lavender.

An Americanized brunch buffet is served at noon on Sunday.

RECOMMENDED DISHES

Rillettes de Maquereaux. Preserved spiced mackerel bits mashed to a paste and served with toast.

Vinaigrette de Lentilles du Puy aux Gésiers Confits. Green lentil salad dressed with vinaigrette and topped with preserved chicken gizzards.

Pavé de Rumsteak Grillé Sauce Vin Rouge. Grilled rump steak served rare in a red wine sauce.

Jambonnette de Lapin Farci à la Graine de Moutarde. Stuffed rabbit sausage with mustard seeds.

Hachis Parmentier Servi à Volonté. Shepherd's pie—minced meat and mashed potatoes baked in the oven, served "unlimited," as much as you like.

Dos de Saumon sur le Grill au Beurre Blanc. Thick slice of grilled salmon with white wine butter sauce.

Rouelle de Gigot d'Agneau au Beurre de Romarin. Thick, round fillet of leg of lamb seasoned with rosemary butter.

Jarret de Porc, Choux Braisés à l'Ancienne. Knuckle of pork and cabbage braised and served in a white sauce with onions and mushrooms.

Gâteau Moelleux au Chocolat Noir, Coulis de Poire. Soft black chocolate cake topped with a pear puree.

Tarte Tatin de Tradition. Upside-down apple cake with caramelized fruit.

Côtes du Frontonnais (Château Camuzac), Bourgogne Irancy, Madiran.

MENUS-CARTES | Lunch 65 francs, dinner 112 francs.

Le Zéphyr

MME. PATRICIA LALOUM
M. MÉZIANE AZAÏCHE
CHEF: M. STÉPHANE BARON

1, rue du Jourdain, 75020 (off rue des Pyrénées) |
🚋 Jourdain
☎ 01-46-36-65-81 | Fax 01-43-58-00-06
Ø Saturday lunch and Sunday; two weeks in August; and
ten days in December
$ $ $ | VISA MasterCard
🍴

Le Zéphyr is tucked away in a quiet neighborhood in northwest Paris. Its name, meaning a fresh breeze, gives you a good idea of what the cuisine is like but does not describe the superb art deco brasserie decor, dating from 1928.

When Méziane and Patricia acquired this "stuffy" haute cuisine restaurant, revived the old decor, changed the name, and modernized the menu, local residents were aghast. It was not long, however, before the fabulous food began attracting a stylish clientele from all over the city.

The historic interior has huge windows, mirrors, decorative glass panels, sconces, moleskin banquettes, an antique coffee machine, and neo-Cubist frescoes by Hazard. The menus, inspired by chef Stéphane Baron, offer both classic and sophisticated modern dishes described as "creative—always recherché and nouvelle." The daily slate, which changes once or twice a week, is varied enough to satisfy any appetite. The à la carte list is so enticing—with staples such as a trio of foie gras; a *gratinée* of snails in Roquefort butter; a "cappuccino" of red haricot beans, oysters, and chorizo sausage; and an exquisite daube of beef cheeks and tender slices of duck confit with potatoes—that one is hard put to it to make a choice.

During the summer, one can enjoy a refreshing frozen fruit dessert parfait on the terrace under the trees.

RECOMMENDED DISHES

"Cappuccino" de Haricots Rouges et Chorizo aux Huitres. Salad of red beans, spicy sausage, and oysters in frothy whipped cream.

Foie Gras de Canard Mi-Cuit et son Pain Brioché Maison. Semicooked duck foie gras baked in a sweet roll.

Terrine de Lentilles Vertes au Haddock et Saumon Fumé et sa Mousse de Raifort. Green lentil salad with smoked haddock and salmon accompanied by creamed horseradish.

Parmentier de Queue de Boeuf au Céleri et Jus de Vin Réduit. Shepherd's pie of minced oxtail and mashed potatoes flavored with celery and a reduction of red wine.

Pavé de Biche en Poivrade à l'Orange, Crêpes de Chataîgnes. Grilled deer steak in an orange vinaigrette with pepper and white wine, accompanied by a chestnut pancake.

Carré d'Agneau Rôti en Persillade et sa Pipérade aux Olives. Roast rack of lamb parsleyed and served with a Provençal dish—scrambled eggs with peppers, onions, tomatoes, and black olives.

Paupiette de Raie à la Créole et Lait de Coco. Slice of skate stuffed with rice, sweet peppers, and tomatoes, rolled up and sautéed with coconut milk.

Côte de Boeuf Grillée au Thym et à la Fleur de Sel. Grilled rib of beef, flavored with thyme and salt (for two).

Saveur de Marrons Glacés, Poires Rôties au Cognac, Sorbet Poire. Candied chestnuts and pears cooked with cognac, accompanied by pear sherbet.

Crème Brûlée à la Noix de Brive et sa Glace Café. Cream-based custard flan with crushed walnuts, caramelized under the grill and served with coffee ice cream.

🍷 Pinot noir d'Alsace (Albert Mann), Fronsac (Château Villars), Macon-Lugny (Les Charmes).

MENUS | Lunch 72 francs, lunch and dinner 160 francs.

PART TWO

RATINGS OF THE BEST BISTRO DISHES

THE DISHES THAT follow represent a cross section of the most typical bistro cuisine. These are the great bistro classics you are likely to encounter in either the modern innovative or the old-fashioned traditional restaurants listed in our guide. You will discover that each version of a dish is as individual as the chef who creates it. Some renditions have become "signature dishes" of a chef, while others are a specialty of the bistro.

We have singled out the first few listed as our favorites—in boldface in descending order of preference—followed by other outstanding versions, in order by arrondissement.

Andouillette
Pungent, cooked chitterling pork sausage.

Le Passage 11^e

Le Relais Chablisien 1er

Auberge Pyrénées Cévennes 11^e

Le Petit Boileau 16^e

Le Petit Marguery 13^e

Chez Pierre 15^e

Caves Pétrissans 17^e

Baba au Rhum
Rum-flavored sponge cake.

À Sousceyrac   11^e

Chez Georges—Le Jeu
   du Mail   2^e

La Côte de Boeuf   17^e

Chez Pauline   1er

La Tour de Monthléry
   1er

Blanquette de Veau
Veal stew in a thick white cream sauce.

Chardenoux   11^e

Chez la Vieille   1er

Benoît   4^e

Mauzac   5^e

Le Relais Chablisien
   1er

Ma Bourgogne   8^e

Au Vins des Rues   14^e

Boeuf Bourguignon
Beef stewed in red wine with bacon, onions,
mushrooms, and herbs.

Chez René   5^e

Chez Pauline   1er

La Grille   10^e

Chez Pierre   15^e

Lescure   1er

Le Vieux Bistro   4^e

Aux Charpentiers   6^e

Chez Dumonet
   (Joséphine)   6^e

Ma Bourgogne   8^e

Boeuf à la Ficelle
Beef tied with a string and poached in broth.

Cartet   11^e

Marie-Louise   18^e

Benoît   4^e

Au Vins des Rues   14^e

Boudin
Large, soft pudding sausage.

Auberge "d'Chez Eux"   7^e

Auberge le Quincy   12^e

La Fontaine de Mars   7^e

Chez Paul   13^e

Au Bascou   3^e

Les Amognes   11^e

L'Avant-Goût   13^e

Le Bistro d'Hubert   15^e

Brandade de Morue
Puree of salt cod.

Cartet   11^e

L'Oeillade   7^e

Aux Charpentiers   6^e

Astier   11^e

Au Vins des Rues   14^e

Carré d'Agneau / Selle d'Agneau
Rack of lamb and saddle of lamb.

Le Pamphlet   3^e

Chez Toutoune   5^e

Le Bistro d'Hubert
   15^e

L'Anacréon   13^e

Le Vieux Bistro   4^e

Chez René   5^e

Auberge "d'Chez Eux"
   7^e

Au Petit Tonneau   7^e

Dame Jeanne   11^e

Le Bistrot de l'Étoile
"Niel"   17^e

La Côte de Boeuf   17^e

Cassoulet
White bean casserole.

À Sousceyrac   11^e

Benoît   4^e

Restaurant du Marché
   15^e

Le Gastroquet   15^e

Le Dauphin   1er

Baracane   4^e

Allard   6^e

Chez Dumonet
   (Joséphine)   6^e

Auberge "d'Chez Eux"   7^e

La Fontaine de Mars   7^e

Auberge Pyrénées
   Cévennes   11^e

Auberge le Quincy   12^e

Champignons
Mushroom dishes.

Au Petit Tonneau   7^e

Le Troyon   17^e

Restaurant du Marché
   15^e

L'Ami Louis 3e Le Boucoléon 8^e
Cartet 11e Le Petit Marguery 13^e
Le Villaret 11e La Côte de Boeuf 17^e

Chou Farci
Stuffed cabbage.

Le Florimond 7e Aux Charpentiers 6^e
Chez la Vieille 1er Marie et Fils 6^e
La Tour de Monthléry   L'Oeillade 7^e
   (Chez Denise) 1er L'Avant-Goût 13^e
Le Petit Boileau 16e Les Coteaux 15^e

Clafoutis
Deep-dish batter tart with fruit.

Marie-Louise 18e Aux Charpentiers 6^e
Au Petit Tonneau 7e Le Réveil du Xe 10^e
Les Fous d'en Face 4e Jean-Pierre Frelet 12^e
L'Ardoise 1er L'Anacréon 13^e
Mauzac 5e Le Café d'Angel 17^e

Cochonnailles / Charcuteries
Assorted pork appetizers: sausages, terrines, hams,
rillettes, head cheese, cold cuts, etc.

La Régalade 14e Chez René 5^e
Auberge "d'Chez Eux" 7e Le Calmont 7^e
Le Petit Boileau 16e Le Réveil du Xe 10^e
Cartet 11e Auberge Pyrénées
La Tour de Monthléry   Cévennes 11^e
   (Chez Denise) 1er Chez Paul 13^e
Mauzac 5e Les Coteaux 15^e

Confit de Canard
Duck, cooked and preserved in its own fat.

La Fontaine de Mars   Baracane (Bistrot de
   7e l'Oulette) 4^e

Auberge "d'Chez Eux"   7e Chez Catherine   9^e
Le Grizzli   4e Le Bouledogue Bistrot
Chez Dumonet (Joséphine)   10^e
   6e Chez Pierre   15^e
Le Calmont   7e Restaurant du Marché
   Lescure   1er 15^e

Coq au Vin
Chicken stewed in wine.

À la Biche au Bois   12e Allard   6^e
Chez Maître Paul   6e Auberge "d'Chez Eux"
Marie-Louise   18e 7^e
Auberge Bressane   7e Ma Bourgogne   8^e
Le Relais Chablisien   1er Le Père Claude   15^e
Chez René   5e Chez Pierre   15^e

Côtes de Boeuf
Ribs of beef.

L'Ami Louis   3e Clémentine   2^e
Les Fontaines   5e Au Bon Accueil   7^e
Auberge "d'Chez Eux"   L'Oenothèque   9^e
   7e Les Amognes   11^e
La Côte de Boeuf   17e Le Zéphyr   20^e
La Tour de Monthléry
   (Chez Denise)   1er

Crème Brûlée
Rich custard dessert topped with caramelized sugar.

Willi's Wine bar   1er Casa Olympe   9^e
Le Réminet   5e Le Parmentier   10^e
Les Jumeaux   11e Le Square Trousseau
Chez Catherine   9e 12^e
La Bastide Odéon   6e Café d'Angel   17^e
Le Boucoléon   8e La Boulangerie   20^e

Crème Caramel / Crème Renversée
Custard baked in a mold coated with caramel.

À la Biche au Bois   12^e
Chez la Vieille   1er
La Tour de Monthléry
    (Chez Denise)   1er

Allard   6^e
Chez Pierre   15^e
Marie-Louise   18^e

Daube de Boeuf
Braised beef stew with vegetables.

Chez la Vieille   1er
Chardenoux   11^e
Baracane (Bistrot
    de l'Oulette)   4^e
Le Parmentier   10^e

Le Passage   11^e
Les Coteaux   15^e
Restaurand du Marché
    15^e
Le Zéphyr   20^e

Escargots de Bourgogne
Vineyard snails in garlic butter.

Allard   6^e
Le Vieux Bistro   4^e
Chez Maître Paul   6^e
Les Coteaux   15^e
Chez Georges—Le Jeu
    du Mail   2^e
Benoît   4^e
Au Bourguignon du Marais
    4^e

Ma Bourgogne   8^e
Le Bouledogue Bistrot
    10^e
Auberge le Quincy   12^e
Chez Pierre   15^e
La Côte de Boeuf   17^e

Foie Gras
Fatted duck or goose liver.

L'Ami Louis   3^e
À Sousceyrac   11^e
Auberge "d'Chez Eux"
    7^e

L'Ardoise   1er
Le Pamphlet   3^e
Chez Dumonet
    (Joséphine)   6^e

Le Bouledogue Bistrot 10^e

Le Hangar 3^e

Les Amognes 11^e

Auberge Pyrénées Cévennes 11^e

Les Jumeaux 11^e

Le Repaire de Cartouche 11^e

À la Biche au Bois 12^e

Restaurant du Marché 15^e

Baptiste 17^e

Foie de Veau
Calf's liver.

Le Pamphlet 3^e

Auberge Pyrénées Cévennes 11^e

Le Vieux Bistro 4^e

Le P'tit Troquet 7^e

L'Oenothèque 9^e

La Villaret 11^e

Chez Pierre 15^e

Le Troquet 15^e

A & M Le Bistrot 16^e

La Cave Gourmande 19^e

Gâteau de Riz / Riz au Lait
Rice pudding.

Chez Pauline 1er

Chez René 5^e

Moissonnier 5^e

Au C'Amelot 11^e

La Villaret 11^e

Le Troquet 15^e

Gigot d'Agneau
Roast leg of lamb.

Chez Dumonet (Joséphine) 6^e

L'Ami Louis 3^e

Au Bascou 3^e

Le Bouledogue Bistrot 10^e

Les Fontaines 5^e

Le P'tit Troquet 7^e

Cartet 11^e

Chardenoux 11^e

Jean-Pierre Frelet 12^e

L'Avant-Goût 13^e

Le Père Claude 15^e

Restaurant du Marché 15^e

La Boulangerie 20^e

Gigot de Sept Heures
Lamb braised for seven hours.

Wadja 6^e	Chardenoux 11^e
Velly 9^e	Le Square Trousseau 12^e

Gratin Dauphinois
Seasoned, sliced potatoes baked in cream and crusted on top.

Cartet 11^e	À Sousceyrac 11^e
L'Avant-Goût 13^e	Le Petit Boileau 16^e
Au Petit Tonneau 7^e	Le Bistrot d'à Côté
Le Passage 11^e	Flaubert 17^e

Hachis Parmentier
Meat and potato casserole (shepherd's pie).

A & M Le Bistrot 16^e	Le Passage 11^e
La Régalade 14^e	Le Villaret 11^e
Le Parmentier 10^e	Le Square Trousseau 12^e
La Boulangerie 20^e	Le Gastroquet 15^e
Le Pamphlet 3^e	Caves Pétrissans 17^e
Mauzac 5^e	Le Zéphyr 20^e

Jambon Cru
Country ham, salt-cured or smoked (or both).

Auberge "d'Chez Eux" 7^e	Chez l'Ami Jean 7^e
Le Grizzli 4^e	L'Alsaco Winstub 9^e
Berrys 8^e	Auberge Pyrénées
Restaurant du Marché 15^e	Cévennes 11^e
Les Fous d'en Face 4^e	Auberge le Quincy 12^e
	Les Coteaux 15^e

Jambon Persillé
Parsleyed ham in white wine aspic.

Le Relais Chablisien   1er

Chez Pierre   15^{e}

Auberge Bressane   7^{e}

Au Bourguignon du
   Marais   4^{e}

Chez Pauline   1er

Chez Georges—Le Jeu
   du Mail   2^{e}

Allard   6^{e}

Ma Bourgogne   8^{e}

Cartet   11^{e}

Lapin à la Moutarde
Rabbit in mustard sauce.

Astier   11^{e}

Le Terroir   13^{e}

La Tour de Monthléry
   (Chez Denise)   1er

La Côte de Boeuf   17^{e}

Lièvre à la Royale
A complex preparation of wild hare, boned and stuffed with foie gras and truffles, then braised in brandy and red wine.

À Sousceyrac   11^{e}

Le Petit Marguery   13^{e}

Chez Pauline   1er

Au Bon Accueil   7^{e}

Le Pétrelle   9^{e}

Restaurant du Marché
   15^{e}

Maquereaux
Mackerel fillets poached in white wine.

La Grille   10^{e}

Le Gastroquet   15^{e}

Lescure   1er

Cartet   11^{e}

Le Petit Marguery   13^{e}

Le Terroir   13^{e}

Navarin d'Agneau
Lamb or mutton stew garnished with potatoes
and vegetables.

Chez Dumonet   Le Grizzli 4^e
  (Joséphine) 6e Le Petit Boileau 16^e
Astier 11^e

Oeufs en Meurette
Eggs poached in red wine sauce with bacon,
mushrooms, and onions.

Le Relais Chablisien 1er Ma Bourgogne 8^e
Au Bourguignon du   Chardenoux 11^e
  Marais 4e Les Coteaux 15^e
Moissonnier 5e Chez Pierre 15^e
Le Calmont 7^e

Petit Salé
Lightly salted pork tenderloin.

Au Vins des Rues 14e Allard 6^e
Aux Charpentiers 6e Auberge Pyrénées
Moissonnier 5e Cévennes 11^e

Pieds de Porc (Cochon) / Pieds de Mouton
Pig's trotters / Sheep's trotters.

À Sousceyrac 11e Cartet 11^e
La Tour de Monthléry   Le Bistrot d'à Côté
  (Chez Denise) 1er Flaubert 17^e
Moissonnier 5^e
Auberge Pyrénées Cévennes
  11^e

Pot-au-Feu / Boeuf Gros Sel

Beef stewed in broth with root vegetables and bone marrow.

L'Avant-Goût   13^e

Auberge le Quincy   12^e

Chez la Vieille   1er

Le Baratin   20^e

La Tour de Monthléry
   (Chez Denise)   1er

Les Fous d'en Face   4^e

Aux Charpentiers   6^e

Chez Paul   13^e

Le Bistrot de l'Étoile
   "Niel"   17^e

Poulet Rôti

Roast chicken.

L'Ami Louis   3^e

Chez Pauline   1er

La Rôtisserie d'en Face
   6^e

La Bastide Odéon   6^e

Le Père Claude   15^e

Le Bistrot d'à Côté
   Flaubert   17^e

Purées de Pommes de Terre / Pommes Écrasées

Mashed and crushed potatoes.

Le Hangar   3^e

Marie et Fils   6^e

Les Bookinistes   6^e

La Rôtisserie d'en Face
   6^e

A & M Le Bistrot   16^e

Quenelles de Brochet

Poached pike dumplings in cream sauce.

Cartet   11^e

Auberge Pyrénées
   Cévennes   11^e

Chez la Vieille   1er

Moissonnier   5^e

Chez René   5^e

Auberge Bressane   7^e

Raie aux Câpres

Skate in black butter sauce with capers.

Les Amognes   11^e

Le P'tit Troquet   7^e

L'Ardoise   1er

Le Bistrot de l'Étoile
   "Niel"   17^e

Ris de Veau / Ris de Agneau
Calf or lamb sweetbreads.

Les Amognes	11^e	L'Oeillade	7^e
À Sousceyrac	11^e	Le Square Trousseau	12^e
Chez Pauline	1er		

Rognons de Veau
Calf's kidneys.

Les Jumeaux	11^e	Velly	9^e
L'Anacréon	13^e	Le Parmentier	10^e
Marie-Louise	18^e	Chardenoux	11^e
L'Ami Louis	3^e	Le Terroir	13^e
Chez la Vieille	1er	La Régalade	14^e
Benoît	4^e	Café d'Angel	17^e
Les Fontaines	5^e	L'Étrier Bistrot	18^e
Au Petit Tonneau	7^e		

Saucisson Chaud
Hot Lyonnaise garlic sausage.

Cartet	11^e	Auberge Pyrénées	
Le Vieux Bistro	4^e	Cévennes	11^e
Benoît	4^e	À Sousceyrac	11^e
Moissonnier	5^e	Les Coteaux	15^e
Chez René	5^e	Marie-Louise	18^e
Auberge Bressane	7^e		

Tabliers de Sapeur
Lyonnaise panfried version of gras-double tripe.

Moissonnier	5^e	Les Coteaux	15^e
Chez Paul	13^e		

Tarte Tatin
Upside-down apple cake with caramelized fruit.

Au Petit Tonneau   7^e

Le Vieux Bistro   4^e

Chez Georges—Le Jeu du Mail   2^e

La Fontaine de Mars   7^e

L'Oeillade   7^e

La Boulangerie   20^e

Terrines
Homemade pâtés served in earthenware terrines.

Cartet   11^e

Chez la Vieille   1er

Le Petit Boileau   16^e

L'Anacréon   13^e

Benoît   4^e

Au Petit Tonneau   7^e

La Grille   10^e

Chez Michel   10^e

Le Parmentier   10^e

Le Repaire de Cartouche   11^e

La Régalade   14^e

Le Père Claude   15^e

Baptiste   17^e

Caves Pétrissans   17^e

Marie-Louise   18^e

Tête de Veau
Calf's head.

La Grille   10^e

Caves Pétrissans   17^e

Chez Pauline   1er

La Fontaine de Mars   7^e

Chez Michel   10^e

Les Coteaux   15^e

Le Gastroquet   15^e

Marie-Louise   18^e

Tripes

La Tour de Monthléry (Chez Denise)   1er

La Bastide Odéon   6^e

L'Oeillade   7^e

Cartet   11^e

Auberge le Quincy   12^e

Tripoux
Auvergnat preparation of veal or mutton.

Le Réveil du Xe 10^e

Le Calmont   7^e

BISTROS OPEN ON SUNDAYS

1er

L'Ardoise
L'Argenteuil (dinner only)
Le Dauphin

3e

L'Ami Louis

4e

Benoît
Les Fous d'en Face
Le Vieux Bistro

5e

Moissonnier (lunch only)
Le Réminet
Chez Toutoune

6e

Les Bookinistes (dinner only)
Aux Charpentiers
Chez Maître Paul

7e

Auberge Bressane
La Fontaine de Mars
Au Petit Tonneau

12e

Le Square Trousseau

13e

Chez Paul
Virgule (dinner only)

15e

Le Bistro d'Hubert
Le Père Claude

17e

Le Bistrot d'à Côté Flaubert
Le Bistrot de l'Étoile "Niel"

20e

La Boulangerie

INDEX OF BISTROS